The Hottest Place on Earth

a novel by Alfred Cool

In a time in which global climate change has raised awareness about the negative effects that large amounts of man-made pollution have on land, air, and water, the policies of the Bush administration focused instead on more immediate, economic concerns, rather than establish long-term solutions with the intent to significantly mitigate contemporary and future environmental problems.

--President Jimmy Carter to G.W. Bush 1977-2009
Presidential Policies and Involvement in the Debate over the Arctic National Wildlife Refuge

By 2022, it will simply be cheaper to build and provide a gigawatt of wind power than the cheapest fossil-fuel alternative and solar will be just behind. Bottom line: renewable energy can power Canada, create jobs, generate wealth and fight climate change.

--David Suzuki, January 2017

ISBN-13: 978-1546972006

ISBN-10: 1546972005

For Dave Rhodes, his wife, his children, and his
grandchildren.

"U-235. This ore," Corey held the packet up and wiggled it in front
of my face, "is the shit."

Chapters:

1. Geiger Counter Downs

I was in Port Radium, on Great Bear Lake, for six weeks before rumors evolved into proof the isolated mining camp had a sinister past linked with Hiroshima. The first time I met Corey, our reclusive geologist, he turned my suspicion to outrage …

• • •

Corey's reputation was hard to nail down. I heard he was a frat rat who was usually intoxicated on Quaaludes. But didn't that breed tend to puff up in cardigan sweaters, abuse alcohol, and seek social status at country clubs? Our Corey hung about the camp as a skeletal loner rattling his bones beneath a dusty lab coat, self-medicating himself to temper his reality. In my estimation, he had potential.

He met my expectations the first time I really met him. He was in his early twenties, as was I; his voice was weak and his shoulders slumped — mine were not. He presented as innocuous and clean-cut, whereas I was brash, opinionated, and tended to rebellion. After weeks in isolation, all chameleon disguises become transparent. There is no place to hide, everyone knows everyone else's propensities, and all are on raw display. Corey's solution to simplify life's challenges was pharmaceutical and personal, so I did not judge him. Equally in his favor, Corey was friends with the twins, Genna and Morag. Any familiar contact with them was off-limits for the rest of us, therefore, their bunkhouse, a place we called the sugar shack, was never out of our minds. For his connections, Corey garnered universal envy and spiteful gossip, but I doubt he ever got laid.

On this particular day, my room partner, Michael, and I had met the plane and were unloading the light supplies. Any non-perishable cargo that arrived with the company plane that a man could lift, I delivered. Michael was thin and strong, had long, greasy brown hair, perennial stubble, and he was a French Canadian. About my age and my height, he was on the run from the law — I was not, although I placed in the "brush with the law" category. Michael

5

always carried a folding knife and was unafraid of the thugs running the back alleys of Winnipeg.

"Careful with that, Michael," I said. "It's probably vital to mining operations I deliver it intact and pronto." The package was marked "RUSH" and was destined for the geology office.

After so many weeks in camp, I had been responding to the boredom by talking, at times, like a telephone switchboard operator. Somewhat more disturbing was the fact I was aware of this but never bothered myself trying to curb the inclination. Camp life had become long days of self-survival. My only focus was to make it to the end of the four-month contract term. I was only half-way through my contract, so it was still a toss up whether I'd get out before going bonkers. That is the exact kind of personal information you keep private in an isolated camp, but, like I say, there was no place to hide.

Michael stopped with the box held firmly in both his hands. It was also clearly marked "FRAGILE" on six sides. He spun around, dropped it, then fired off a sardonic mock-Nazi salute at me.

Later that afternoon, I made the delivery to Corey's lab. It was after three p.m. before I finished a lengthy bout of frustrated flirting with Morag, who occasionally worked in the cook shack. However, the time I invested was as wasted as ripe fruit rotting on the vine because, lately, when in my company, we were chaperoned by the camp cook's obese wife.

I slid the bus to a stop at the geologist's office. Corey had rooms in one of the larger, almost-abandoned warehouses, re-purposed from the original miner's two story bunkhouse. Built on the lakeshore, it stuck out like a sore thumb on a hand full of arthritic digits. The building was another example of the many dreary, abandoned structures at the site. Constructed of timber and yellowed plywood, torn black tar paper sheets hung off the exposed outer walls. Pockmarked patches of grey asphalt shingles nailed up to the eaves replaced missing siding. Two feet of snow covered most of the roof. Blown-snow berms, built up against the outside of the structure, reached to the bottom of the crosshatched windows on either side of the cracked, weather-beaten door.

I looked in one window. Besides the cardboard boxes piled high, I saw the windowsills and glass sections were grimy with the omnipresent black dust that pervaded camp life. I knocked once on the door, turned the knob, and then kicked the base of the door to snap it free of the ice buildup. The routine was standard operating procedure at the mine throughout winter. Having announced my arrival, I stepped inside.

A single bare bulb illuminated the room. It hung on a white household extension cord tied to one of the exposed rafters below the tatters of the unfinished, vaulted ceiling. This end of the bunkhouse was a cavernous room where rough boards were shelves nailed to exposed wall studs. Three tiers on each wall encircled the room, each shelf had been stocked with core samples. Edison's invention threw little light to the corners, so it took some time for my eyes to adjust to the dull twilight. I heard a faint cough from down the hallway, caught before it grew into a crescendo of hacking. An epidemic of dry cough, flu, and bronchitis was circulating through camp.

The geo-geek hesitated, framed by the inside doorway. I had the distinct feeling he studied me. He snapped a light switch on the wall before he walked into the cavern. Fluorescent fixtures attached to the bare rafters high above us flickered, flashed, and eventually flushed the room with harsh, white-blue light.

"Oh, it's you. What do you want?"

"Delivery. This is the geology lab, right?"

"Right. Sure. Yes, geology, in all its professional glory."

We approached each other and met at the desk in the center of the room. One on one, Corey appeared frail and sickly. His bloodshot eyes watered, and his complexion reminded me of Madam Tussauds' "Rue Morgue" display. His fingers were thin and jittery. He wore a parka over a grimy, once-white lab coat. When we spoke, it was cold enough to see our breath.

I looked around the dismal room again. Black dust covered rolls of maps, stacked cardboard boxes, and the shelves full of long, black core samples. The place looked more abandoned than occupied.

"Guess you don't get much of a budget for interior decorating. It's freezing in here."

He looked past and around me. "Eddie is coming over to fix the acetylene heater. I was hoping you might be him. You can put that package down there. Thanks."

I was careful to place the crushed corner of the box away from his line of sight. I needed to find someone who travelled to

Edmonton regularly to bring back contraband for me and the guys, so I took this opportunity to sound Corey out. "Y'know, some curtains, a little dusting, a stereo might brighten up this place. How's things on the outside, anyway?"

"The same. Boring. Depressing. Better off here. Smashed the box did you?"

I decided to take a shot in the dark, "Is Nixon still an asshole? Must have happened on the plane."

"Bumpy landing, I suppose? Yes, as a matter of fact, he is. They're going to impeach him and then fry his ass, I hope. Johnson, Nixon, Ford, they're all implicated in JFK's assassination." He looked at me long enough to make me feel uncomfortable about the parcel.

I said, "Makes a crushed box corner seem trivial. And Agnew needs to go, too."

Corey agreed. "Murdering students on campuses, throttling the free press, escalating Vietnam. Five years for weed possession. Disco. What else do they need down there to dump the creeps? I've been trying to get that instrument in here for a year."

"Another one of their fixed elections, I guess. You know what The Who said, 'Meet the new boss ...'"

"We'll have to return it now. '... same as the old boss, we won't get fooled again.' But we always do. My name is Corey."

Finally, we had synchronicity. I shook his shaky, out-stretched hand, thankful we could end the double-helixed threads of this conversation. I looked around again. Two desks pushed together were stacked with dusty boxes and crowded the center of the room. A wooden desk chair with a broken leg leaned against the shelving in one corner. Long cobweb strands, illuminated in the light, hung from the rafters, attached like silk threads to dozens of the core samples. The dusty geology of forty years of mining at Port Radium lay stacked on these wooden racks. I noticed what appeared to be an odd-looking tuner on the desk.

"I'm Al. Nice place you have here ... When do I meet Quasimodo?"

"Pleased to meet you. Genna and Morag told me about you."

"They did? What'd they say?" I was hopeful for a favorable evaluation. After all, they were the only available, young women within hundreds of square miles of frozen tundra.

"They said you were a company man and would repeat

everything you heard to Jimmy."

"What do you know, they nailed me." We stopped shaking hands. I pointed at the tuner that looked like a 1940's mantle radio. "What the hell is that thing?"

Corey's response surprised me. "I don't have many friends in this camp. Morag and Genna are my friends, but they're a-political. Why don't we cut to the chase … They say you can be trusted. If I show you something, you have to keep it between us. But if something happens to me, would you tell someone about it? Would you do that?" His voice had a definite edge.

"I guess … But why me?"

"Genna told me you had journalism aspirations. Is that true?"

"That's what I'm saving for."

"This might be your blockbuster story. I mean that."

Corey looked at the tuner. He tried to blow the thick layer of black dust off the meter, but the sticky grunge was unaffected. The entire camp had the same layer of grime on it. The stuff was pervasive and required effort to wipe off any surface, which few of us bothered with because the dust, like our personality traits, always returned by the next day. There was no mystery involved, mining and dust go together. Corey spit on the meter glass and then used his lab coat sleeve to clean off the grime. A single black knob stuck out below the meter.

"It's a Geiger counter."

I bent down to look more closely. Beside the knob was a black lever with a range of three settings other than OFF.

"Wow," I said, "that's pretty cool, but why is it here?"

Corey looked at me. "Are you kidding?" I shook my head. "Okay then … The twins trust you, maybe I can too. I'll give you a private tour of Port Radium." He opened a desk drawer and took out one of the gritty, small plastic sample bags strewn inside. "Watch and learn."

He pulled a small tray out of the bottom slot of the Geiger counter. Each label of the other positions might as well have been hieroglyphics. The first position read "1X mR/h."

"The sensor is here." I watched him pull a pencil-thin tube out of the front of the counter, above the small sample tray. Cory plugged in the machine. The meter glowed pale yellow. The thin, black needle jumped full across the meter then bounced back to

9

remain stable on the left, at exactly "0 mR/h."

"Okay, it's self-calibrated to zero and initialized." The machine clattered steadily, like a coffee percolator on full. "That's only background gammas and betas. I've already calibrated the machine to ignore the background rads."

"Sorry? I'm a bit out of my element ..."

"*Isotope*, would have been funnier. I'm talking about the core samples, the radiation in the walls, and this goddamned dust. The everyday stuff around camp."

That simple statement and the unnerving ticking launched my anxiety attack. He placed the small sample bag on the tray. He watched me as he snapped the dial to the position "1X mR/h." A wild, rapid-fire, burping-ticking sound filled the room, exactly the same soundtrack I'd heard in every B-quality sci-fi movie.

"Holy shit! Weird science ... Is that radioactivity?"

He turned off the machine. In the sudden silence, he grabbed my arm. "Quiet. Not one word. Ever. We could both lose more than our jobs if you say anything to anyone about this."

I reassured my paranoid co-conspirator that I could keep a secret. I began to feel this desperate addict had unlocked the door to a modern version of Dr. Frankenstein's laboratory.

Corey said, "I hate this place, but now I need the job for my medical coverage. If I quit, they cancel my plan and I'm on the street. Each notch on this switch invokes a heavier filter for accurate readings of higher concentrations of uranium in the sample."

I felt like I had poked the sleeping bear, but I was fascinated. I leaned in to peer at the sample. There was only a small amount of dust in the tiny bag.

"That's right," said Cory. "It doesn't take much to produce that kind of reading. There's more; that was only level one. My contract says I'm supposed to make sure no one ever sees this level, let alone what I'm going to show you. This counter can measure extreme radiation levels. This is a government unit, the best they had in the forties, and is still accurate today. This unit came from the US military. At least, they used them all the time. After the war, the CIA called the shots here until the mid-sixties. Anyway, watch the needle."

Corey removed the packet, turned on the counter, and it repeated its zero calibration. Again, the silence in the room was replaced by the intimidating clatter.

"The black numbers are the lowest on the register, reading the lowest when the needle stays left, the green counts on the second level, that's the "5X mR/h" setting, the red is the third, the "10X mR/h" setting, which is the highest level of radiation detection and measurement this machine can manage. What you would measure the day the bomb dropped in Hiroshima. Are you ready for the Twilight Zone?"

Talley-ho, Madame Currie, bring me into the twentieth century. I nodded.

Corey suppressed another slight cough before he placed the packet onto the tray. As before, at the first position, the counter rattled and the needle zipped across the meter, where it remained tight to the right extremity. Corey snapped the switch to the second level; the noise increased but the needle only quivered. Corey stared at me. He snapped the switch to the final position and pointed to the red scale on the meter. The loud burps remained constant, but the needle quivered then vibrated over the 84 percent tick.

"Do you see that?" I nodded, unknowledgeable about what I was looking at. "A few months of exposure to anything past half-way on the first scale means cancer. We are way beyond that. This sample is one of the most recent from Eldorado. The closer you get to the Eldorado shaft, the hotter everything is, and they vent that radon in between our bunkhouses! Soon, tons of this stuff is going to come out of Eldorado every day. Again. Breathe down there, or near any of the mine vents in camp, and you die up here." He snapped the lever back down through the levels, and then turned off and unplugged the machine.

When the noise stopped, Corey said, "That ore was used to fuel the bomb dropped on Hiroshima."

"What?"

"U-235. This ore," he held the packet up and wiggled it in front of my face, "is the shit. The Nazis stole 3500 tons of yellowcake from Belgium to start their atomic bomb program. The Americans got sixty tons from us to start theirs."

He let that sink in. I was shocked. "Did you say tons?"

"Yes. And our side admitted to dumping mountains of this stuff into the lake, right in front of the bunkhouses. I cannot imagine what they actually dumped, if they admit to that much, and how much more over the last twenty years. They must have loved the

11

isolation of this site. 'Manhattan,' do you know what that is?"

"A drink ordered at swanky cocktail lounges?"

"Funny. Making the first atomic bombs was just getting started, and Port Radium's U-235 was 6 percent to the ton. The Congo yellowcake was only 1 percent per ton. This whole area is still so hot with radiation, but especially dangerous with radon, that if anyone bothered to measure the air above ground, they'd shut us down today. And they should! They originally sent forty miners into the mine. I heard thirty-eight of them already died from lung cancer. Breathing the dust kills you, radon gets into your lungs on the dust, then burns holes in there. Shit, man, thousands of the miners that work underground in uranium mines, all over the world, die from lung cancer."

"When I took this job, I was told this was a silver mine."

"Sure, there is some silver here, but in 1910, the going rate was $75,000 per gram for radium and in the thirties they were getting $25,000 per gram. At those rates, processing silver was a lower priority. They used small amounts of it in hospitals, but mostly, women hand-painted radium on jewelry and clock faces because it glowed in the dark. Radium is found in uranium; they were handling uranium with bare hands. How many of them died of cancer? After Hiroshima and Manhattan, they used enriched plutonium to fuel nuclear bombs. Nagasaki was a plutonium bomb. We should have been off the supply grid in 1945. But our government kept Eldorado producing U-235 for the Cold War until 1960, at least. Then Echo Bay took over. They wanted the silver and the copper. Now we're going to bring up lots of silver ore from Eldorado again. The stuff I showed you in the packet has silver in it, too. Problem is, are they extracting the uranium from the silver? No. That is a completely different chemical process, which is way more expensive. We are shipping the uranium and the radon with the silver ore. Have you been to the tailing pond yet?"

"Not yet."

"Well, don't you have a surprise coming? By the way, the sample you saw is dated." Corey lifted the packet from the sample tray and read aloud, "1975. Thirty years after the war ended; in fact, this year. But these samples measure the same as the samples from '42. U-235 takes a while to decay, like forty-seven million human generations, literally. So far, no one cares about this part of the planet or the amount of this shit already dumped in the lake. Most of the rest of the bad news stays frozen under the permafrost. I read a report in our university library that Great Bear Lake is considered 'the most pristine lake inside Canada's borders.' Not anymore, and if it is, man, do we have problems." He returned the sample bag to the drawer and closed it.

"Wait a minute. I thought Canada was a leader in clean nuclear power. What is it, the Candu reactor? "

"Such a joke. India is already re-configuring their Candu reactors as part of their plan to blow the crap out of Pakistan. Canada is proliferating potential nuclear arms throughout the world. I wish it was the Can-Don't." Corey became thoughtful for a minute. "Why do you think we have a night shift?" He did not wait for my answer. "Eight miners go into Eldorado on three different shifts, the same fucking hole where so many have already died. They mine the silver. Then we process and condense the ore in our crushing mill where more men work. The dust gets spread around." He swiped his finger across the bench, leaving a glistening trail in the grit. "Then it gets shipped out by convoy to Fort McMurray, Uranium City, and finally Port Hope, Ontario. If mom and pop only knew what was in their coins … Who knows? Maybe they are extracting the U-235 back in Ontario where they're set up. Even if they are, they never get it all." He held his blackened finger up between us. "This dust is everywhere. This is what kills us, man. Where do you think it comes from? I mean, for Christ's sake, it's in our air, our food, our drinking and shower water, the walls, and where we work."

"And these management assholes know it's this bad?"

"Of course. I provide them with readings on a daily basis, which is why I'm under a gag order. But that's the least of my worries. You've met the new security around here, right? Schläger is a very dangerous man."

"Yeah, the Nazi guy you flew in with?"

The sound of a creaking door came from down the hall. Corey and I froze. Corey motioned I was to wait while he went to investigate. When he came back, he looked worried. "That was probably just the wind, but I'm sure that door was locked."

His voice was just above a whisper. "Anyway, your choice of the word 'Nazi'? There's truth in that. So, after three days of working in those conditions, they send the miner's back over to work at the

Echo Bay mine. It's a little less dangerous for radon in that dust, but it's still deadly. They flood Eldorado with lake water every three days to cool it down then pump the water back into the lake, then they send the miners back into that shit pit. JT and Jimmy came up with that plan."

Jimmy, JT's only child, lived in Port Radium, but we saw him only on rare occasions. JT owned the company working the mine for the Canadian government and was our employer, the only employer in Port Radium, although he had never appeared in camp since I arrived.

"I heard we were doing that. I didn't really know what to believe."

"Believe it. It's the same thing they've been pulling off for the last thirty years, sending the miners into the killer hole for ore."

"So, what you're telling me is that Jimmy is sending miners into the radon-poisoned dust. And he knows he is doing this? Do the miners know how bad it is?"

Corey shook his head. "You know the camp rule, no one talks about radiation, radon, or uranium. It's a firing offence."

"They go underground without knowing about the hazards. And we concentrate the ore at the mill. Do those guys know? And what about Uranium City and Port Hope? What about the people moving this crap across the country? What about them? This kind of hazard would never get past WCB. We have to tell the government."

"This *is* the government! Echo Bay leases this site from Canada. No one looks very hard at us because we're officially mining for copper and silver. No one tests for radiation or radon gas anymore." He stopped to let that sink in. "There's a kicker. This counter is the one we use to test samples before Jimmy goes underground. He won't set foot in either mine if the sample reads above level one, which it will drop to for half a shift after they drain the mine and before the miners finish drilling. We sample accurately for management."

Corey looked over his shoulder toward the hallway. His nervous reaction was telling.

"The company owns two other counters, CD V-700s. They have a famous known flaw. When the sensor is over-exposed to high radiation, like if one of these sample bags is left nearby for an hour or so, then it reads low, like almost zero, due to saturation. The sensor chokes out, I guess, is one way to think of it. Both our counters stay in Eldorado and Echo Bay for the miners to see every shift. If it reads zero, they go to work. The sensors are always saturated and always read zero, so the miners always go to work. Jimmy plays the same game with WCB and the mine inspectors when they come through here. If they bother to check the readings at all, they see it reads almost zero and leave satisfied. Anyway, I'm the technician who provides the readings, so the inspectors can pass this site as safe for work. I'm not supposed to know what I do about the V-700, but I've done my homework. This same sample would read zero in the mine." His hand went up to his mouth to suppress a strangling burp-hiccup. "Anyway, I don't want people to work in Eldorado. It's way too dangerous."

I could hardly believe my own ears. I said, "So the ore still leaves Port Radium and enters the manufacturing world or the Canadian mint this goddamn hot? And Jimmy and JT and the Canadian government know all this?"

"That's right. There have only been damaging reports, but government management suppressed them. Settle down," Corey commanded and I listened. "Yeah, it's that bad. Once it leaves here, no outsiders check the ore, far as I know. We are potentially sending cancer out to maybe hundreds of thousands of innocent people, and have been doing this for decades. Awesome thought, eh? The real joke is Canada promotes itself as so 'nuclear' clean. Remember, you promised not to say anything."

"I'm getting it, but there are promises and there are promises. This ain't no little white lie either, is it? I can't believe these owners are willing to do this to all of us to make a few bucks."

"Look, this is one promise you'd better keep. If the office finds out you know about this, and might leak something and shut this place down, then Schläger will come after you, and maybe Genna and Morag, too. This isn't about *a few bucks*. JT and Jimmy have New York Stock Exchange plans. I've heard them boasting about it. Don't be stupid. It would be easy for them to take you for a one-way plane ride and drop you a hundred miles north of here. The wolves and bears would take care of you after that. No one would ever find your bones. Take my advice, don't sign up for another contract, and stay as far away from the mine and the plant as you can."

Now I was worried, too. "This will be our secret. Ho-ly fuck

..."

"Remember, the closer you get to Eldorado, the more radiation in the buildings, the air, the ground. That old mill is still dangerous hot. That's why it's off-limits. I'm surprised there hasn't already been an insurance fire. Maybe JT is saving that for his final act; that's his style. When you leave here, scrub your hands thoroughly, get under the nails. And don't shower very often, either."

I was outraged. "Shouldn't they have all this stuff stored in a lead-lined room or something?"

"In a way they've done that ... the entire camp is painted in lead-based paint."

My co-conspirator launched into a violent and protracted coughing jag. When he was able to talk, he said he had work to finish, by which I understood him to mean it was time for his self-medication.

"Take care of that cough, man, it sounds bad."

I left Corey to his dark nightmare. My emotions reeled as I ground through the gears driving back to the sugar shack to plug in the bus block heater for the night. I was angry. The bench Geiger counter told the truth. The thought occurred to me that the sample, one of dozens I saw in the drawer, and the core samples too, should never have been left out in the open like that.

Before dinner, I considered a long shower, but Corey had warned me off. I remained distracted and distant until I was roaring drunk later on at beer night. I managed to stifle my yapping because, for the first time since Michael and I had flown into camp, Schläger came to the beer trailer. He took a table next to us, drank a slow beer, but never once looked at us. I remembered the creaking door at the geo-office.

Back in our bunkhouse, Michael watched me punch black dust out of my pillow. I told him about Corey's *tour*. After he finished punching the black dust out of his pillow, Michael said better than I ever could, "I knew that JT was an asshole."

That night, I dreamt a terrifying nightmare: I was an innocent miniature of myself, just one terrorized peep away from being discovered, devoured and forgotten, having wandered into the midst of giant, angry demons colluding with wicked sorcerers.

2. Cookie

I never intended to start this story half way in, and neither was I trying to be artistic or creative. Maybe it's the nature of this story, just like my revelation, that causes events to jump up at me this way, as if they had a life of their own. I will have to ask you to persevere with me; I know, I owe you backstory … but this incident is more important. The next thing that happened was Jimmy fired me …

• • •

When I had time to think about it, I walked right into their trap.

Two days after I met with Corey at the geology lab, I was working through my mine deliveries after lunch. I raced the engine and ground across the transmission gears until I found an accepting gear, maybe the third. I gripped the wheel, released the clutch, and bunny-hopped the school bus over twenty feet of frozen snow and ice until it stalled. I was embarrassed and thankful for few witnesses. The neat stack of boxes I'd arranged for my delivery route had bounced, rolled, and tumbled into a chaotic jumble of parcels along Beulah's aisle. I restarted her engine

I had named her Beulah because I felt I could work with her, talk to her, and coax a better relationship out of her by giving her a woman's name. I still had much to learn about driving, and yes, I was that young and stupid about women, too. In addition, while I was stuck working in this isolated mining camp at Canada's Arctic Circle, even just thinking a woman's name re-reassured me that the better half of humanity still existed.

The neo-Nazi, Schläger, surprised me when he manifested out of the sun's blinding glare at my side window. Schläger slowly waved both his arms in wide arcs over his head as if he was guiding a 747 into a parking slot.

None of the gang I hung around with in the camp knew why Schläger was here. *What did he do, besides hang around and fill the role of JT's bootlick and hired thug?* I slid the window open, and Schläger stopped waving his arms.

"You must come to the manager's office. Now," he shouted at me. His thick German accent sounded like a put-on, which was another thing that irritated me about the man. He walked around the front of the bus, keeping an eye on me all the way. It was -22F outside, so I waited until he knocked on the glass door panel before I opened the bi-fold bus doors.

I had arrived in Port Radium hours before the bite of a vicious, weeklong blizzard, six weeks ago. Besides the Draconian managers, many things about this archaic uranium mine grated on my nerves. I already felt bushed. Long hours, isolation, tough working conditions, a poor diet, and surviving in a bunkhouse with forty other men contributed to my current state of agitation. A summons and escort to the manager's office was never a good sign and would do little to improve my mental state. And I did not like Schläger or men of his ilk.

"I'm trying to get up that way, but the transmission is broken," I explained to the nimrod.

Schläger stepped onto the lowest step of the bus, so I closed the doors behind him, screwed up my face to prove I was trying, and punished the full range of gears again until Beulah treated us to another series of bunny-hops. The violence and bucking threw Schläger around hard enough to knock off his yellow hardhat. We lurched again when I stomped on the gas, and Schläger's head snapped backward and banged against the stanchion. Anti-climatically, Beulah stalled. I felt satisfied this demonstration proved her transmission was faulty.

I looked at Schläger as if to say, *I told you so.*

Rubbing his head, he said, "Really? Here, I will try."

"You can try if you like, but you won't win the argument. You'll never get 'er up this hill."

The loaded and baited bear trap was set.

I gave up my command post reluctantly; it had taken weeks of long days to win the driver's seat. I moved to allow Schläger to sit in my place, whispering a quiet apology to Beulah. After I received vindication, I would remind Schläger of the nasty, purple-red bump forming on the side of his head. However, contrary to my expectations, and smooth as soft ice cream, Schläger drove us up the icy incline. He switched through the gears like a pro at the Nürburgring. Never did Beulah slip or buck and neither did he grind a gear on our way to the office. She was two-timing me.

"It runs okay, but there is not much clutch left."

"See! I told you."

A couple of weeks earlier, Jack had promoted me from

surface laborer to bus driver. It was a cushy job and meant I would be out of the weather, but more importantly, I had my own, personal heater. It was a nice setup for anyone working outside during the month of March at the Arctic Circle. It was my job to meet the company supply plane and drive the miners to and from work every day. What gave me pause about taking the job was the fact I had never actually learned to drive a standard, especially a four-wheel drive bus on sheets of ice up and down narrow, unprotected roads gouged along and through steep crags. After an infinitesimally short moment of concern for my passengers, I decided I could learn on the job. I hated to admit that Schläger was correct; I had destroyed Beulah's new clutch in just three days. I should have been honest with Jack, but that heater … Well, it still dipped to -45F overnight, so I had no choice.

When we arrived at the office, I knew Schläger would keep Beulah's keys, just like I knew management was gunning for me. Lately, I had been complaining often and loudly about the food served in the cook shack. I wanted to start another food revolution and have the cook and his crew swapped out for someone familiar, at least, with kitchen fundamentals, but I under-estimated Jimmy's pushback. He and JT sniffed out and locked onto recalcitrance like a couple of pit bulls on a poodle in heat, silencing all of the 140 men in camp, except me, giving voice to justified complaints. I was an unemployed man walking.

I watched the mine manager exit his pickup and quickly descend the wooden steps to the office. He was a dead ringer for a stern, "Moscow Square" Joseph Stalin. He did not look back at us but entered the office while Schläger parked Beulah. If I was the target in the crosshairs of Jimmy's scope, I knew Stalin's presence was a sure sign I was about to draw hostile fire.

When I stood at the reception counter, Carl, one of the two twerpy office clerks, said, "Jimmy wants to see you right away."

"That's why I'm here."

Bill, Jimmy's assistant, popped his head out of the office door, "Jimmy's ready."

Carl's voice quivered when he said, "We're on our way in now." I thought Carl looked distracted and flustered. A recent camp rumor circulated that Carl was having an affair with Bill. Camp gossip replaced our lack of newspapers, TV, movies, radio, phones, or a library. Rumors of homosexuals in camp were making the rounds lately, and we all ate it up. Camp boredom was an epidemic, and the weight of no mental stimulation dragged out the weeks and crushed the spirit. Trivial gossip, though it meant nothing to most of us in town, became monumental to everyone on Great Bear Lake.

What's this snooty twit's problem? I'm the one bein' canned.

The egg had not rolled far from the nest. Neither JT nor Jimmy was likely to take personal responsibility or accept fault if anyone else was within shouting distance. With few exceptions, the men thought of Jimmy as a smarmy know-it-all, attached firmly to his father's coattails with his lips puckered. Jimmy put on airs about working his way up through the ranks, but everything he had JT had given him. Whenever I dealt with Jimmy, I found it almost impossible to withstand his arrogance and proverbial, dismissive smirk. Jimmy's lifetime of failures nurtured his insecurity; that and trying to prove himself capable of ascending to higher standards than JT ever reached. In camp, this unnecessary and contrived pressure translated to the burden of subservience for the rest of us. In our eyes, he diminished his own worth for that reason. That, and the fact Jimmy was a bully.

Both Carl and Schläger escorted me into Jimmy's office.

I realized I might have taken my complaining too far. Though I was half-expecting this confrontation, my stomach churned as I anticipated the next few minutes. Firing someone was a process in Port Radium. First, it was leaked around camp they were having another of their management meetings. Next, they would call the poor sap with his figurative neck on the chopping block into the office for the confrontation. The interview always occurred when the sap's friends were at work, and the company supply plane was scheduled to arrive, unload, and return to Yellowknife the same day. The sap would disappear from camp, vaporized as if he never existed. It was all pre-arranged and sanitized. I was surface labor, ergo, I met the plane and had often witnessed terminations happen exactly that way.

I never expected sympathy or fairness, and my status was self-inflicted; I was the unofficial voice of the vast majority of men who complained about the food to each other. Taking up the cause meant mean firing, that I might be unable to pay my university tuition for the coming year, but I was equally unable help myself.

Carl minced in front of me, and Schläger goose-stepped behind us both. In the office, he faded off to stand and smirk at me from a corner. Carl held the door, and then closed it with a definitive bang after Schläger had passed through. Carl took a chair close to Bill, really close. Bill draped himself on the chair in front of the camp's only short-wave radio set. A thick layer of acrid cigarette smoke dissected the office, reminding me of pictures of the oil slick wafting on the summer surface of our sheltered LaBine Bay. I braced myself, staring into the condescending face of the under-lord, feeling like the martyr at a brown-shirt rally in 1934 Nuremberg.

Jimmy's face remained as wooden as his desk. His haircut was foxhole short, his military jaw was set, and his beady eyes judged me as if he were about to order me out and into the raking crossfire of enemy machine guns. I stood in the center of the room, waiting for someone to speak. Stalin, the most approachable member of the management squad, moved from in front of a window, allowing the blinding Arctic sunlight to fall full upon me.

Jimmy started. "You don't like it here, I understand. You have lots of complaints?"

"No, it's fine."

I lied. I needed to keep this job. If I quit or left camp before I finished my four-month contract, even if they unjustly terminated me, I would depart without so much as a bus token in my pockets and arrive back on the Edmonton streets as broke as when I'd left. My future was on the line, and I hated the thought that Jimmy, of all people, stood between me and my slim hopes of a career in journalism.

"That's a lie. I've heard that you complain."

I scanned the room. Stalin arched a single eyebrow, as if to ask, "I'm here to discipline someone complaining about the food? The kitchen staff won't even eat what they feed the men."

My gut told me I was finished, but I contrived one last, desperate ploy. I did what they did; I mixed beaches of lies with a grain of truth. "The food you provide is top of the line. But the cook, well, that says it all," I said.

I think they recognized the familiar gambit and embraced my conformity.

As if my leg hovered over the trip wire in their bear trap, the next moment was critical to my future. My words hung in the room

21

as foul as a rotting albatross carcass; an unkind mix swirling with the cancerous pall of second-hand cigarette smoke. These men were incapable of respecting dissent; I needed to shift their focus away from me. My strategy was to make them think we shared common ground by igniting their pre-disposition to bias and bullying anyone different from themselves.

The room went silent. No one would deny the cook was incompetent. Anyone without the constitution of a Serengeti bush dog could expect to suffer recurrent attacks of Irritable Bowel Syndrome, which, from time to time, we all endured. In fact, our Cockney cook, Les, was so proud of his military service and his East London roots, he seemed to put his heart into ruining plausible food for the precise reason of crippling strong constitutions. I assumed it was a tradition of Empire.

Stalin said, "Everyone hates Les's cooking, don't they, Jimmy?"

This comment served to knock Jimmy completely off his tangent and launch between the management team a round of sidelong, doubtful glances. Jimmy put voice to the question plainly formed across his smug face. "Can you do better?"

I had to think fast. When I was fifteen, I worked as a carhop in a drive-in restaurant in Vancouver. That experience, and the little I learned in "Cookie" Calvert's three-month home economics course in high school, accounted for all of my formal culinary training. However, this was the wrong time to haggle over details of my *curriculum vitae*. "Damn right I can," I stated. "I've worked in restaurants and attended cooking courses."

I blurted out my reply, slathered with saucy self-confidence. And why not? I had misrepresented myself when Jack asked me if I could drive; I lied and got that job, so I hoped the same strategy would work here. In reality, cooking my own breakfast and sifting flour ranked as the highest level of expertise I had ever attained in any kitchen. But, I reasoned to myself, how hard could it be?

Jimmy's stern scowl disappeared and his face tended to neutrality. He liked where this was going. "Wait outside," he ordered. "Close the door behind you."

I left the office, not quite fired, not quite trapped, and not quite reprieved. With my ear pressed to the outside of the office door, I listened to every word spoken inside.

Something felt different.

Jimmy said, "We keep him in camp, work him until I decide to dump him. He can work off the cost of that clutch and never get a cent from me, no matter how long he lasts in this camp. He can't possibly fuck things up in the kitchen worse than they already are, so we have nothing to lose keeping him around for a couple more weeks." A pause, then, "All right, call him back in."

Jimmy's estimation failed me as a vote of confidence. However, my immediate career path appeared navigable and my future as a journalist still possible.

Carl called me back into the office. This time I sat in the high-backed, wooden dining chair that had materialized in front of Jimmy's desk. His smile was bleak but when he looked at Bill his expression became self-satisfied. Bill stared at Carl, who mooned back at Bill with puppy love eyes. Schläger glared at me as if he were starving and I was meat on a spit over an open fire. The bump on his head had matured, now approximating the size and color of a miniature, moldy Mandarin orange.

The *politburo* loomed over me, exchanging glances among themselves until they converged on Stalin. He stood in front of the window again, blocking the direct sunlight. He was the first to break free of their eyeball circle to ask, "So, you have experience cooking?"

"Like I said, I worked in a restaurant in Vancouver."

Whap! Clank! Jimmy had me snared in his trap.

There were only two ways out: I could quit, which would be the equivalent of gnawing my own leg off to crawl away to a pitiful demise; or I could play along. I was in a state of disbelief that *dumping* me meant the 5,000-foot drop Corey had warned me about. Corey was convinced Schläger assisted camp troublemakers off the plane when it was a mile in the air and over the lake.

Jimmy said, "Okay, kid, you're hired, if you can do the job. I'm firing you as our surface crew driver. You're our new second cook, or you're on the plane with Schläger. Which is it?"

Jimmy looked pleased with himself. I had to agree, though my self-survival alarm reverberated in my head as if I was in Big Ben's belfry at noon. I snatched a quick look at Schläger. I was never getting on a plane with him; his unnerving sneer rattled me. *My God, would they really have me dig my own grave and then kick me into the hole?* I had no choice; I would figure a way out of this situation later, but first, I needed a temporary reprieve from the gallows. My only *get-out-of-jail-free* card was to demonstrate my counterfeit claims of culinary skills. On the plus side, Les set that bar so low in this camp, even I could do a better job of breakfast. Somehow, I had become management's hope for temporary gastronomical relief from the British cook, and they were willing to take that chance.

At about that moment, the enormity of my exaggerations struck me, and I paled beneath Jimmy's inquisitional stare. *What did I just do to myself?* The call to the food trough for 140 hungry and judgmental men, each of whom would stare me in the face and mercilessly judge my efforts, occurred three times a day.

I said, "Let's take a step back here. What's the pay rate?"

Jimmy looked at Carl, and then Carl looked at Bill. Schläger looked at Stalin, now smoking, who stared at me. Bill took the lead. "The position is second cook. You get a raise to $5.27 an hour, plus three hours a day mandatory overtime, and night shift differential. You work seven days a week, but you get Sunday afternoon off, without pay."

Negotiations had ended; I knew a circling pack of predators when I saw one. "So, I get a raise? That'll do fine."

Jimmy said, "Go tell the cook you start tomorrow. Schläger, give him the bus keys, so he can return it to Jack. That is all. Leave the door open on your way out."

That was how I became the second cook in Port Radium. Despite the disturbing notion I dragged a bear trap with every step I took, this was a win-win for me. Genna and Morag, the only two single women within hundreds of miles, worked in the kitchen. I would be rubbing elbows every day with the famous red-headed twins. After I left the office, my hormones were on high alert and, curiously, I hoped my next two and a half months would slow down so I could enjoy a sociable pace.

I drove Beulah away from the office, to the top of the ridge, where I enjoyed the view of the vast ocean of ice on Great Bear Lake. The privilege I felt before Nature diminished my recent humiliation before men. Millions of square miles of dangerous, near-pristine, white wilderness surrounded me. I felt humbled, but significantly free and back in charge of my destiny. What had become a *stalag* was once again an opportunity on the shores of a frozen sea, the bridge across my personal River Kwai, where I would find a meaningful future. I wondered at Mankind's ego at the feet of Nature's timeless dominance. I scoffed at us all for being a self-absorbed race, abusing Nature's raw, breathtaking beauty for our own fleeting, hollow moments of profit. The limitless, solitary North inspired me.

Besides, my new job was inside and therefore out of any real danger, I thought. Denial is a treacherous weakness of the misinformed.

3. "Royt, cookin's an art then, innit Liz?"

I'm still holding on presenting the backstory ... I think you need to know how I came to be exactly where I was in the universe at the exact moment of my enlightenment, a state worthy of attaining and which might exclude my returning here as a frog or a snake ... Besides, you have to meet Les.

• • •

I watched a black dot as it meandered across the ice, half a mile from shore — a wolverine.

What the hell is it doing out there?

After it disappeared behind an ice ridge, I put the bus in gear, though I was unsure of which option I chose, and ground through most of the rest of them all the way back to the cook shack. I had time to think while I destroyed the last remnants of the clutch. *Something was odd about this management group. Schläger was a bona fide creep. And if they didn't like gay men, wasn't that Bill and Carl connection pretty much Fire Island on Pride Day?* I decided the farther I kept away from the office lunacy, the better for me.

I walked into the cook shack to inform my favorite chef that Jimmy had reincarnated me as a cook. The first person I met was Jan. "I'm the new camp cook, which means I'm your boss," I said, thinking Jan would get a laugh out of that.

"That's the stupidest thing I've heard today. You're lying." Her provocative green eyes flashed in the glint coming from the stainless steel fume hoods.

"I am not. I just got the promotion. Where's the limey? I have to inform him I start in here tomorrow."

"The *loymey* is royt be'ind you. You botherin' the girls? Do Oy 'ave to call Liz?"

"Hi, Les. I'm your new cook, and I start tomorrow. Jimmy said to come and tell you."

"Oy don't believe it. Wot's this 'ere, then? Okay, Jan darlink, you can run along now. Find Liz — she 's lookin' for you. This lad an' Oy 'ave some'in' to talk over in private."

Jan looked at me with a flirty sort of questioning look before she left us. Les and I sat across from each other at the table nearest the kitchen. "You start, you barmy, cheeky git."

"They were going to fire me today, but they found out I've worked in a restaurant in Vancouver. I told Jimmy I was a cook, so he sent me here."

"Sent you 'ere? For wot?"

"Like I said, I'm your new cook. I start tomorrow."

"Jimmy said that, did 'e? You? You start in 'ere? Tomarrow, is it then? As my second?" He paused, having run out of all possible questions and amazement, slapped both his smallish hands flat down on the table, rolled his eyes full across the ceiling in a dramatic, Shakespearean gesture, and said, "And in this 'ere restaurant ... Did you ever so much as flip an egg?"

"No, not actually. I worked myself up from cleaning trays to a carhop. It was my job to clean the food trays near the kitchen, but I saw a lot of what goes on. I was fast at cleaning trays."

"Royt, so, can you cook as well as you droyve?"

"'Bout the same, I guess. That clutch failed because of 'bad parts.' Ask Eddie." Everything about everybody gets around camp.

"Oy 'll do no such think. Well, then, at least yer honest. Oy only 'ave one piece of advoyce for you." He kept eye contact with me, tilted his head to the side, and yelled, "Liz? Cookin' 's an art then, innit?"

From the pantry, I heard a distant, female voice, "Royt you are, Les 'oney." Her affirmation came back muffled as if her mouth was full. Les seemed pleased. "If Jimmy says it's on, then welcome to moy crew. We'll see you tomarrow at foyve eye am. You start your troynin' then. If you last the week, you can fill in as my noyght shift cook. Oy've been workin' both shifts for two months now, and Oy need some 'elp."

"Five a.m.?"

"Royt. One think about the kitchen, mate, we are always first up and last to bed. Get Ernie to find you yer whoytes and be ready for breakfast tomarrow."

I spent the rest of the afternoon explaining to Michael I had to keep some sort of job, even this job, and that was why I made the choice.

"Maybe so, but only 'you hoo' boys work in the kitchen."

"Well, how do you explain the women working there? And the cook and Liz are married, too ..."

Michael again pondered my change of status, and then said,

"I know that, but still…"

He stuck to his guns at beer night and in Dave's room after that, when we brought out the guitars and had more beers. Dave toasted me with an impish smile. "About time we had a real cook in this camp."

I cursed myself again for my big mouth. To be fair, I only signed on to work my contract and go home. The rest of what I found in camp was a dark surprise. Despite what I heard eavesdropped through the office door earlier that day, I was in denial about being a company target, my job change having anything to do with Corey, or my destroying the clutch in the bus. I drank too much beer, which felt like almost enough, and stayed up with the guys far too late to be trainable when the morning alarm kicked me in the head.

But *troyn*, I did. Les introduced me to the walk-in fridge, the stock room, the freezers, and the pantry, which I dubbed "Liz's office." The door to the garbage shed off the rear of the building was broken, so we kept it shut and locked by wedging a 2x4 against the inside doorknob. The shed door was the only other kitchen entrance, besides the main door into the dining hall.

We were about to review the order sheets and menus when I interrupted Les's cheery, staccato blithering and stopped in front of a photograph tacked to the inside of the backdoor frame. Someone had taken a snapshot leaning over another idiot's shoulder. At the end of an outstretched arm, where the whites turned to flesh and bone, the dumber of the duo dangled a slab of red meat from his fingers. The man was teasing a wolverine standing in the pile of garbage bags inside the shed. The black, hairy blob bared more teeth than a pack of hyenas challenging a lioness for her kill. Two beady, red reflections from its piercing eyes confirmed the true origin of the spirit and character of the menacing predator in the photo. Wolverines are fierce enough to chase a polar bear off a dead seal.

"Did either of these two simpletons live through the encounter?" I asked Les as I tapped the photo.

"That's Petunia, our pet wolverine. She's a beaut. Oy used to feed 'er every doy. She's the one 'as got away from the trappers. She's still around 'ere somewheres. We're supposed to 'ave garbage pick-up every doy, but Errol lets the garbage poyl up, so the wolverines come in. She was always a bit grouchy, Oy must say."

We finished my orientation when we visited the two huge, metal sinks where the camp bull cook, Ernie, hand-washed every pot, pan, dish, cup, all the cutlery, and the food trays three times every day.

On my second shift, I assisted Les at breakfast. Our plate count confirmed 143 men had drifted through for breakfast. Just as I had done, each approached us incredibly hopeful and left terribly disappointed. We suffered menacing stares and threatening grunts and growls that began with the early birds before 6:00 a.m., and lasted through the bedraggled appearance of the surface crew at 7:25 a.m. Michael was one of the last to arrive.

"I want French toast."

"Good fuckin' luck," I said, serving him instead my final reserve of professional equanimity after a horrible morning feeling the brunt of the men's chagrin.

When he came through, as one of the earlybirds, Deputy Frank had threatened me. "You burned my eggs," and then he delivered a string of curses with the most intimidating scowl of which I was ever the focus. He refused my apology. Despite my efforts, I seemed to break almost every fried egg I flipped, and yes, in some cases, my timing was off and I burned some egg orders. I was already developing a growing resentment for the men, who demanded only a decent breakfast. As expected, the rest of the week was less a tasteful presentation of divine morsels and culinary delights and more a blur of pots, pans, colloquial insults, and thickly accented truisms from Les. Gems such as, "British tut'lage, innit, Liz?" were abundant.

My stress escalated as Les piled duty after duty onto my shoulders. I don't recall a single conversation with anyone other than Les and Liz during that week. Jan had the annoying habit of avoiding me altogether to sneak off for lengthy cups of coffee with Sean. The twins were a fast-fading mirage as they worked elsewhere throughout most of the day. They prepared management's daily fine dining experience in the sugar shack, where the "upper class" could enjoy a glass of wine along with their meals and sexual fantasies. I discovered both girls only performed cameo appearances in the cook shack to borrow or return cooking pans and utensils. I also discovered I was more interested in Morag than Genna.

As for my professional culinary experience, had I deigned to clean or stack trays, I am sure I would have been comfortable in my element. Now, as a second-class egg-flipper, I sublet that menial task to Ernie. From the lay side of the grill, my former trench-mates, the palate-sensitive surface crew, judged me by my product. Scores of angry faces filed past me that week and confirmed my suspicion. Even as I doled out Les' sad version of breakfast, I knew I was going to have to produce *Can-eye-djun* dishes as soon as I started working alone.

Finally, I completed my training shifts and Les set me free. Anointed in sweat and bacon fat, I graduated as Les's version of Second Cook, Port Radium, NWT. I vowed to forget everything he taught me. My first solo breakfast was the next morning, a Sunday.

However, Saturday night came along first, and it culminated only after we were roaring drunk. At midnight, we sang as loud as we could every song on *Rubber Soul*, twice. I joined Murray, Dave, Michael, Don, Eddie, mouthy Frank, myself, and four hangers-on tearing up the bunkhouse, howling until past three a.m. I had to be at work at five a.m. to start the bacon, so I packed it in early. When my head hit the pillow, I passed out immediately. I sank into a blissful, deep sleep and lingered in the sack an hour past my personal reveille.

I jumped up in a panic, still in my greasy whites from the day before. I ran through the bunkhouses, along boardwalks, up tiers of slippery steps two at a time, only to arrive breathless and miserably hung-over outside the kitchen door. A lineup of a dozen cold, angry men waited, gauging me during my approach. Deputy Frank was at the front of the line. He glared at me while I completed the pantomime of patting each of my empty pockets. *No key!* I thought about returning to my room to search for the keys, but Frank's glare put the kibosh to the idea; instead, I broke a window and clambered through. Frank was my first customer. There was no coffee, the grills were cold, I was late, and at first, I had only crackers and milk to offer the men. The deputy stood at the counter and stared at me, giving me insight in to how the captain of the Titanic felt. From the bridge of my personal disaster, I felt as if I could almost reach out and produce a serving of ice cubes from the deputy's cold stare.

I had to turn this thing around. I hypnotized myself with a silent mantra: get in gear, get going, and get the job done. Under the relentless pressure of the deputy's loud, sardonic comments, I sped through my morning routine: I cranked up the griddles and slathered them with oil, made the fastest urns of coffee I could, and then heated the pre-cooked and sliced potatoes. The grill would be difficult to clean later, but this was an emergency.

The aroma of seventy sizzling slices of pre-cut bacon and five pounds of sausages on the griddle eased the tension in the room. I ran to put out milk for the coffee and six loaves of sliced bread beside the toasters, three white and three whole-wheat loaves. I brought butter, peanut butter, and jam. Next, I pulled six flats of eggs from the fridge. I rolled the raft of sausages and flipped the bacon strips, poured my own cup of coffee, cursed myself for being hung over, and dreaded the lengthening lineup of hungry, petulant men. I cracked four eggs for Frank, broke three yokes, burned them all while taking other orders and flipping bacon and rolling sausages.

I served Frank his eggs. That transfer of burnt mush was a pivotal, personal moment, which passed when the lineup of derisive men forced him away from my serving station. Having dismissed my apology, he would have to be content serving his verbal, blunt epithet to me.

I moved on. Somehow, I fed everyone, and I mean everyone. I estimated only ten workers, the guys I'd partied with the night before, the administration, and our crack kitchen staff failed to show for breakfast. I made it through the hours and guiltily left Ernie a mountain of burned pots, dirty trays full of dirty dishes, and greasy utensils. I left the kitchen at eight a.m., moments after Les and Liz came in to begin their shift.

As usual, when she arrived, Liz organized the girls from the open pantry door. She snapped them into action like a bloated Welsh corgi running sheep across the rolling, green fields behind Cardiff. Casually sipping from a cup of coffee, Les asked, "Royt, 'ow 'd it go then?" When I saw Morag, I stopped short and ignored Les. She stared back at me with eyes that could melt lake ice or send you into a millennial deep freeze.

"Perfect," I tore off my apron. "Everyone got what they deserved. The early birds had to wait for the coffee, though."

"They'll live. Enjoy your afternoon off. You're on for nine tonoyght through to breakfast tomarrow. Expect eleven for dinner at two a.m. I'll leave burgers out for you to 'eat up for the noyt shift."

"Royght."

I dragged myself into my bunk too tired to shower and fell asleep as Michael woke. He left the room after I threatened to bludgeon him with my boots for talking to me and stinking up the air with cigarette smoke.

Sometime in the late afternoon, I woke up again and felt much better. I socialized over a gallon of coffee with John, Michael, and Dave, then grabbed a brief nap when they went to dinner and beer night. Then I went to work again.

I reviewed my list of duties: put out lunch fixin's for the night shift, cook for eleven miners at two a.m., peel one hundred pounds of potatoes and fifty pounds of carrots by hand, peel and slice thirty pounds of bacon, and rummage around to find whatever still-edible vegetable I could feed the men that night. Of course, I would finish the last three hours of my shift short-order cooking breakfast for the rest of the men in camp.

First, though, I had to find something the night shift could take to work for lunch. I searched high and low for anything to put out for them. I knew there was no exotic cuisine; I only looked for food I thought any isolated work camp should have readily available for working men. The only leftovers I found was the vat of stew. I had to do better.

I discovered a tube of baloney, French's mustard and stale, but not yet moldy, loaves of white bread. The last of the whole wheat was gone. I put the last quart can of raspberry jam out. Someone, Liz probably, had squirreled it away at the back of the top shelf in one of the cupboards in the pantry. I went through the entire fridge and freezer. I was meticulous; there was no treasure trove of food stashed there that I could find. I went into every nook, cranny, and shelf in every storage room. I did my best but failed to find the stash Morag and Jenna kept for management.

I greeted each man standing in the breach, ready for the barrage, but none of the night shift miners complained. I thought that a little sad. I watched them fold up stale baloney sandwiches in wax paper. Most of them made toast and jam. It felt wrong to send men into the dangerous underground night without first providing a feast appropriate for a warrior.

After that single hour of service, I locked the doors. The cook shack was my domain alone until two a.m. I had two hours to loll around and drink the rest of the coffee. I had come a long way since I'd met Michael and Dave on the flight just two months earlier.

My life had taken a weird turn, and there still many were more miles to travel before I became a journalist. With time to reminisce, I looked back in time, to seek the path to my future.

4. Cold. Goddamn Cold.

Okay, now for a little backstory … Did I mention it was cold? As for the rest, I'll leave it up to you to decide whether I'm a lyin' son-of-a-bitch.

• • •

My detour through Canada's nuclear history began with a job interview in Edmonton, on a bitterly cold day in early February. The merciless, icy north winds that ripped down Jasper Avenue attacked with deadly intent. Such bitter, cruel gusts are iconic Canadian winter fiends, which, for months and without end, stampede through the country like vengeful marauders bludgeoning the unfortunates in the interior of our continent. Winter's sole aim is to ravage southwards across thousands of miles of frozen sovereignty, raking us with its powerful, angry and perpetually icy claws. Even to a Canadian, the months of restricted daylight and freezing ice particles can become tedious, though we say we love it.

Canada was a different country in 1975. The decade began with a bang, literally. In November 1971, Nixon underground-tested a nuclear bomb on the island along the Aleutian Chain, Amchitka. The test was on BC's doorstep and just 577 miles from America's nearest superpower and Cold War rival, the Soviet Union. The announced yield was five megatons, the largest underground nuclear test in US history. The ground lifted twenty feet, pushed by an explosive force almost four hundred times the power of the Hiroshima bomb. Subsidence and faulting at the site created a new lake over a mile wide. The explosion registered a seismic shock of 7.0 on the Richter scale, causing rock falls and turf slides.

The same decade I applied for my summer job in Port Radium, local hockey people around Brantford, Ontario were taking notice of the "next one." A soon-to-be Canadian winter icon, Wayne Gretzky was 14 years old. The Montreal Canadians were about to take the Stanley Cup away from the Philadelphia Flyers and keep it for four more years, and in Pittsburg, the Steel Curtain defense was mauling every other NFL team. The hippy scene had wound down and dispersed to the country. The pet rock craze was about to define the scope of Western imagination, and Saigon fell. The first vaccine for chicken pox had existed for a year and Sudbury boasted the tallest smokestack in the Western Hemisphere. Nixon resigned during the 1974 world oil crisis while Canada, an oil-rich nation, suffered from "stag-flation." The spectacular abundance of cod, which for millennia had layered the ocean floor from the mouth of the St. Lawrence River to the Grand Banks, was all but gone from over-fishing. A hole in the ozone was developing over the Antarctic, and the residents of Salmon Arm, BC, would have to wait a few years before Pierre Elliot Trudeau fingered them from his luxury railroad car. A horrible plague, called "disco," threatened to destroy the musical creativity in the world, and a winter storm would take the SS Edmund Fitzgerald to the bottom of Lake Superior with all hands lost. In 1979, the US House Select Committee on Assassinations would finally state that the Kennedy assassination was "probably" a conspiracy.

My issue was more immediate. I stepped off the bus into a bitter wind that mercilessly grated across my exposed skin, and I needed to be out of that penetrating blast. At -23F, I struggled to believe it was noon in the Alberta capital. I was born and raised on the west coast of BC, so I was on a steep learning curve discovering the nuances of extreme wind chill. Only the week before, I had returned to BC flat broke from months on the Costa del Sol and now wanted to kick myself hard for being in this situation.

I still had an hour to kill before my interview with Echo Bay Mines, who needed surface laborers to work in the "north." Turned away from the wind, I drove my already numbed fingers deep into both front pockets of my Levi's, just as I had ten minutes before, and produced the same seventy-eight cents. I could purchase, with this borrowed sum, bus fare back to where I was crashing and a pack of gum. I had no choice but to duck back into the Hudson Bay store, linger inside fake shopping, and avoid the store dicks.

How much more north *is there in Canada, anyway?*

I had hitched to Edmonton from the west coast to stay with a friend who worked at the university, in the Geology department. Finding a logging job in BC in the spring was a sure thing, but spring was months off yet. Over the past months, travelling southern Europe had been fun, but I had run out of money in Spain and returned to Canada two months early. Until I landed this job interview, I thought I'd made the wrong call coming to Edmonton to find work in the dead of winter. The night before, the TV weatherman called this deep freeze a "Siberian High." I called it criminal, watching frozen crystals dance in the amber streetlight cones. The dreary, foggy world seemed to hang as lifeless as the icy, sagging branches of the trees thick with frozen snow.

A few days earlier, my friend had left the Edmonton Journal by the coffee pot before he'd left for work. Already folded to the Help Wanted pages, I read the circled ad: "Hiring: surface labour only. Apply at Echo Bay Mines. Call for an interview."

A woman with a husky, sultry voice answered when I dialed the number. "Good morning, Echo Bay Mines."

"Hi. I'm responding to your ad in the paper for laborers?"

"It's surface labour only. There is no chance to work indoors or underground and our silver mine is at the Arctic Circle. Do you still want an interview?"

"If the job is still available, I sure do."

"Honey," she said, "this job is always available. Be here Monday, at 1:00 p.m. and Mr. Zigarlitz will interview you. What's your name, sugar, so I can book your appointment?"

And that was it. I had an interview with Mr. Cigar Lips, after which it sounded like I would fly even farther north. That night, I told my friend I guessed the receptionist must be Mrs. Potato Head as we studied the map of Great Bear Lake he brought home from work. Port Radium was on LaBine Bay, diagonally across the lake from the only other place name on the map, De☐line or Fort Franklin.

He said, "You're not applying for 'coffee and rum under a blanket at a football game' north, but more like 'Franklin's search for the Northwest Passage, kill, then eat your sled dogs and hope you freeze to death before you starve to death' north. You're going way, way up there."

I knew the temperature could and did drop to -70F at the Arctic Circle. "Pleasant thoughts," I said. "Thank you for sharing that insight."

Undermining his concern, he handed me a rye and water, and said, "Your blood needs thickening up."

Monday morning, I committed a major mistake: for the interview, I wore a light green T-shirt that announced across my chest, "Down with 3 Mile Island" in white, Tolkien-esque rune letters across a giant, dark-green marijuana frond. Stupidly, I challenged winter's worst wearing only my Levis, my worn leather tennis shoes, and my Buffalo wool Cowichan sweater. As a future teammate of the silver mine's surface crew, I imagined an occasional dash out into the cold, then a hasty retreat to a heated staff room and a hot mug-up. There, I fantasized, we would pass the time in warm camaraderie, forging new friendships while roughing it on the endless, frozen tundra.

On serious consideration, I doubted there would be actual outside work in the man-killing weather at the Arctic Circle. *Are these owners that heartless?* I expected they would understand the mining would just have to slow down in times of seriously inclement weather. My plan was simple: get off the streets, eat like a king for a while, and save up a pile of cash. Then I would return to the coast, fling a small portion of my earnings around to treat my friends to a fun night, and begin taking journalism courses in September.

Half an hour later, it was time to make the mad dash to the interview. The instant I left the Hudson Bay store, my jeans froze around my legs. I pushed on; tears caused by the cruel wind froze on my face. Around the first corner, a wind from the rear pushed me four long blocks to the interview address. Once there, I was horrified to learn I had arrived at "104th Street" as opposed to "104th Avenue." I was going to be late. I had to retrace my steps eight blocks and then some. My gaffe meant I had to run into the wind.

Convinced I already suffered from frostbite, any bravado I had about surviving the cold with style soon dissolved. I was deep in it now and arriving at my destination meant nothing less than putting out a Herculean effort. My vision was bleary from squinting. My nose burned when I inhaled. If I opened my mouth to breathe, my teeth hurt. My cheeks stung alarmingly. Though I had tucked my ears under my black toque, the lobes burned from the cold. My hands and fingers ached and the wind sliced through my clothes. I still had seven more possibly lethal blocks to navigate. Somewhere, during my epic journey, my eyesight diminished to cloudy images, objects appeared indistinct, and I almost stepped in front of a twenty-ton ball of blue cotton batten that morphed into a honking city bus. The driver was kind enough to avoid plowing into me as he sped through the crosswalk six inches in front of my beet-red nose.

When I finally fell through the revolving door at the correct address, I almost took a knee on top of the wide mosaic of a polar bear adorning the vestibule floor. I teetered there, bent over, and tried to recover, amazed at my miraculous self-rescue. Scant minutes more, I was sure, and instead of mundane elevator music piped into the lobby, a choir of angels would have sung for me.

I stood straight, and as my eyes responded to the heavenly warmth, I saw the foyer was crowded. I could not allow my potential employer to see me in this state; I had to stiffen up a bit. I approached the tenant listings board and read the small, white letters directing me to the Echo Bay Mine offices on the third floor. *Damn! No public bathroom.* There was no elevator service, either, but that suited me; running the stairs would give me the chance to thaw out.

When I pushed open the door, I was unprepared for the blonde beauty coming into focus at the end of my expanding tunnel vision. She turned from the filing cabinet to greet me. Her smile was in bright contrast to the brown wallboard and bland furnishings of the Echo Bay offices. She wore the standard business attire of a sensible top and skirt, nylons, low heels and a sweater. However, I would have none of this, and imagined her in a low-cut, red evening dress, black belt, and black choker necklace, a single pearl dangling on her milk-white neck. The office was pungent with a mix of stale cigarette smoke and her perfume. Perhaps it was the influence of my recent European vacation or my near-brush with death that caused me to drift away to images of Venetian nights of seduction on a terrace overlooking a piazza. In the background of my fantasy, an obese Italian couple performed a dramatic aria, while something about the receptionist made me think of bondage, furry handcuffs, and "feather boa" teasing. Though I had never been to Venice and was as ignorant of opera as I was of unorthodox sexual appetites, I remained distracted by my fantasy of hot nights and restrained sex.

Never taking her eyes off me, the receptionist cleared her throat and adjusted her black-frame glasses. Still quite numb and unable to muster up any moxie to snap out of it, I stared at her breasts. "Jesus fartin' pepperoni," I said. "That's cold out there." My élan had spluttered into full stall.

Like so many ice crystals, my words hung frozen in the air for several awkward seconds. Enthralled, I watched her take her chair behind the reception desk, lift her hand, point at her cleavage with her index finger, then lift my eyes until I gazed into her own. She was a bull terrier sizing up a rat. "Well, Mr. Cool," she said. "You sure aren't living up to your name. You're ready for the interview then?"

I nodded mutely, wondering if I had stumbled around an existential corner and into a different reality.

"All righty, I'll see if Mr. Zigarlitz is ready for you." She reared back and bellowed like an elephant startled by a tigress, "JT, are you ready for the new kid yet?"

From the inner office, behind an imitation mahogany door, I heard a deep male voice boom, "He's bloody late, but send him in anyway."

Rasping her nails, and with the coy hint of a tease playing on the whimsical tones of a coquettish flirt, she said, "You may go in now. Good luck. A word of advice: don't mention the war."

5. "Don't Mention the War."

Still withdrawing from my hypothermic delirium, I floated across the floor of bland, worn linoleum, wondering, War? What war?

Inside Mr. Cigar Lips' door, my drifting reality crash-landed. An obese man occupied the far side of the mahogany plateau of his desk. His posture approximated that of a linebacker on the line of scrimmage. Already under siege by his grey years, he waited, propped up by his chair and both hands, his stout fingers spread wide on the desk. He leaned forward, squaring me off, as if we were on the Plains of Abraham, he Wolfe, and I Montcalm. I gathered my defenses for either an interview or a confrontation.

JT, as I later knew to call him, sucked noisily on the stubby remnants of an extinguished stogy. He was appraising me. His salt and pepper crew cut was mostly devoid of pepper; the scrub looked like a bath brush atop his pugnacious, fleshy face, held in place by a jelly mold of three tiers of neck rolls reminiscent of a bull elephant's leg. His sagging countenance spoke volumes of the tragedy of a life of alcohol and tobacco abuse. A radish-red hue along the full length of his bulbous nose suggested clogged arteries complicated by liver disease. His bulging, jaundiced eyes meandered aimlessly in deep, wrinkled sockets until they ceased their orbits and focused on me.

Apparently, his hearing was still acute but my sensibilities were not. I had accidentally repeated out loud the receptionist's last words.

JT greeted me with a booming voice that seemed to come from a labyrinth leading to Hell itself, "War? What's a pissant like you know about war?"

I flinched. Confirming my insignificance, I responded like a three-time felon in front of a hanging judge. "War? No, I'm here for the job."

He yelled back at me, "Job?"

JT animatedly beat his chest like a challenged gorilla, doing a reasonable job of expressing his corporate prowess. He never took his eyes off me. He hollered to the receptionist. "Mary-Ellen, who is this little shit? And where is my damn lighter?" Evidently, my entrance had knocked JT's stylus off the single track he was capable of maintaining.

Mary-Ellen returned his favor and yelled back, "Your lighter is where it always is, on your desk beside your pen set. So is his application." I could now guess what it must have been like in the trenches at Vimy Ridge, when cannons fired across the heads of the men in the front lines. "That's Mr. Cool," the receptionist volleyed again. "He wants a surface crew job. The job in the paper? For the mine at Port Radium?" I heard her mutter, "You deaf old goat. It's your own damn mine."

"Why the Christ didn't you say so in the first place?"

After JT fired back his deafening rejoinder, I pointed to his lighter. JT waved his giant paw in the air to dismiss the helpful intentions of my index finger. He grabbed the lighter with a swift violence, but he kept his accusing eyes on me. When he lit the end of the cigar butt, he singed part of the growth out of his left nostril and a substantial portion of his left eyebrow in the process. His expression never changed, though the cigar end glowed an alarming shade of red beneath his nose.

"One day I will fire that bitch."

Almost simultaneously, I heard *that bitch* mutter back, "I have to quit you, you old bastard."

Distracted from my resumé on his desk, JT struggled to regain focus. He took it in hand, but the direction of his thought, it seemed to me, wandered off from my bulleted, if short, list of qualifications. His smokestack was on full burn. He initiated my interview with a menacing growl, enquiring of me, "What makes you think I'd hire you, anyway?"

I considered telling him my qualifications were that I had already worked for several first class assholes in my day, and had already walked away from many more that paled against him in comparison. However, my growling belly and financial destitution kept me on point. I said, "Because I'm willing to give 'er a go?"

"Well," he considered, "that's something. Nowadays, most of you young pups want a free ride."

JT relaxed a little after venting his contempt for my generation. He appeared to mellow behind the clouds of cigar and nose hair smoke. He leaned back in his president's chair, looking me up and down with judgmental eyes. Though his eyes were set uncommonly close together, I thought I caught a fleeting benevolence in the arch of his eyebrows. I wondered if I might have prematurely misjudged the man.

I squirmed in front of him and nodded toward the interview chair. JT shook his head, grumbled something inconclusive, and re-furrowed his brow. The old badger was going to make me stand in his presence.

"What makes you think you can come into my office asking about the war?" His eyes lifted to a large photograph of a camouflaged B-52 on the wall behind him and mine followed his. "That's where I got my lighter, from the men in the 8th. It means a lot to me."

I wanted to help the old boy out a little, so I corrected him. "No, I came here for..."

"The war," he boomed, flying off topic on his own azimuth. "Since you're asking, I revered Lemay. We all did."

JT nodded to a framed black and white photograph hanging on another wall; it captured a dullard in an American Air Force uniform glowering over a map table. An impressive amount of braiding and medals plastered his chest. In order to earn himself so many accolades, the general campaigned with resolve and vigor, sent many to the slaughter, and welcomed far fewer of them back home. The photograph captured a smallish figurine of the Crucifixion that hung on the wall behind the General.

I recognized Ol' Iron Pants, Curtis E. Lemay: the ridiculous, unlit cigar anchored decisively in his mouth; his sullen, whiskey-bloated face; the mean eyes. He appeared to be planning the next carpet-bombing raid in front of the implicated Jesus, whose Sunday morning absolution, at least in the General's world, released him of all responsibility. Lemay was renowned for developing one single military concept: for decades, he promoted his meager understanding of military tactics in resolving global conflict by carpet-bombing whole civilian populations into subservience. JT was a mirror image of the general.

"Lemay blew the Krauts back to Hell," said JT. "He was the 8th Air Force, men did their duty back then."

From the other side of the door, I heard, "Here we go ... I warned you."

JT was adrift in reassuring memories of millions of tons of phosphorus incendiaries raining down on hundreds of thousands of German and Japanese women and children. Although results suggested otherwise, occasional and unsubstantiated reports in the red, white, and blue press, suggested Lemay's raids occasionally also pulverized military objectives. JT sighed, "Those were the good times."

I tried to advantage JT's nostalgia for mass murder to return to my job interview. I launched into a fake, "good old boy, back slapping, rib sucking, Southern Cross" tirade. "Yeah, those Nazis and their families sure had it coming, didn't they, JT?" I threw in the familiar use of his initials to soften up the demented old war wound. I've had better ideas.

He exploded. "I hate being called *JT*. To you, I am Mr. Zigarlitz or 'Sir.' Is that understood?"

I was sure the senile old battle cruiser wanted to add recruit to my censure. I faltered, straightened, and nodded. I even considered saluting, but held off because the only uniform I had ever worn was server's garb in a restaurant in Vancouver. He rolled the last of the smokestack around his lips while he blustered. I watched a ball of grey cigar ash avalanche down his suit coat, leaving a grey trail in its wake.

"What does that mean, 'Down With 3 Mile Island'? Nuclear power will save this earth. That damn communist Churchill gave the A-rabs the oil, but we have the nukes, you dumb little shit. You want some guy named Mohamed to tell you how to live?"

Satisfied that my wagging head meant "No," and that he had communicated his religion and politics to me, he ranted on, "Hitler wasn't so bad. But he was on the wrong side. That man in the picture on the wall was a war criminal, too, but we won, so we made him a hero, and he built military tradition. Your type could learn a thing or two from him. He had the guts to design and order hundreds of missions, and we might have changed the war in Europe if the bleeding hearts in the White House hadn't gone yellow and listened to the commie press. But, oh no, Roosevelt let the Brits put a stop to it. And I'm telling you now, that same attitude is going to hurt us in Vietnam."

• • •

Because of a social studies essay I'd researched in high school, I could fault JT on three counts: by 1945, the OSS already had control of much of the American press; many of the powerful players in the

Alfred Cool

CIA were re-purposed, high-ranking Nazi SS or scientists, promoting from inside the US military, like army ants at a picnic, their paranoid Fascist hatred for Russia and their love affair with propaganda and war; and the US dropped twice the tonnage of bombs on Indochina and North Vietnam than during the entire Second World War in Europe and Asia combined. And still the little men and women in sandals, black shirts, and funny hats kept fighting for their homeland.

War is a time of sacrifice and gross inefficiencies. Therefore, the US Air Force dispatched Lemay overseas two years after the brave British, Polish, and Canadian aviators had already won the Battle of Britain. Stationed well behind the front lines, Lemay's single exposure to gunfire conflicted with military policy that restricted senior military staff leading their men at the front and dying in battle. Lemay never repeated that mistake. Unfortunately, because he had participated once and seen enemy fire, Lemay promoted first strike tactics for the rest of his life. After that one raid, Lemay ordered others to fly his missions of attrition, an ill-conceived strategy that had proved futile during World War I. The tactic preceded Napoleon and exposed the incompetence of so many generals who sacrificed so many fathers, sons, and brothers. Wars generated by politicians, monarchs, and corporations fought by millions of brave, if misguided conscripts, never resulted in a cessation of aggressive politics, but only in unending, tragic slaughter on bloody battlefields. The single outcome of the tactic, other than an accrual of profit to one side and the transfer of debt to the other, was the development of genocide as a tactic of modern warfare, its effectiveness measured in the carnage always endured by civilians.

Smoking cigars and swilling whiskey, Lemay was a relentless and ferocious aggressor from behind his desk. Undaunted by potential casualties, fearless and on the attack, he boldly advanced plastic miniature airplane toys across a large table-map of Europe. Time after time, the belligerent general and his staff ordered thousands of naive youth under his command into the exploding ack-ack rounds and deadly fire of the remaining Luftwaffe fighters that blew 25,000 Allied airmen out of the skies. Fate of war, blind luck, and Lemay's acceptance of promotions enabled the US press, in need of war heroes to sell War Bonds, to describe Lemay's particular lunacy as heroic.

Old Iron Pants no doubt caught wind of an exclusive,

flagship military project, code-named Manhattan. It was right up his carpet-bombing alley. Unbloodied, loftily detached, and insulated from the horror of fiery genocide, Lemay politicked valiantly for the US to deploy more nuclear weapons. Historical records prove the Japanese tried to capitulate during Stalin's grab of Manchuria, started months before Hiroshima and Nagasaki were bombed. History proves Truman went "Old Testament," and ordered the bombs dropped before any surrender was accepted, having invested so much money and presidential credibility in the Manhattan Project. Besides, his war counsel wanted to mete out punishment as the terrible revenge for the world to witness.

Lemay was disappointed and dissatisfied that the US had deployed just the two nuclear bombs on human populations. Even as the mushroom clouds formed, and with an eye on Moscow, Lemay recommended to President Truman that the US proceed with a Japanese solution, specifically, "killing a nation" with more nukes. Lemay offered to turn all of Japan into radioactive rubble, make the country the Pompey of Asia, buried beneath thousands of years of radioactivity. Truman denied Lemay that opportunity, but promoted him to Commander of the Strategic Air Command (SAC), where he festered through the Cold War and two presidencies, then mushroomed up again as one of the Chiefs of Staff for John Kennedy. Common sense, humanity, and hope for the future reigned during JFK's shortened presidency, exposing Lemay as a dangerous, embarrassing, nuclear war fanatic.

Before he hung up his Cold War guns, Lemay joined the flood of war merchants and military ghouls promoting the obliteration of America's next targets: Russia, Indochina, China, and even Cuba. It is a substantial telling point that Lemay and his crones blustered and slung influence around the White House during the Cuban Missile crises of 1962. Lemay lasted through the presidency of Johnson, and was on the GOP ticket with KKK candidate George Wallace against Nixon in 1968. From behind his stateside desk, Ol' Iron Pants was fighting the Cold War with allies; he was the new Stuka for the entrenched military-industrial complex, already the new juggernaut with which the world would have to reconcile. But the Wallace-Lemay ticket smeared ugly, stinking handfuls of entrenched, deep-south racism in the faces of too many federal voters. When an assassin shot Wallace, the single bullet that put him in a wheelchair for the rest of his life also capped the carpet bomber's aspirations for a political career.

The lengthy and vast body of decimation produced by this worker-bee warrior and his military cabal produced a grotesque bastardization of Roosevelt's Four Freedoms intentions. In pursuit of freedom, the US military has since tried to save the world, in WWII, in Korea, through their own war on drugs, throughout the Cold War, in Laos, Vietnam, Beirut, Panama, Libya, Afghanistan, and several times each through Iraq and Iran, into Syria, Central Africa, Palestine, and Israel. Unfortunately, but by design, US and Russian nuclear armament proliferated through the decades, as has the worst version of "lemonade from lemons" spin-off – the nuclear power industry. Since 1945, the CIA and US politicians proved themselves efficient at starting wars, but inept at winning or ending them. The one exception is the US military triumph over the tiny Caribbean island of Granada, whose national bird is a critically endangered dove.

• • •

JT rattled on, "Soon as we whupped 'em over there, we went to Japan, carpet-bombed 'em, then dropped the A-bombs. That finished the Japs. We ended that war in victory, too."

To me, honoring Curtis E. Lemay, a mass murderer and a "war criminal" by his own admission, was akin to giving Stalin a merit badge for his gulags. My stomach grumbled again, reminding me of my own mission. JT hesitated, furrowed his brow again, and then wiped his red, sweaty forehead with a blue polka-dot handkerchief. His face had reddened, a possible indication of a pending stroke.

"I would have enlisted with the Brits when the Yanks sent Lemay to England. That was late in '42. If they had left him in Europe past August '43, he might have ended the war sooner." He looked up at me as if his words answered one of my unarticulated questions. "Say, why aren't you fighting in Vietnam? You're the perfect age. Stiffen you up. Do you good."

"That's a US economic war for oil. I'm Canadian. Says so right there on my job application."

He was bellowing again, "You pump red blood, don't you? What are you, a coward? Freedom is freedom, son, and you better get used to it. Are you a commie? I won't have any pinkos in this company."

From the reception area, Mary-Ellen screamed her guts out. "JT, your next interview is here."

"No sir," I said, scrambling to recover. "I'm here to work hard for you as a red-blooded, whiskey-drinking member of your crew."

I had figured out that much during this interview: I had no chance at the job if I didn't try to appease this semi-calcified throwback by suppressing my politics, which tended to making love, not war. I had no investment in what I had just said to JT, beyond my hope of finding work so I could return to school. I thought it enough I was willing to go.

"That's what I like to hear." Bingo! "You leave tomorrow. Four months in; no breaks. We loan you your airfare, but if you quit or are fired, the cost of the flights comes out of your pay." Ol' JT could sure zero-in if his money was involved.

"You ain't a queer, are you?" Adamant, I shook my head. "We don't need any of that kind up there …"

Tough financial terms, but empty pockets are a heavier burden. "Got it, JT."

My gaff was monumental. JT spat the dead stub of his cigar onto his desk. He jumped up. An alarming, angry vein throbbed on his forehead. "I told you I hate that! — What are you, some sort of BC smartass troublemaker? Is that your game? Because if it is, I'll throw you out of here myself, and I don't mean through the door."

I looked at the window and his meaning was clear. JT's rage was palpable, but before he could hit the after-burners, the receptionist appeared at the door. "JT!" He fumed at her, which diverted his wrath from me. "I already have his flight booked and the paperwork finished. Let's give him a chance, okay? What do you say, sugar lips?"

His gaze still riveted on me, JT said, "I'm watching you, BC boy. You little mother licker, I'm watching you." As an afterthought, he chastised Mary-Ellen. "And don't you call me that."

JT slumped into his chair, scowling and his eyes bulging. He plugged a new cigar in his mouth and patted his chest pockets again, looking for his lost lighter. I caught Mary-Ellen's sideways glance and backed out of the office. Once outside the door, I sidestepped out of JT's line of sight. Truly, in a teapot, was there ever thrown a more self-absorbed hissy fit than that display by a tempestuous egotist?

The next applicant sat on the reception area couch. He was lanky; he had a jail tan, and shoulder-length, stringy brown hair. He looked hard and dour. The yellow lettering embroidered on the front of his greasy, black baseball cap said *CAT*. For years, the Caterpillar Company produced these hats to give to their employees. The brand signified job stability and quality industrial machinery. I had the feeling this man was of another breed. Under the brim, he had thick eyebrows, which shadowed his eyes. He looked up at me, smiled, and asked, "'How was it?" His accent was thick, which made deciphering his words more difficult because he also spoke with a quiet tone. When he smiled, his face brightened up to genuine friendliness.

"I softened him up. JT's mellow now. He was a bit gruff at first. Be sure to ask him about the war; he likes talking about it." Far as I knew, the Frenchman was my competition and I needed the job.

The receptionist appeared at JT's doorway, "Michael? Mr. Zigarlitz is ready for you now."

"That's pronounced Me-shell," he said.

From inside the office I heard JT holler, "Send that frog in here. Jesus H. Christ, Mary-Ellen, are you finding these guys in prisons? Who's this, Charles-fucking-Manson? If you want a job, get your ass in here and let me look at you. Stand up! did I ask you to sit down? What makes you think I'd hire street trash like you, anyway?"

The receptionist closed the door on *Me-shell's* interview. She said, "JT's in a bit of a mood today. We received the estimate to fix the 'cat' that went through the ice at the mine last month ...'"

"I didn't find him so bad."

She looked up at me with raised eyebrows. "… because he's a cream puff compared to his son and the mine manager. They're quite a bit more conservative. Now, you'll be flying from the downtown airport, leaving at 6:00 a.m. tomorrow. Okay?"

"Perfect. I don't have any winter clothes besides these." Mary-Ellen appraised my west coast garb. "Can I outfit in camp?"

"Oh sure. They have everything you will need. Sign these waivers and this agreement to forfeit your airfare regardless of the reason for job termination before reaching the four-month maturity of your contract…"

Her lapse into well-rehearsed legalese halted my involuntary re-visit to my 'balcony in Venice' fantasy. "Contract? I'm signing a contract?"

"Oh, didn't JT mention that? Yes, we have these simple formalities to finish with here." She winked at me. "It is a four-month contract." She twitched her nose and pursed her lips. "If you quit or are fired before the term expires," she adjusted her breasts with the subtle twitch of an upper arm, causing the mounds beneath her sweater to roll, "we recover the airfare and your room and board from your final cheque." I didn't process a thing she said. When she passed me a pen, she grazed her fingers across my hand ever so slightly. I signed.

"Oh, yeah, Mr. Cigar Lips said something like that. How much is that airfare, then, so I can budget this out?" I returned the pen to her and was disappointed there was no further contact.

"It's pronounced 'Zuh-gar-litz' and we're sensitive to that. It is a $2,500 return ticket."

I failed to absorb her distinction in pronunciation. Instead, my libido crashed into a wreck at the base of my financial cliff. "What? Where am I flying? I can fly from Vancouver to Heathrow return in First Class for $600."

"You're not going to Mexico though, are you?"

Under the spell of her intoxicating perfume and bewitching eyes, I swirled again in momentary confusion, lost in her adorable ignorance of geography.

"You're going to Port Radium in the Northwest Territories. Twenty-six miles south of the Arctic Circle. It's 1200 miles due north of Edmonton. And you're flying on our plane, so we set the fares. Most employees work out the contract anyway, so who cares how much we charge? That's a picture of the camp on the wall."

I tore my eyes away from her and looked at the color photograph. It depicted a helter-skelter collection of broken-down and dilapidated sheds strung along the snowy shore of an impressive, flat expanse. Several larger, multi-storey bunkhouses and other buildings populated a nearby ridge. Boardwalks and stairways connected the buildings scattered across the ridge; an abandoned-looking, multi-storey bunkhouse and a huge building with a tall smokestack were also jammed onto the flat at the foot of the ridge. Three men in heavy Arctic outerwear stood knee-deep in snow in front of one rectangular shoebox-like building, behind which the snow-covered ridge blended into the shores of a sea of white. A black roadway dissected the flat at the base of the ridge behind the men. A complete waste of color film, the caption read, "JT and Jimmy, Port Radium, November 1968." The other man was a dark-skinned, smiling native. His eyes were deep-set and phalanxed by an array of criss-crossed wrinkles, the wind and sunburned face of the Northern experience.

I frowned at the commercial signature, the menagerie of waste. The camp was rusting and rotting in the midst of industrial mining flotsam. The site, surely once unspoiled and mysterious, except to local hunters and gatherers, had metastasized a tumor on the shore of the bay. Behind the camp, unending, frozen folds of pre-Cambrian bitumen dwarfed the enterprise, and the Canadian barrens spread out for what could be Nature's definition of infinity, without so much as a single road or another building in sight.

"What's all this white here," I asked, "and this huge yellow patch here?"

"That's Great Bear Lake. Fantastic trout fishing in the summer … That's our silver mine, but that picture is from years ago; things have changed a lot since then, we have a curling rink now. You'll find out when you get up there; that yellow is the tailing pond. Here's your ticket."

Pond hardly fit the description of the vast area of diarrhea-colored sludge that dominated a quarter of the photograph. However, her blonde curls overwhelmed me again as she hustled me out the door. So fast did she eschew me into the hallway that I had less than seconds to reconsider spending the next four months in the shit-hole depicted in the photograph. I was no senator's son, but neither did I want to step decades backward in time to 1940s' mining. And I swear, when I caught her winking at me, my pheromone reaction skyrocketed again.

I vaguely pondered the cost of furry handcuffs, thinking my interview had gone well enough. A terrible din emanated from JT's office; Cigar Lips was givin' it to Me-shell. But Mary-Ellen's wink and flirty smile had actually made me believe she was interested in me. I enjoyed this thought until I stepped again into the freezing Edmonton wind and swore aloud when the gritty, frigid gust tore into me. Straight from the desolate bowels of Port Radium, just fourteen miles south of the Arctic Circle, the wind cut deep enough to make me wonder what I had just done to myself.

While I waited for the bus, I fought a losing battle to retain anything like full acuity. I joined others hiding from the torturous wind behind the poorly sheltered bus stop. I knew this was a snapshot of my immediate future. Just five minutes later, my bus arrived, but I was already frozen. When I flopped down onto the seat in the warm interior, I curled into a quasi-fetal position and tried to be brave. Before I lapsed into a comfortable, drowsy daydream, I overheard two elderly women talking behind me. Bundled up like babushkas in Minsk, they discussed the approaching cold front and blizzard.

One granny said, "This weather is supposed to stay with us for the rest of the week."

The other granny replied, "It might finally turn cold."

With more than a little dread, I thought, *I'm going to be on Great Bear Lake tomorrow ...*

For the rest of the bus ride, I drifted into a near-hypothermic, sexual fantasy: lusty Mary-Ellen and I snuggle, safe from the howling blizzard outside; her clothing already dissolved in the warm confines of the deserted mechanic's shop; she seduces me in front of the red, glowing coals of the 45-gallon drum stove; our champagne is cooling on ice I hacked out of the lake; we roll on a thick, warm bed of luxurious polar bear rugs for prolonged moments, unbound by furry handcuffs.

Other than the cold, the blizzard, and the ice, I knew in my heart the fulfillment of my fantasy was in grave doubt, but still, I held hope our connection would prevail.

6. The Flight

In 1975, the Edmonton skyline boasted a dozen high-rise buildings taller than six floors. Edmonton had two airports: the International airport, the newer of the two, opened outside the city limits in 1960. The conveniently-located City Centre airport, had a shorter airstrip, few warehouses, and no coffee shop.

At five thirty a.m. the next morning and six weeks before I knew about radioactive dust particles and radon, Jimmy, doors opening mysteriously while the plane was in the air, and British-style culinary arts that would put a hyena on the run, I borrowed ten dollars from my friend. "Anything," he said, "to get you out of the house." During the drive to the airport, the cab driver tried a joke. "It's so cold; I had to kick a hole in the air to get outside." I tipped him anyway.

I sipped Sanka from a Styrofoam cup and evaluated the pros and cons of my situation. My surroundings put me in a skeptical mood, but at least I had a job.

The waiting room was a drafty, plywood shed tacked onto a warehouse. The shed creaked under the strain of the blustery airfield wind. Swaying lights hung from electrical cords, throwing dim shadows across unpainted clapboard walls, creating the impression we were on a boat in tossing seas. The airtight wood stove provided only marginal heat. Personally, I was thankful for any sort of shelter from the wind and cold. I crossed the small waiting room and took a chair against the opposite wall. Michael had arrived before me. He snapped his head around and stared at me when I walked in the door. I think I saw a little disappointment in his dark, sunken eyes. He looked like he had spent the night the same way as me, self-medicating and dreading the next four months. I watched the string-bean Frenchman who twitched constantly. He watched the door and chain-smoked pungent Gitane cigarettes. Each time the door squealed open on its rusty hinges he snapped to and then sank lower again as if weighed down with a heavy burden of disappointment.

Far from faulting him, I was doing the same thing. Perhaps yesterday my little coquette, Mary-Ellen, radiated some residual vibe to "Me-shell." I measured him and waited, a Lancelot poised to pounce to the rescue of his Guinevere, the moment she brought to

52

that miserable shanty her dazzling, warm smile. *Jesus Christ! Did she hustle him too?*

Our small gathering included the most irritating Gollum-like character, who attended to loading and prepping the airplane. He was a withered snag of a wiry, wind-burnt, bespectacled, older man, who bubbled with energy, frothy comments, and affable cheer. I begrudged him all that. The man floated within his green, over-sized goose-down coat, snow pants, insulated boots and fur-fringed hood, dispensing chirpy finality to each chore or sentence by clapping his over-size mitts together. If he took those mitts and disappeared inside his billowing down parka and winter pants until our plane departed, I, for one, could have survive the pre-flight without him. I supposed Handy Andy knew everything about how to load the cargo on the plane, what was missing, what was not, how much fuel was in each tank, and where each wrench, nut, and bolt fit. But his real value to the company had to be his willingness to run outside at this hour and in this extreme cold.

The bleary-eyed woman who sat at the receptionist's desk was a stark contrast to Andy; she chain-smoked cigarettes at her station, a stale woman with Bassett Hound eyes, she looked bored to tears with her job. I thought she might benefit from a blood transfusion and a shot of adrenalin. She slouched behind stacks of disarrayed papers and a schmozzle of invoice chaos. Singularly unimpressed with us, she avoided eye contact as if we were bound for contagion quarantine. She too wore a puffy, pea-green, down-filled parka, which protected her against the frigid blasts of Arctic-infused gales that escorted Andy the many times he opened the door to or from the hangar.

The two pilots were constantly in and out of the office as well, engaged in nitpicking over the flight manifest like a dowager and a concubine arguing over a will. They marched through the waiting room with fake smiles and out-of-context aloofness, as impressive as security guards in a government liquor store. They conferred between themselves over their clipboards and refilled their coffee cups with instant coffee and powdered milk. When the captain complained about the sour coffee to the chain-smoking office clerk, she said, "So go find better." Confused over how to respond to her disdain, the captain discharged his frustration in the form of a short but huffy rebuke directed at our chipper Mr. Crank-It-Up. At the captain's petulant outburst, we returned deafening and awkward silent stares in defense of our Handy Andy, which forced both pilots out of the waiting room. Another gale ripped through when they left, and I cursed Andy.

We were experiencing a departure delay. From comments the pilots passed, I gathered Step 'n' Fetch It should have put blanket cowls on the engines the previous night. The co-pilot complained to the office clerk, who certainly was unimpressed, "These cold nights always screw up our flight plan."

I had ample time to scan the group that I would crew with for the next four months. Another of us fools ready to board this ship was a dark, tightly wound coil of a man. He was perhaps two inches shy of six feet, a fighter who might weigh in as a middleweight. His witch-nose hooked downward precipitously between high cheekbones and sunken, roving eyes. He impressed me as moody and dangerous. He sat by himself, smoking, a Diamond Back rattlesnake of a man in a state of pre-explosion. He appeared to be keenly observant, though he did avoid eye contact with anyone from behind his nicotine-stained fingers cupped near his mouth. This lone wolf could be anything from a family man to a cold-blooded killer. He made Michael look like a sunshine lollipop man, and whoever Michael was he was certainly not that.

A forklift motor revved before it left the garage. When it reappeared, it blew in with it a toxic, bitter cloud of exhaust. The latest infusion of carbon monoxide brought with it another of the pilots' cameo appearances. The senior of the two explained Andy was taking heated engine oil out to the plane. The waiting room dropped twenty uncomfortable degrees in temperature while the warehouse door remained open. The standing room adjacent to the airtight stove proved a popular place to wait.

A young man and woman completed the last of our intrepid Argonaut manifest. They had set up shop on the low wooden bench nearest the stove. Puffed up in their winter coats, insulated coveralls, and snow boots, their faces looked like a couple of cashews in puffs of cotton batting. They were prepared and might have known something about the future I did not, but I knew something about her he did not; she was dumping him. They didn't speak or touch each other; their eye contact was furtive, and she sat with her body turned slightly away from him. She was pleasant enough looking, a

Canadian lass, likely of Scottish descent. Reddish-blonde hair swirled about her turned-down hood and a smattering of freckles graced her fair skin. She had large, blue eyes and a small, worried mouth. He was a big-puppy-dog-boy version of a man with a kind smile, clear brown eyes, sandy hair, and piano-player hands. I guessed he'd made the high school football team, but only as the second-string quarterback. Neither of them smoked. He doted on her, but she rolled his attentions away with a cold shoulder. They were engaged in a tragic ritual, an emotional man drifting away in a sea of rejection insisting bravely the once-familiar woman in her lonely lifeboat preserve herself. It looked to me like she was uncomfortable in his company. Boarding a flight to the Arctic seemed a curious time and place to sort out a failing relationship.

Still two hours before dawn, the thermometer outside the window that provided a view to the runway confirmed Edmonton would awake to -33F. I checked the wall clock again; it was 6:30 a.m. and well past the departure hour. The paperwork and inventory were re-confirmed when Andy reappeared, having finished slamming the forklift around in the hangar. The plane engines were still silent. I wondered idly if they would de-ice the wings as I opted for another disappointing cup of Sanka. I bumped into Michael at the steam geyser rising from the whistling kettle.

"*Salut*," he said, raising his white Styrofoam cup. He reeked of rum.

"Hey. Made it through the job interview, eh?" I felt a wry smile develop.

He laughed loudly when he blurted out his dark recollection of the interview. "*Tabernac*. What an asshole is that Cigar Lip."

I was sure he cranked the volume on purpose. Everyone in the room stared at us. We had denigrated the highest of priests, JT, the living legend at the rim of the frozen hole in the tundra. The icy looks of disgust on the faces of Handy Andy and the clerk told me we were marked, doomed before we left the runway as "those two guys."

Michael looked at me, pushed his cap back, and raised his eyebrows to half the height of his forehead. "What?" he said. "He is a prick, isn't he?"

"The truth hurts, eh?" I raised my cup to acknowledge Michael's opinion.

Our moment and the glacial silence around us shattered when one of the plane's engines backfired and stalled. I looked out the window. Andy raced out the door, called to action by the start-up procedure. Again, the engine coughed raggedly and then stopped in a disheartening, phlegmy flub. The pilot slid his cockpit window open and looked out. The engine stuttered again and then began a slow confidence-crushing, wheezing hack that became more like the intermittent barking of a frightened dog. The engine struggled and stumbled through RPM fluctuations, and then its partner returned from the far, frozen bank of Lethe to agonize through the same doubtful thralls. Finally, the almost-steady roar from both engines became more consistent, if decidedly worrisome.

A gust of frigid air propelled Andy, our ever-blossoming vine of positive expectations, back into our shanty, where he announced with a coy smile, "Okay, m'lords and lady … your carriage is loaded, warmed up, and ready for her royalty now. Please depart through gate number one." He smiled at us, bent into an exaggerated bow, and swept his arm toward my uninviting future. We filed out, escorted by the receptionist's string of invective; she appreciated neither Andy's theatrics nor the open door

From behind me, I heard Michael ask, "What's wrong with you? Do you think we are Kings of England or something?"

Strings of blue landing lights bordered and illuminated the extremities of the icy runway, converging to a distant point in the dark. For the second time, I cursed the icy kiss of the prairie morning. I tossed my personal gear and my guitar onto the plane, then climbed the four-rung, steel ladder into the rear door of the ancient DC-3. I was past the point of no return and inside the dim, green, cavernous cargo area, the no frills belly of the beast. Andy's assurance the plane was warm must have been in reference to the motors, because the seats were still frozen into their collapsed position and the seat belts were inflexible with the cold. My breath added to the buildup of a substantial fog bank inside the plane, created by other bodies that now occupied the confined polar air. With depleted hope for success, I fumbled with frozen hands in hopes I might snag onto a heater release valve, but no such valve existed.

I looked around and caught Michael's eye. He rubbed his hands together, turned both palms up, and shrugged. Cold alcoholic plumes steamed out of both his nostrils. He curled up into as tight a little *croissant* as he could to maintain his body heat and fell asleep. The young couple took seats across the expansive aisle from me. They were unbothered by the cold, and I envied them their serenity in the down-filled comfort fluffing up around them. She had settled into her toasty parka, absorbed by something beyond the opacity of her frosted window, which prevented her from seeing outside. He posted unappreciated guard on her. *Oh yeah, they're breaking up.* Resigned to a meaningless death by hypothermia, I followed Michael's lead. I curled into a tight ball and tried to conserve whatever small measure of body heat remained in my core.

An invigorating breeze blew steadily through the passenger area, quite unnecessarily refreshing the cargo hold. I broke out of my position, about to unleash my protest when another traveler joined us. *Well, who doesn't mind waiting for the late guy?* Andy mercifully slammed the cargo door shut. The waiting co-pilot secured it.

Over the drone of the engines, the fully bearded, stocky, smiling late guy yelled, "Sorry. Sorry. I'm late. My fault. Thank you for waiting." He took a seat.

As the co-pilot moved up front to take his seat seat in the cockpit, I coiled back into my survival ball of freezing flesh. The plane started to move. The co-pilot turned around to yell at us from the open cockpit door. "We're taking off now. Seat belts on and no smoking until we reach altitude. We'll be at Yellowknife in five hours. The heater comes on after we're airborne."

He turned away from us to engage the pilot, who appeared worried; both men began adjusting dials and twisting knobs. We taxied out to the runway where the roar of the engines doubled in volume, the plane vibrated, and we bounced along. To my delight, the engines sounded like they were growling at each other, though I wondered if we were underpowered for lift off with the passengers, the crew, and the plane half-full of cargo. We turned at the end of the runway and the co-pilot checked quickly to confirm we were not dancing in a conga line, then the pilot cranked the motors on full. We lumbered and shook down the pre-dawn, skating rink runway into the teeth of the North wind. A mile or so later we achieved approximately five-feet of lift off, clearing by two feet most of the highest prairie undulations between Edmonton and Port Radium. As we skimmed over the frozen wheat straw, I watched vehicles on the feeder highway into Edmonton catch up and pass us. If a jet was a Thoroughbred, our loaded, bloated DC-3 was a workhorse.

Thankfully, the pilot shared our collective, and my frantic, desire for more altitude. He was pugnacious in his effort to pull the control column back through his chest while the co-pilot trimmed ailerons in a similar effort to coax more lift out of the wings. I waited for the sudden drop, searing pain, the white flash, and our premature demise. But to my surprise, the tired war relic attained the few more feet required to clear the clutch of warehouses at the end of the runway. When we gained that smidge of altitude, a little cheer and applause erupted from all of us in steerage. Echo Bay Air had made it off the ground again.

It was still dark. We soared over Terra Firma, rising above the patchy ground-fog layer. Through the frosty windows across the aisle, I glimpsed a radiant, rosy dawn glowing past the wing tip, a distant crimson-orange sliver-thin slash on the horizon. When I looked down through my window, I was amazed at how quickly we left the cityscape behind. We flew over frozen and increasingly more remote collections of farm buildings, connected by fewer stretches of lonely roads. Soon, even these oases disappeared, and below us there were only thousands of square miles of soul-testing isolation and enduring winter. Despite heroic efforts and truly epic sacrifice, Canadians never conquered this land, they outlasted it.

We flew ever northward. By the time we gained a thousand feet in elevation, the frenzy in the cockpit had abated. The pilot adjusted the motors down a notch from racing panic to a more reassuring drone, and the co-pilot rewarded us by signaling it was okay to smoke. On cue, the smokers lit up in the still-deafening roar.

We climbed to five thousand feet, which seemed excessive above the pancake landscape of northern Alberta. We flew away from the Canadian Rocky Mountains into the land of the frozen muskeg and rolling stone waves of the barrens.

Located at the sub-Arctic tail-out of the western extremity of the Canadian Shield, Port Radium was one of the most isolated communities in Canada. When the magnificent sun conquered the eastern horizon, an overwhelming ocean of Canada's white, frozen wilderness unfurled below us. There was a point, somewhere down there, where we would leave Alberta and fly into the Northwest Territories. I felt my excited sense of adventure grow in the immense vastness of this wilderness, as I turned to a clean page of experience. In a land of indistinct borders or authority, all things were possible. This was freedom. I exhilarated when I imagined how hooded Death, also free in the northern wilderness, might reach for me with frigid talons, and that it was up to me to avoid the inevitability of that heartless grip. I was young and therefore immortal and undaunted by fears of any final disaster. I knew I would not, could not die, and whatever lay ahead of me would be an adventure.

7. "Dusty" Rhodes

I snuck furtive glances around the cargo bay. My fellow passengers either still stared out their windows or tried to sleep. There was little hope of having a conversation over the roar of the engines, so I succumbed to my lack of sleep and the slightly warmer air emanating from somewhere down by my ankles. For a fitful hour, I fell into a lolling doze, but I was only able to nod off, and I startled awake every time the plane swayed on an air current. Finally, having shifted through so many positions, none of which worked for me, I gave up on my futile attempt to recover an hour of sleep.

I would have killed for a Sanka. Though half my window was clear of ice and the cabin was still uncomfortably cold, I could no longer see my breath. The sun was a brilliant yellow orb; the sky was a deep, almost liquid blue through the opaque windows. We were still three hours out of Yellowknife. I rubbed the sleep out of my eyes. I yawned to pop my eardrums. I also needed to relieve myself, but the company had sacrificed the toilet to cargo space. Everyone waited with crossed knees until we arrived at Yellowknife, and would wait again until we reached the Arctic Circle.

Michael had joined the late guy in the last rows of passenger seating, where they chatted like old friends. There was an empty seat in front of the late guy, so I unbuckled and joined them. I was stiff with cold when I stood up. I made my way to the back of the plane through the haze of cigarette smoke, past the sullen, chain-smoking hit man. His eyes darted toward me once, then something outside his window drew his attention, and he was captivated again.

I unfolded a seat and sat down in front of my two fellow Echo Bay-ers. I nodded at Michael and held out my hand to the late guy. "Hi. My name is Al."

He looked me in the eye, shook my hand, and we met. His grip was strong, but never meant as a test of strength. I knew he could have snapped my fingers like so many swizzle sticks. "I'm Dave Rhodes. Nice to meet you, Al. You two know each other?"

"Yeah, we know each other. Hey, Michael, did that office tart con you too?"

"I thought she was going to be here. Did you, too?"

60

We both laughed at each other's expectations. We shook hands and became friends.

Dave said, "At one time Mary-Ellen was junior's main squeeze. She's an expert at recruiting, eh?"

"Who's *junior*?"

"JT's kid, Jimmy. He's still trying to make a name for himself. He has a lot to learn; I'm glad I don't have much to do with him. Michael said you brought a guitar?"

"Yeah, I play a bit. You?"

"Sure. C'mon over to my room tonight. You too, Michael. I'll introduce you around."

New friendships in remote camps can be so spontaneous you wonder where these people were your whole life. Truth is, there are millions of us camp tramps around the world, and we come in all shapes and sizes. I wanted to know more about Port Radium. "Sounds like you know your way around this place?"

Dave said, "I just finished a four-month term. I'm comin' back from a week of R and R, seeing my ol' lady in Sudbury. That's where I'm from."

"I worked for a month in Sudbury when I was sixteen, on a wire gang for CN. How the hell do you breathe that air?"

Dave smiled at me. "You get used to it."

"Sorry, man, I didn't mean to run your town down. I met some great people while I was there. How'd you wind up here?"

"I used to play major junior hockey for the Wolves. When the NHL didn't draft me, I went into the mines. I like the work. All I ever wanted since then was to be a hard rock miner underground and move a few mountains around. No other life for me. It gets into your soul."

It was a simple story, but I could tell Dave had a big heart and meant what he said and said what he meant. I understood. I had experienced two years of logging camps in BC's coastal mountains. I knew how that kind of work and lifestyle could seduce you away from a normal life. People think the money is the hook, but the real seduction is the sweat, the challenge, the camaraderie, the dangerous, hard work, beating the survival odds, toughening up, and the heady smells of the diesel, the pungent cedar, and the spruce. The binding mortar of the lifestyle is the power: bull-strong engines crank enough torque to strain miles of deadly snapping steel cable lines used to heave impossibly heavy loads. Strong men use their machines to harvest necessities from our spirit mother, Nature. The reward for months of high-risk labor, sweating under the searing heat or soaked, knee-deep in mud during torrential rains, is the return to town with a pocket full of cash and the will to spend every penny of it. For me, the life was compelling, although it was time to find my way back to school. But here was a miner being friendly, the hardest rock of the hard rocks. If miners are like fallers, Dave's friendliness was unusual. The aloof, moody hit man was more typical of the profile: purposeful, quiet, powerful, perhaps dangerous loners. You left these men alone; there were too many who believed their own legends.

"We land in a couple of hours in Yellowknife," said Dave. "Either of you guys been there?"

Both Michael and I shook our heads. The plane was so loud, sign language was a reasonable first option. We strained to hear each other, so we spoke in elevated voices. "We only have a pit stop there. They let us off the plane for fifteen minutes. Sometimes they load more passengers or cargo, then we're off again."

I said, "More cargo? We barely lifted off the runway in Edmonton."

"Don't let that fool you; this bird is no falcon, but she can pack heavy loads. They built 'em to carry about three tons of cargo. And this one does that. A lot. You two are surface crew, right?" Michael and I nodded our heads. "So, you'll be unloading trucks."

"What trucks?" asked Michael.

"Convoys of semis drive up the rivers and across the lakes from Yellowknife. The lake ice is at least five feet thick, so they plow out a winter road and truck in the heavy mine equipment and bulk supplies. That's how they transport the ore out in the winter. Sometimes as many as eight trucks arrive at once. An outfit run by a guy named Denison rebuilds the road every year. They say he's famous …"

The hit man spun up and out of his seat and came straight toward us. Dave reclined in his seat; Michael and I turned our knees straight so the hit man could squeeze by, although there was nothing behind us except a wall of freight and the narrow aisle to the back door. It turned out, he only wanted to threaten us. Before he launched his assault, Dave tried to intervene and deflect him. "Hi, Frank. In for another contract?"

Frank ignored Dave, glared at Michael and me, and said, "I want you two to shut up. I'm trying to sleep." Frank was impressive. I was prepared to zip it for four months if that would convince him to leave. Michael stiffened.

Dave said, "Hey, Frank, we didn't know you were sleeping. Sorry. These are two new surface guys. They don't know you're the camp deputy. Meet Al and Michael."

The Deputy looked us over, but remained fierce. "I'm only trying to make the flight pass faster, that's all." He returned to his seat. The scars on his knuckles and the deep, red gash through his left eyebrow bore the evidence of a hard life. Frank probably had to outlast WWII in Europe, or survive essential services duty, as had many of the older men I had worked with in the woods. Men like Frank knew only a hard life. I wondered if there was serious stuff on his mind, and I asked Dave.

Resignation in his voice, Dave answered, "He's okay once you get to know him." The chauvinist bond was thick, intact, and resilient.

We talked about other things, taking care to lean in a little, careful to leave "Deputy" Frank undisturbed. I asked Dave about claustrophobia in the tunnels.

"I never get that ... I find it peaceful down there. No one around. Just me, my muck-stick, my jackleg, and no foreman. I drill my holes, set my charges, move my mountains, and go home. I like the life. It can be dusty, noisy, wet, even dangerous, but it's not coal dust, at least."

"What's a jackleg?" I asked.

"A 180 pounds of compressor, drills, and hoses I haul around all day. You've never been underground, eh?"

"Nope. So do you move something like that with a forklift?"

"Forklift?" Dave laughed at me. "No room down there; just "armstrong" moving and cartage. And for this outfit, I'm surprised we're not using sledges, chisels, and coolies to pack the ore out. I guess at one time they did."

"Coolies ... really? Way up here?"

"Well, actually, local native men transported the ore until the fifties. A lot of 'em died from it, too."

"Died? How?"

"Radiation poisoning; the dust gets in your lungs. Uranium is poison. Most of the camp is knee-deep in the tailings. Why do you think they named it Port Radium?"

"No idea, but how great is it my choice is between working my way out of debt in the worst hole in the world or going hungry on the streets?"

Dave said, "A guy has to eat, and us married guys have families."

We talked among ourselves during the rest of the flight to Yellowknife, the only commercial airport between Edmonton and Port Radium, or as far as I knew, the North Pole. Michael was in and out of the conversation, drifting off to snooze away his hangover and then startling awake after fitful twitches to listen in again. He wasn't much of a talker, anyway. Dave and I covered the full gambit: money, women, pot, the Vietnam War, Nixon, Trudeau, the Arctic, Americans, logging, mining, JT, Great Bear Lake, music, and the camp food.

When the plane descended and began our long approach into Yellowknife, Dave said, "I don't think this camp will be anything like what you're used to, from what you say."

"That might be disappointing, because if it ain't top of the line grub, then what is there to do in camp? And for four months?"

"It sure ain't top of the line. In camp, like I say, a couple of us get together for music. You too, now. We need someone who knows more chords. And then there's beer at night. The company runs a club at the curling rink, but we can buy beer in the bar."

"There's a curling rink and a bar?"

"Yeah, the working guys' bar is half a storage trailer. You can take beer back to the bunkhouse, but only open bottles, so you have to drink it right away. I don't go to the curling rink. It's a little too exclusive for me. Besides, it costs twenty-five dollars to join, and I never seem to come up with the cash. I'm more of a hockey guy, I guess."

"How'd you mean?"

"Well, when the bosses want to screw someone over, they set it up at the rink. Or, if they want to bribe mine inspectors or Workers' Comp. They fly 'em in and throw a party at the rink. That kind of stuff. If I have a problem with someone, I'll settle it on the ice and then it's over. But I don't usually have problems."

I believed that about this man, too. "What about the women

in camp? Are they available?"

"Not much female action in Port Radium, but there are a couple of single girls around, Morag and Genna, the twins. They work mostly in the sugar shack and the community hall at night, frying up burgers and chips, then they head off to the penalty box. That's what I call the sugar shack. That's their bunkhouse, and none of us are allowed. They'll fire you on the spot if you're caught sniffing around — no one gets laid in Port Radium." He nodded forward, toward the Scottish lass. "Is she with him?"

"He thinks she is."

Dave nodded. "Some guys only eat at the community hall. Not sure if it's because of the girls or the food."

What with the current vacuum in my love life, this sounded slightly hopeful, if only because we were all isolated together. "So, WCB comes through camp once in a while?"

"Yeah, but only for the bi-annual Echo Bay gala bonspiels." He laughed at his description. "The company sends this plane to Yellowknife, gets everyone drunk there, brings 'em to camp, they throw a few rocks down the ice, drink like fish. Rumors have it, JT pays them off in camp. Then they fly 'em back. If they cared to actually look at what goes on in this mine, we'd be shut down by now. I know; I worked in enough union mines around Sudbury to tell you this place is bad, really bad."

"So, why are you here, then?"

Dave looked past me. We were just two people yakking at the back of the plane; no one was interested. Even Michael had dozed off again. Dave took a package of Export 'A' cigarettes from his shirt pocket and held it in his hand. "Don't tell anyone you saw this, okay? It's important no one knows."

"Sure. What? You smoke. Who gives a crap?"

He held up an index finger. "Give me a minute."

Dave opened three middle buttons on his shirt and revealed a horrific gash that started just below his sternum and reached to his navel. A second, horizontal scar ran across his stomach almost to his lower left ribcage. Both gashes had healed, but neither had healed over. He took the cigarette package and pushed it into the vertical injury, then pinched the opening closed with the cigarette package inside. His stomach wall had a three-inch deep gash in it, from top to bottom, and he was still hard rock mining. He held his hands up, looked at me with the cigarette package still in his guts. "Look, ma, no hands."

Surreptitiously, he retrieved the cigarettes and buttoned his shirt again. "I can get damn near anything but a new TV through customs."

I laughed a little to hide my queasy stomach. "Were you in 'Nam or something?"

"Underground accident two years ago. An ore car jumped a track and pinched me against another ore car. They thought I was a goner, but us Wolves are tougher than that. Missed all my vitals, except my spleen. They took that out. The cut across here," he traced a finger across the horizontal scar, "was the scary one. I guess I was pretty close to done, but I made 'er. When I tried to come back to work, the company refused to re-hire me. They said I was a liability. I was out of work and Compo was threatening to cut me off. My parts work fine, my ol' lady can vouch, but WCB said I was too much of a health risk to go back underground. They wanted me to sell stereos or something. It took me a while to accept that only Echo Bay, the bottom of the barrel, would hire me. No medical checkup required here, no real WCB inspections, and no union records to check. If you can swing a muck-stick, you can work for this outfit. Management don't give a crap as long as the ore cars are full. I figure if I do two contracts here, they can't deny me in Sudbury. I'll prove myself. That way I can have a job and be with my woman again. She needs me to be there now. Without her and mining, I got nothing. Hey, we're almost at Yellowknife."

Below us, the ground was still a blank, white canvas: no roads, no fences, no telephone poles, no farms, nothing but white. I had never been in a land where an articulated horizon failed to exist. On the B.C. coast, the distant expanse ended in a cut of blue sky above ranges of mountains or the ocean. Instead, the distance below us faded upwards into a ghostly mix of white-blue until it became obvious one was looking at sky.

The co-pilot waved at us to belt in for the landing. We flew over a broken-down, windbreak fence, and then dropped so abruptly my stomach rose to my throat. We glided over a plowed cement-slab runway and rejoined civilization. The tower appeared to speed by us as we thumped down hard on the frozen, frost-heaved airstrip. We bounced once, and then thumped down again.

The Hottest Place on Earth

At the airport, we all flew off the plane into a wind brisk enough to turn the Franklin expedition back. The cold snapped at my ears and face as I hippity-hopped with the other passengers through the blinding bright glare toward the waiting room. I squinted hard, barely able to make out objects through my tears. I was always super-sensitive to reflected sunlight and hoped there wouldn't be too much of that in Port Radium.

My waiting room experience was a blur of warm relief and machine coffee. On my return to the plane, a crippling gust of north wind bent me almost double. I wasn't sure how long it took to contract frostbite, but I was sure I verged on the threshold by the time the rest of the passengers returned and the co-pilot closed the cargo door. The pilots never killed the engines, so we took off right away into the rising wind. I slurped what remained of my cold coffee; the top half had become a brown stain frozen onto the Yellowknife runway. I returned to my first seat thinking I might sleep during the rest of the flight.

Out my window, I caught a quick glimpse of the small community. It worried me that there was so little there. With a population of around six thousand people and five times as many dogs, the village was unimpressive as Canada's gateway to the Arctic. Still, it unnerved me to watch Yellowknife shrink away behind us, fading beneath the icy, misty, non-horizon.

My eyes burned with missed sleep, but I tried reading anyway. I couldn't concentrate, so I tried to fall asleep, lulled by the gentle up and down motion of the plane and the insufficient heat wafting across my ankles. I attained only more disappointing twitching. Defeated, I looked out my window and wondered if Guinness had a world record for staring at blank pages.

8. Port Radium

I moved back to the seat in front of Dave. For the rest of the flight, I snatched looks outside for Denison's ice road, but saw no sign of it. After two and a half hours, we dropped into a low, wide circle to dip our wings over the eastern shore of Great Bear Lake. The orange sun lingered over the foggy curvature of the western horizon like a celestial Japanese lantern.

Dave said, "This time of year, the sun rises and sets in five hours."

During our flight, the sun negotiated a shallow arc around us. It was still high enough in the southwestern sky to create long stripes of severe orange glare. Dave told me that the earth wobbles on its axis out of its winter solstice position until the sun breaches the dawn horizon directly north of camp, and sets twenty-two hours later at almost the same spot. At this latitude in late June ("There's no real dark of night," said Dave. "We paint our windows to keep the light out so we can sleep."), twilight descends for two or three hours. The opposite lack of daylight occurs at the winter solstice in December, when the wobble causes the North Pole to point away from the sun. Today, it was only 2:00 p.m. and the sun appeared ready to dip back below the horizon. It was the middle of winter at the Arctic Circle. I couldn't see the far shores of the lake, and even if that were possible, sky meeting land or ice would have been an indefinite blur, even from this altitude. The surface was a massive expanse of snow-drifted ice, and the land was an infinite furl of undulating barrens covered in frozen snow.

Dave said, "We land here, on the ice."

"Really? This fat duck lands on the ice? Won't we skid around or something?"

"No way. The snow's so cold it grips the tires like sandpaper. Everything grips until May, when breakup starts. Then everything turns to muddy goo around camp and everything is insanely slippery for a month, then it stays really dusty and hot. In the summer, the plane lands at the airstrip five miles east of camp. Where we're landing is where they arrive with those supply convoys of semis you'll be unloading over the next four months."

Below us, Port Radium, a black scar in the otherwise white

landscape, was even more disappointing in real life than in Mary-Ellen's photo, which had failed to capture the palpable isolation. I used a familiar cartographical reference to process the vastness of the barrens; the Arctic Circle dissects the most northern reaches of the lake. I was far from the temperate BC fjords, my green river valleys, and snow-capped mountains. I knew these next four months would require a few personal adjustments.

I already had reason enough to dread this camp: radioactivity and lung cancer, lousy food, rare or no female company, old bunkhouses, a dirty job, and bitter cold. My contract would end and I would be long gone before the two intense summer months of biting-fly torture and the dread of the beginning of the next brutal ten-month winter.

The camp looked like a prison. The power plant stood out as an antiquated and irresponsible polluter. Its smokestack huffed thick, grey plumes of exhaust into the center of the bunkhouses. On the western edge of camp, along the lakeshore, huge aluminum fuel tanks rusted on the small peninsula that jutted into the bay. Dave pointed out the frozen, snow-covered mounds just behind camp, which he said were tailings dumps. Mary-Ellen's photograph made the camp appear as a quasi-sanitized and almost acceptable industrial site. But this camp was deceptively more vile: radioactive tailings piles were everywhere and were much larger than they looked in the photograph. The fuel tanks and three dark green Quonset huts behind the fuel tanks were built on tailings piles. The roads were capped and leveled with radioactive tailings, as were our bunkhouses, Dave told me. The largest tailings dump in camp, the Murphy dump, filled a half-mile long, deep ravine immediately behind the cook shack. Radon was vented in four places in camp. Dave said, "During the summer, most of the chemical sludge in Garbage Lake leaches into Great Bear Lake."

Until we flew over the camp, and the shambles of buildings broke that expanse of white, it felt less like we were about to land and more like we were about to crash somewhere down there under the white-wool landscape. We swung way out over the lake to circle around. If the altimeter was faulty, trying to land in the ivory opaque fog could be a disaster. Then I saw the black smoke from the diesel pots on the ice. Two rows of fuel pots smoldered below us and described the borders of our ice runway. My perspective altered immediately. We were only feet over the ice and were about to touch down.

When we first circled over camp, Dave pointed out Silver Point. Half-buried in snowy, wind-swept berms, rows of black, forty-gallon drums, stacked three high, lined the shore to the end of Silver Point. "First the transport trucks, then the Fort MacMurray train takes the concentrate away in those containers to Uranium City or Port Hope for more refining," said Dave. "They fly the drums out to the train when the ice road melts. I'll bet over a billion dollars came out of here since the war."

The frozen surface of the lake gobbled up the last few feet of our altitude and we slammed down hard on the ice. We bounced off the surface and then slammed down hard again. From a distance, the ice looked flat, but even as thick as it was, it was far from rigid. Our weight caused it to flex, dip, and roll. The ice surface sank under us, and then it sprang back as the plane fought a bow wave of water formed beneath the ice. I, for one, was glad thick ice was incredibly resilient.

Dave continued to orient me as we turned around at the end of the plowed runway and taxied past the smudge pots to the center of LaBine Bay. Two ancient trucks and a runty black school bus idled there, each vehicle spewing clouds of thick white-grey exhaust. The camp buildings loomed above us and evoked a Hitchcockian trepidation — as if the entire site were a "Bates Motel." Both of the one-ton trucks were painted red beneath their rust. One truck was a flatbed, the other a miniature dump truck. Road salt dusted the sides and front of the school bus, its windshield thick with the same grime. The drivers and their swampers stayed in the vehicles.

When the pilot killed the engines, we threw our belts off almost as a group, eager to disembark. Below the ridges of LaBine Bay, the middle afternoon light had turned to a murky, purple twilight. The co-pilot bustled down the aisle to open the door for the ground crew and confirmed it had warmed up to -45F during the day. We deplaned into a wind that was stronger than it was at Yellowknife, and it was much colder.

I wanted my first gulp of Arctic air to be memorable, so I inhaled deep lungfuls and coughed up the bitter exhaust that still billowed from the airplane engine. The wall of cold body-slammed me as two members of the surface crew approached us.

Inside his filthy snowsuit, leather mittens, boots, and from behind his goggles, I saw the fleshy face of a twenty-something, obese, ugly man. He raised his yellow goggles to his forehead; his eyes were at first piggy and then snaky when he squinted at us; his thin-lipped mouth was half-hidden behind an uneven, scraggly, blond beard. He watched us unload our personal gear, but another member of the surface crew joined to help us. He babbled incessantly and finished every sentence with a brash, phony laugh. The fat guy watched a frosted yellow forklift chug down the lake ramp and across the ice to expand our welcoming committee. The forklift rattled to a stop near the airplane door, and the man who exited yelled, "Get a move on, Errol, you too, Mike. I gotta re-fuel the plane. They're flying right back to Yellowknife."

Errol, the fat man with goggles, scowled back at the forklift driver. Errol's swamper, Mike, was a much larger man, dressed the same as Errol but without eye protection. His black beard fuzzed up thickest under his jaw and down his neck, the epitome of a hulking, suspendered, in-bred, Arkansas hillbilly.

Michael tried to speak to him. "Can you drive us to the office?"

Errol wasted no time confirming himself a jerk. "No. Mike fuckin' can't," he said. "You new guys walk; miners ride." Errol tried to dismiss Michael by turning away. "Big" Mike stepped forward and tried to menace us, but failed to convince either Michael or me. Dumb is unfortunate, but never intimidating. I noticed when both Errol and Mike nodded in deference toward Dave and Deputy Frank.

Michael was about to call Errol on his aggression. Michael stiffened, slung his bag over his shoulders, tapped Errol on the back, and said, "Hey, Miss Piggy, I bet you just love pork chop night, eh?"

Errol, the fool, turned around, aggressive and insulted, but made no move toward Michael. Really, one look at Michael could stop you in your tracks.

It was entirely the wrong climate for a Mexican standoff. I caught Michael by the arm without Errol seeing me do so. Michael's arm felt like it was made of steel. "Easy, friend, we've just landed."

Michael glared at Errol, and muttered, "...*calice de tabernac* ..." He sounded more than a little dangerous. "In town, he is down, talking at me that way." Michael said to Errol and Mike, "Are you two as gay as those pilot? It looks that way to me. We don't give a fuck if you hold hands."

I was unaware *Québécois* called homosexuals gays. I bumped into Michael from the side, and said, "Yeah, some welcoming party all right. No marching band or champagne either, just a couple of idiots. C'mon, let's grab our stuff and head up."

I hauled Michael out of there and away from Errol and Mike. Deputy Frank took the ride. Dave declined Errol's offer, choosing instead to show Michael and me the route up to the office. The young couple was already on the bus. We followed Dave across the ice, humping our gear past the roar of the power plant, through the rows of warehouses and garages, our footsteps crunching in the frozen snow until we began the long climb up to the first bunkhouse, the vibrating steps creaked under our weight.

The two-story bunkhouses looked identical, a maze of elaborate plank stairs and boardwalks connected the buildings. Dave told us one-half of the building on the highest part of the ridge, farthest away from the men's bunkhouses, was the penthouse. It was the guest house and was off limits to us. On general principles of defiance, I promised myself I would reconnoiter and invade that bunkhouse in the near future.

"The office is over there and that's the community hall and there's the cook shack. That," Dave pointed up to a sizable, unattached building past the cook shack, larger than a bunkhouse and overlooking the ridge, "is our hospital, but nobody is ever there. The house beside it is the sugar shack." Before he dropped out of the expedition, Dave asked, "Well, now you've met your fellow grunts, how do you like the job so far?"

I said, "Either Errol or Mike could wear the tail end of the horse costume at Halloween."

Huffing up the many steps and through the bunkhouses winded me. Michael smoked all the way. We were sheltered from the worst of the wind by the ridge, so the cold was only slightly less biting as it had been on the ice. I built up a modicum of warmth with the workout, but my face and scalp felt frozen and my earlobes burned from the cold. Even though we passed through two bunkhouses during our trek, I worried about possible frostbite complications with my aching hands.

Dave stopped at his room in one of the bunkhouses, where he reminded us to swing by after we sorted ourselves. Michael and I carried on towards the office with our gear. At the crest of the ridge, the wind assaulted us again, forcing us to bend into it for the final two hundred yards. Michael made a colorful comment about wind at "Portage and Main," which I failed to understand. I chanted a silent oath directed at Errol; silent, because my teeth hurt from the cold when I cursed him out loud.

We descended two more flights of steps before finally arriving at the office. By then, I wanted to run into the relief of the heated building. The room reeked of decades of stale cigarette smoke the pale green paint could not absorb. Michael was a quick second act behind me. The clerk was busy at his desk five feet in front of us. Our commotion failed to interest him. We gathered ourselves and stepped up to the chest-high counter, where we waited an awkward amount of time for the clerk to deign to recognize us. *Nothing?* I dropped my hockey bag. Even that failed to interrupt the clerk's concentration.

Michael took the lead. "Hey, buddy. We are here now. My name is Michael Foutaud and this is Al (he pronounced my name like Hal). We are new surface crew and we need a room."

The clerk refused to look at us; instead, the officious twerp said, "I'm not your *buddy*. Wait." He placed his pen down, and then took meticulous care to pile several sheets of paper into neat stacks. He scraped his chair when he left his desk and disappeared into an interior office. Michael dropped his gear on the floor. The young couple joined us, and, instantly, the small reception area was ridiculously crowded.

"Is anyone here?" asked the smiling, strapping young buck. I assumed this was his first trip off whatever ranch he had just left, and he was so stunned because he had fallen at least once off the back of the buckboard.

"We're supposed to wait. My name's Al. This is Michael. We prob'ly should have introduced ourselves in Edmonton." I held out my hand.

"I'm Don and this is my girlfriend, Jan." She elbowed Don then flipped off her hood and shook out her hair. I thought I caught a furtive glance from her. As Don shook my hand, she said, "Hi," gushing as if she had a secret to tell. Her eyes were riveting, blue, and clear.

Our meet-and-greet ended when the inner office door

opened and the clerk returned. A man followed him out; it was the angry Joseph Stalin doppelgänger come back to life. He stared at us as he approached, and I sensed he carried the weight of our gulag on his shoulders. "You all start tomorrow." He pointed at Michael and me. "Ernie will assign you two a room, if he isn't already drunk. He'll be somewhere in a bunkhouse. You sign your papers first." He fixed a stare on us that was colder than a north wind direct from Siberia. "I don't want no shit from you two. Got it?"

I had the distinct impression our status had changed to "dismissed." We both nodded our subservience and then shuffled sideways, sliding down the reception counter to duck out of Stalin's direct line of fire. We began to sign our futures away as we plowed through the stacks of forms and waivers the snotty clerk pushed across the counter to us.

I noticed an abrupt change in Stalin's tone when he said, "So, you two newly-weds finally made it here. I'll call your uncle Jack and let him know. Bill, I'd like you to help Jan and Donny get settled in the married quarters."

La-dee-da. Port Radium blue bloods.

But then Jan blurted out, "We haven't set a date yet." Donny's face reddened; discombobulation blazed across it.

Stalin said, "Not married? But I thought you were going to live in the married quarters?"

Cute as a button, Jan repeated, "We're not married."

"Well, that changes things. Don goes in the bunkhouse, Bill, and Jan has to put up in the sugar… I mean, the female quarters."

Michael and I looked at each other briefly. Stalin scrutinized Jan with that old-school charm that reconciles Lemay's mass murders as a lifetime of "achievement," but cannot accept two young people in love co-habiting. "We can't have you two living in sin. JT would never tolerate that."

Jan nodded, batting not-so-innocent doe-eyed lashes at him. Her signals made it clear she was happily compliant. She had this all figured out: it was a ring and the whole cow or no more milk for Donny-boy. Of all of us, Don was the only one confused by what had just transpired.

Michael and I left the office first. It was almost dark, so most of the buildings on the ridge and the bunkhouses blazed with interior lights. We packed our gear back up the stairs to the ridge through the amber cones thrown down by the boardwalk lights. I cursed the wind as we passed by the darkened windows of the locked community hall. Soldiering on, at each bunkhouse, we called for Ernie. Eventually, he popped his head out at Dave's room. Dave plucked away, tuning new strings on his guitar.

"Welcome to my castle. You guys looking for the concierge?" Dave had a private room, a privilege of the highest order in the working man's ranks.

"Yeah. We need bunks."

Ernie was a skinny, sixty-ish, almost bald man. He sported both a rakish comb-over and a week's patchy stubble. He was a bent man who might have been my height when he was younger. When we shook hands, despite his reputation in the office, he smelled only of tobacco smoke. Still, he had the jaundiced eyes of a heavy drinker and an awful set of stained, yellow dentures, which chattered when he talked.

"I can get you boys set up right now. Follow me."

"See you guys at chow? You know where I live, so don't be strangers," Dave said.

"Yeah, you bet."

Michael and I followed Ernie, who chattered away, literally, as he led us all the way back to the first bunkhouse we had entered before we lugged our gear up to the office. This bunkhouse was closest to the dismal buildings along the lake. Ernie seemed excited and chatted non-stop, but I had no idea what he said. His uppers and lowers clicked and popped like a ticker tape as he tried to converse over our tramping footsteps through the long hallways. I was sure all it would take was one small smoker's cough, and he would hurl his dentures.

Finally, we stopped at the last lower-level room, next to the outside door, facing south. We had a fetching view of the top of the power plant smokestack. Ernie pointed out the rooftop of the building where the mechanics and surface crew assembled each morning. Powerful commercial lighting threw long amber shadows across the deserted yard below us. The sky was black. I asked Ernie for the time.

"3:20 p.m. You two flew in together so you might as well bunk together. You were lucky to beat the weather. They say a big one is coming our way."

Michael said, "Flip you for the window?"

"Let's make it easy; you can have it."

Ernie said, "Supper is at five, kitchen is open until six. Don't be late. Welcome to the hottest place on Earth. See you later." Before he left the room in a hurried, stutter-step gait, I asked him about the coming storm.

"Storms can last for weeks," he chattered. "We got through one a couple of days ago." From down the hallway, as an afterthought, Ernie hollered back, "Cleared most of the wolverines out of camp, so you know it was bad." Ernie's phrase, *most of the wolverines* hung in the air like a string of Air Force flares at midnight. As I unpacked, I wondered just how many wolverines lived here on a nice day and why Port Radium was the hottest place on Earth?

9. Me-shell

Michael grunted and then slung his duffel bag onto the bed. He flopped down on the mattress. *"Tabernacle,"* he said, pounding out random lumps with his fist.

"That decent, hunh?" I sat on my bed and rolled my hips. "Not much give." I pounded my fist into my unyielding slab, and said, "Yeah, tabernacle, for sure." We both laughed.

Michael said, "Did you think Mary-Ellen liked you too?"

I looked at him; it was time for the truth. These camp moments come and go in a blink, and you cannot let them pass with a room partner you bunk with or they linger for months. "Yeah, I did. She turned on the flirt for me."

"You?" he said exasperated. "Jesus Christ, I thought I was going to get a blow job."

We burst out laughing at ourselves. "Yeah, she's some recruiter."

"She," said my room partner, "is nothing but a whore and we are two suckers who took her bait."

I looked around the room. Bad painters had managed to paint our large window shut, but had failed to slop enough paint around to cover up the wear and tear and tobacco stains. There was no window blind, so the lights from the yard, which threw our shadows on the wall behind me, would keep our room well illuminated throughout the night. The din from the power plant was arrhythmic, so that would keep me awake, too. The single overhead bulb equated all the ambiance found in the Vancouver drunk tank. Worst of all, the room was stifling hot; the dry air already burned my sinuses.

Michael peeled off his jacket, and I took off my Cowichan sweater. We looked around the room for a thermostat, but none existed. Michael went into the hall to find the controller. Someone had smashed it, so it hung off the wall, attached by wires. He pounded the thing several times, providing insight as to how it came to be in its current state of disrepair. Our choices were full on or full off. At -45F, the latter was not an option.

I checked out the toilets to find the source of the gurgling pipes. There were eight stalls in a row, three with no doors. The toilets and sinks were stained yellow, and the black crack lines looked like a porcelain version of Varicose Veins. *What, these guys crap pitchblende?* Attached to the wall across from the three shower stalls was a long, aluminum trough urinal. A water pipe, crusty with green deposits, leaked a steady stream of water from the rusty joint, forming a rivulet to the main drain in the center of the floor. The rust motif continued in the shower stalls, where each showerhead leaked. The stained, yellow shower curtains were ancient, many of the eyelets torn. I was vaguely intimidated, thinking it might be an act of bravery to shower. The builders had mounted the showerheads at a height of five feet. I wondered what idiot would build showers in a men's bunkhouse that failed to accommodate anyone taller than a pre-history hominid.

Michael came in, looked around, and said, "It's like this whole place is fucked up. It's better at jail."

I said, "It looks like they expect us to crap more than shower."

We returned to our room. Now that I knew the toilets ran and the showers dripped continuously, I heard each drop from my bunk. We sat beneath the interrogating glare from our bare, overhead light bulb. Michael took a Buck knife out of his pocket. He snapped his wrist, the blade opened and he cleaned under his nails. From his complacency, I assumed he considered our accommodations tolerable.

"Nice little pig sticker you have there, Michael. Too bad there aren't any pigs around."

"I don't know, but maybe that Errol is a pig." He pronounced the name like "Url."

"Well, if it comes to that, I have his big goof buddy if you go for Errol. What a couple of idiots."

Michael nodded at me, checking my eyes to see if I was serious. Satisfied that I meant what I said, he said, "Last night, before I left my hotel, I got a call from my roommate. He was my partner in Winnipeg. He is calling me from jail, and he told me the sky was black and blue."

"Black and blue?"

"That means the cops beat him up pretty bad. They arrested him on twenty-eight charge — the worst is attempted murder."

I did my best to hold a poker face. My eye caught the light

glinting off the blade edge. "So, your partner was arrested yesterday on twenty-eight charges? And bloody attempted murder, too. Tell me again when you left Winnipeg."

"There was no blood. Two days ago."

"That's just a saying. Well, you got out in time, eh?"

"Just barely, but they are looking for me."

"I bet you're not the first guy to land here with the law on his tail. We could write a song about it, maybe?"

Michael laughed. "I think you are okay, Al."

Other than his trouble with when to employ the letter "h", he was the perfect camp partner. The closest town was hundreds of air miles away, so it was all about self-reliance in camp. Our partnership suited me fine.

We launched into the same kind of conversation I'd had in logging camps. The "background" talk continues until it stops, ending when you know what you need to know about your room partner and whether you can or will drop the *room* part of it. It is a touchy thing with partners; they can be great or they can drag you down. Camp friend does not necessarily equate with town friend. It sounded like Michael was a serious concern on the streets, a style different from mine, but it was already evident he would have my back; I would return the favor.

We chatted on. I talked about logging, he told me this was his first mining camp. Much of his working background was construction in Winnipeg. Every Québécois I ever met called himself a faller or worked at some time or other in construction in Winnipeg. He never mentioned his former partner again, or his family, girlfriends, or much of anyone he knew. However, I did learn he had a superb French cursing vocabulary, was a Rolling Stones and AC/DC fan (whoever they were), liked *poutine* (whatever that was), and was angry with the way the Montreal Canadians treated Guy Lafleur. Michael was intolerable of derogatory slang – especially the slur – *frog*.

I liked Michael. He was funny and smart, though he downplayed his wit. Our friendship seemed mutual. I had already caught on to his accent, and, I guess, he to mine.

We had finished bragging to each other by the time the crew stomped through the bunkhouse. Errol and his monkey-man Mike slowed down to glare into our room. Most of the guys moved on to showers before supper. The wind had picked up to gale force; it howled and slammed snow at our window. I decided I would pay attention to the weather over the next several months.

What a Jesus-desolate place.

Half an hour later, we followed the exodus toward the cook shack, marching through the bunkhouses, again, and into the long, dark, Arctic night.

10. Dinner, a Spree, and a Beer

The construction crew had attached three modular doublewide trailers together into a single story structure to create the cook shack. The white exterior and flat roof gave it the appearance of a huge cake box. The dining hall, an important venue for the men in the camp, had only a single door for their access. Inside, two-thirds of the interior was the dining hall, and a stainless steel serving counter separated the kitchen from the rest of the hall. Two hundred men could sit for a meal, though current seating was set up for two-thirds capacity. Disconnected from the separate head tables, two long rows of tables ran parallel to either side of the hall; the organization resembled a detached 'π' symbol. The kitchen was at the end of the building opposite to the head table.

Dave said, "The twins usually cater to the managers at the sugar shack, but if the managers are slumming, they eat over there, at the special table." He snickered at his reference. I found it odd that management promoted such strict delineation because this never happened in logging camps – management ate with the loggers.

On the right, walking in, was the chef's domain: the kitchen. Stainless steel and white porcelain counters glimmered behind the full-length, stainless steel serving counter and tray rack, along which hungry men slid their trays past the buffet hoods. Against the back wall, aging sheet metal grease hoods hung over three propane grills. An entrance beside the walk-in fridge, which had been built into an interior wall, opened into a massive pantry. Against the wall kitty-corner to the grills, were two large, stainless steel sinks.

The chef, Les, had a worried face, as did his twitchy second cook, when they greeted the lineup of men from behind yet another cutting surface. Our skinny Englishman chef had once been a cook in Cyprus for the British military, a bad sign.

Michael and I joined the end of the long line of men silently sliding trays with the enthusiasm of the condemned about to walk the plank at swordpoint. The line curled around the outside of the farthest tables, past the cutlery bins and plate stacks. When my turn came to peruse the contents of the aluminum salad bowl full of rusty lettuce and soft cucumber, I ignored the offering. Further along, I tried to identify the smells that came from the other side of the serving counter. As I shuffled toward my first meal in Port Radium, I looked around and watched a kitchen flunky serve our Stalin clone at the special table. Dave was in line, ahead of Michael and me.

When I had passed him to join the end of the line, Dave said, "Hope you like stew."

I observed the dour faces of the few men already served, how they hung over their dinner at the tables. Most had several thick slices of bread piled on their trays. Most dunked bread into their bowls and chowed-down full dripping slabs. Les' wife, Liz, a short and yet enormous woman, carried a laundry-size basket of white bread slices out to the condiment table. She took a similar, but empty, basket away.

Our skinny chef, another bad sign, greeted each worker with a nod, repeating in monotone, "'Ow are you tonoyght, then?"

Having never been in a camp where stew was on the menu, let alone the dinner entrée, I was suspicious of this chef. Where I came from, Salvation Army volunteers in soup kitchens ladled out stew to destitute, desperate souls on the east side of skid row Vancouver. A wealthy corporation would never skimp on men who paid board and who labored for a multi-million dollar operation. I loaded my plate with bread just like the other men had, but also took a fork and knife, which I considered a customary expectation when eating dinner.

When I arrived at the front of the line, Les said, "Oh, oy think yer new, then, aren't you?"

"Yeah. We flew in today."

"Royt then, yer loykely starvin' … 'Ere, have an extra dollop." He held a soup bowl in his hand and ladled up his diarrhea-colored, lumpy goop. I was able to identify kernels of corn and the occasional, lonely chunk of ground 'burger. He passed the full bowl to me.

I accepted it out of politeness, and then said, "So what's for dinner?"

"Wot?"

"What did you cook for supper, I mean besides this?"

"That *is* dinner; it's stew noyght, innit, Liz?"

The rotund woman looked over her shoulder from the condiment table and nodded. She confirmed the chef and the British cliché; when she smiled, she exposed a mouthful of yellowed and crooked teeth.

I turned to look at Michael over my shoulder, shrugged and laughed.

"'Ere. What's the problem then?"

He said it loud enough to draw Stalin's attention. I looked around and saw the chief of the politburo was staring at me, a slice of bread in his hand, and postured to banish any malcontent.

"You expect men to work all day and then come in and eat this slop? You've got some nerve." I walked away, confident that in any BC logging camp my protest alone would instigate a management scramble to change the kitchen staff and keep the men happy.

Behind me, I heard the chef say, "Look 'ere, Lizzy, we've got one of the Royals suppin' wiv us tonoyght."

Idiot.

I heard several men laugh. When I turned to find a table, I saw the loudest ass laughing was Errol. I took a chair across from Dave. I pondered the stew. "I waited all day for this?"

Dave said, "Best to keep your voice down, Cool Hand Luke. Especially when the boss-man is in here. I told you on the plane, the food's not great. Les cycles the grub, so if you look at it this way, you're actually eating several meals at once: four nights ago, this was roast beef, the drippings are in the stew. Then it was shepherd's pie from those leftovers three nights ago. Then he probably made ground burger mush-patties last night from the shepherd's pie, and tonight we're finishing off the cycle of those leftovers as stew. Don't let the boss man overhear you complain about the food; guys are fired for two things here: mentioning radiation and complaining about the food."

"Maybe so, but I'm a little worried where the corn came from, and this smells like it might be a really suspect place."

"Do what we do, eat plenty of bread and then buy a burger later. You can run a tab and fill up at the community hall." He took a big bite of bread and gravy, shrugged his shoulders, and rolled his eyes as if to say, "Not much you can do about it, anyway."

My dander was up. When Michael sat down, he vigorously salted and peppered his bowl in a vain attempt to smother or at least deflect the smell. Michael's enthusiasm possibly revealed a hungry childhood whenever someone placed food in front of him, he ate it.

I had a different idea. I stood up, a piece of stale, buttered bread in my mouth, and carried my tray across the hall in full view of Father Russia. After all, he couldn't banish me to Siberia, I was already there! I poured my full bowl into the garbage, slammed my tray down on the stack, and clanged my cutlery into the rinsing pail.

Outside, I crunched frozen steps through the rising gale to the community hall, where I would gladly put a hamburger on camp credit. My reproachful stomach growled when I discovered all the hall windows were dark and the door locked. It was -55F and the wind was up, so I abandoned plan B and headed for the nearest bunkhouse before I froze to friggin' death. Back in our room, I bruised my ribs flopping onto my cement mattress, adjusted my dusty pillow, which smelled of stale cigarette smoke, and began a letter to my friend in Edmonton.

Minutes later, Dave and Michael came into the room. Dave was laughing. "You started it …" Michael sat down on his bed.

"Started what?"

"After you left, half the guys did what you did, the same way. The boss left. You started a food revolution your first night in camp, man! Not bad. The chef closed the kitchen and kicked us all out. He was pissed. There's gonna be a shovel full of shit coming your way, but most of us did the same as you, so you probably don't have to worry about losing your job. At least, not till you work off your flights."

"I could eat a dead musk ox, hide 'n' all. What time does that community hall open?"

'Usually around seven p.m., an hour or so from now."

"What about the company store? Can we buy food there? I gotta buy work gear, too." Michael nodded at me; we both needed winter work clothes.

Dave said, "Bill gets in there at about the same time."

When seven p.m. came around, Michael, Dave and I hiked up to the community hall for a quick bite, then Michael and I planned to carry on to the store. We agreed to meet later at the pub to slurp down a beer or two and maybe grab a bite of pub food. However, the locked community hall and dark windows were uninviting.

"I guess," Dave said, "there's no burgers if we don't eat their gruel. Never seen the hall closed at night. Management is a bunch of real vengeful assholes and they have a lot of ears around camp. It's been a long day, so I'm going to pass on the pub tonight. Drop by the room later if you want." Dave left us in the biting wind to carry on to the company store.

The half of the trailer that was not the pub was the store. Michael opened the trailer door and we stepped inside. Bill sat behind a table, silent and ready to take our cash. We soon discovered this little goldmine certainly believed in profit: a pack of cigarettes in Edmonton — $0.35, in Port Radium $3.00; a pair of wool work socks in Edmonton — $0.75, in Port Radium $3.00; a large chocolate bar in Edmonton — $.15, regular chocolate bar in Port Radium $3.00. JT missed nothing when it came to setting prices that kept the labor in penury by skimming our paycheques.

With empty pockets, our only option was company credit. I needed a coat, boots, gloves, and a hard hat. Michael waited his turn beside me, while I sold "my soul to the company store." With each item I ordered, JT owned more of my credit-killed future.

"I need a pair of size ten-and-a-half work boots," I said.

"Lemme see if I can get those for you." He never took his eyes off me and never moved a muscle. "Nope."

"Elevens?"

"Nope."

"Well, what do you have here for winter work boots?"

"I could only get two pairs in from Edmonton: eights or thirteens. What'll it be?"

"Michael, what size are your feet?"

"Nine. I think."

"Okay, I'll go with the clown feet. Thirteens, please." Bill slammed the boots on the counter.

"I need a snowsuit and a parka, too."

"I only have one size and only two suits in camp. You better grab 'em now because they go fast up here."

"One each it is ..." I looked at Michael and he nodded. I said, "I'll take a couple of those chocolate bars too, a pair of gloves and a hard hat as well." The pile I accumulated was impressive. Bill said, "Twenty-five dollar deposit for the hard hat; we return that when you finish your contract. Will that be all then?" Bill's manner was more of a statement than a question.

"Sure, how much is that?"

"Let me see, $40 for the boots, $80 for the winter suit, $80 for the parka, $10 bucks for the gloves and $25 deposit on the hard hat, $6 for chocolate bars. That comes to $201 dollars with the deposit. There's a ten percent surcharge for anything bought on credit, company policy, so what'll it be? Cash or company charge?"

That floored me. My gear, board, and the airfare ate up my first two months wages in camp, stolen back by these grifters. We were at their mercy, and they knew it.

"Company charge," I said, defeated. Michael received the same treatment. But those size eight boots meant he would have sore, cold feet for a month or more.

We slipped over to the bar side of the trailer. At least it was open for business. Errol and Mike had spread out at the table closest to the fridge. They still wore their work snowsuits, so their heads looked small and disproportionate to their body girth. They both glowered at us with the same "north face of Mt. Robson" attitude. Michael and I piled our purchases on an empty table. The bartender was one of the kitchen crew I'd heard Les call "young Phillip." He still wore his kitchen whites to operate the beer opener behind the makeshift plywood bar.

We each ordered two beers. The bartender said, "Six dollars each. Will that be cash or credit?"

We responded in sync, "Credit."

Phillip said, "There's a ten percent surcharge for credit."

I said, "Is there any surcharge for sitting down?" Phillip ignored me, so Michael and I initialed credit chits and then squeezed into chairs at our table.

I was in no mood to start small talk with Errol, but he had a bone to pick with us. "You two are workin' surface, eh?"

Michael answered, "We are surface." He pointed at me with his beer and then took a long, decisive swig. I read his message loud and clear.

Errol did not. "Then you work for me. I run the surface crew."

Michael looked at me with baleful eyes, then asked Errol, "How long you been in camp?"

"Three months. Why?" When he talked, Errol's upper lip snarled up as if he had a tick.

Michael took another long swig. This time, he locked his eyes on Errol while he gulped. He finished the beer and slammed the bottle on the table. "I just want to know if you think you will work again or if this was your last day?"

Errol looked confused. He looked at Big Mike, who always looked confused. Errol said to Mike, "Tell him I work every day."

Big Mike was about to chirp, but Michael said, "I am talking to you, Errol."

Errol turned mute, faltering under Michael's intimidating glare, and then turned away to begin a sparse conversation with Mike, snatching only occasional glimpses in our direction over the next two hours.

We kept our eyes on them. I drank more beers, running my bar credit to an astronomical sum; after taxes, I spent the equivalent of the wages I would earn after a day of work. We made $3.75 per hour. It became obvious to me why so few were in the bar. In town, a pint of beer was still only $0.85. I wanted to forget the cost of the flight and the work gear.

When Phillip announced, "It's nine p.m. Last call for off sales," Michael and I split the cost of a case of beer to take back to Dave's room. The kid opened each beer before he placed them in a beer case. After I sat down to finish my last beer, Errol sent Mike up to buy a dozen. Mike brought his case back to their table and sat down again. Neither Errol nor Michael had moved.

Errol said, "Tomorrow, you work for me. Right?"

So, there it was. It's always best to settle this sort of thing right away. Michael looked me in the eyes as he took one of his empties off the table and put it in his new parka pocket. Errol was all eyes. He looked at Mike, who now appeared a little less prone to sticking his jaw out.

Errol said, "Michael, what do you want with that bottle?"

"It's for you." A stone-cold killer, Michael stared Errol down.

I wondered Errol didn't throw his back out, wiping the tough-guy sneer from his face. "No … no, Michael. I was only kiddin'. I don't want no trouble." He held his hands up, as if he were ordering ten donuts. "We don't want trouble."

"You've been looking for it all night."

Now I saw their fear. Mike jumped in. "No, we was kiddin'. We like you."

"Yeah," repeated Errol, "we like you …"

Michael held his stare, "Even so, I don't like you." His

intentions were clear, red snow in the morning.

Errol said, "No problem. We'll leave. We don't want no trouble." Mike grabbed their case, but first Errol placed two open beers on our table. As he nudged past us, Errol said, "Here, have these. We're buddies, right?"

Egg-suckin' dogs. If he puckered up any more, his head would have disappeared down his own cake hole. *Disgusting.* Michael looked at the two beers, shrugged his shoulders, never looked at Errol, raised his hand, snapped open his knife, and began to pick his teeth. Both Errol and Mike flinched, tripping over each other on their way out.

When the door slapped shut behind them, I said, "What a couple of sorry losers. Well, I guess we'll see 'em in the morning. You scared 'em off for now, Michael." I clinked his beer and drank the bottom half of my own.

Phillip said, "I don't get paid past nine and I get up at four thirty."

Once outside, we were both wary of *dry-gulching,* but Errol and Mike were long gone. We hurried through the blowing snow to the nearest bunkhouse, carrying the case of opened beer as carefully as we could. We went to find Dave for a nightcap.

11. Gore

As we approached Dave's room, cheery voices erupted after someone playing an acoustic guitar finished a song with a flourish.

We met a bunch of the guys. "Aussie" Murray, was a young, game Australian, small but wiry, quick with a joke and a genuine laugh, and, soon found out he could drink with the best of 'em. He worked in the ball mill, crushing aggregate into ore and was in year three of his six-year quest to work and party while he circumnavigated the globe. Eddie "the Wrench" was a Métis from the Red River area. He was a dark-skinned, hollow-eyed truck mechanic, who had thin, small hands but long fingers. He was a magician with a set of tools, hungry to play blues on the guitar, but was unable to transpose his desire into dedication, so he was the frustrated wannabe musician in the group. Eddie played lap-drums after three beers loosened him up.

The only two native men in camp were regulars at Dave's shindigs. Young John Mantla was a Slave Lake Indian chief's son. John was soft spoken, was shorter than me but huskier, was my age, strong, and bright enough to stay out of big trouble. I surmised he had lived much of his life in the company of older people, because he rarely spoke unless asked a direct question. In our group, if he said anything, he gave short, concise answers. John's smile was warm and friendly, though rarely available, and his eyes were both gentle and clear. John's partner, "Silent" Sam, was a generation older, though he and John treated each other like equals. Sam was weatherworn. His face was red, tired, and scarred from chicken pox. He grew the stringy black beard of a man who had rarely shaved when he was younger. Sam was reserved, stocky, muscular, and had thick hands, he was a bull of a man. The first thing I sensed about him was anger boiling just below the surface, but that might have been insecurity in the company of so many white strangers.

Of course, "Dusty" Dave Rhodes was there with his big, friendly smile, and his scooching way of familiarity and respect for personal space. He was our master of ceremonies, and he looked comfortable in that role. Besides John and Sam, Michael, Ernie, Murray, and Eddie, there were others, but no miners. Don was elsewhere, busy worrying over Jan.

Dave was playing his guitar again. Live music turned the night into a shindig. It was a good time that became more raucous after we finished the first dozen beers. We drew lots of attention; more men in the bunkhouse joined our nonsense, hanging out in the hallway and at the door. Dave had a lava lamp, because, he said, "Pink flamingos won't fit in my suitcase." The dyed goop in the lamp threw odd, liquid shadows onto the walls.

Dave strummed up Country Roads. He replaced the words so that "Arctic winds are blowing" and "timber wolves are howling at midnight" in places where John Denver sang about the ancient Blue Ridge Mountains. Dave's lyrics worked well. We sang along or tried to until we learned Dave's version. Even the people in the hallway sang. It became our anthem, and we never failed to sing it at least a couple of times any night the feel-good happened. During a music break, I told the story in hushed tones of Michael, Errol, and Mike.

Michael said, "Anyways, that's fuck all." I think he was embarrassed.

Dave said, "Yeah, they want to keep the ball and bat and take it home with them. They're short-timers now, I think."

Eddie said, "Naw, dey 'ave a mont' to go yet."

Dave said, "Short-timers compared to me and these new guys, though, eh?"

"Dat's for sure."

Dave said, "Hey, Sam. I got a martin." Sam looked up, interested. This was something he could relate to, his invitation to belly up to the bar, so to speak. "I got him the day before I went for R 'n' R. I clubbed him with this." Dave held up a bloody crescent wrench.

Murray said, "Right. They do advertise a multiple range of uses."

"Wanna see?" asked Dave. "Ernie stored him in the freezer while I was gone; he's mostly thawed out now." Sam nodded. Dave fiddled with his window latch. Dave's room was on the opposite side of the bunkhouse from the lake. The snow accumulated during the winter storms buried all the lower windows on Dave's floor. "Since the snow built up, these little buggers have been running around down here, waking me up with their squeaking and scratchin'. I used your trap," Dave said to Sam, "and got one with Ernie's sardines."

Ernie piped up, "The cook was going to toss him in the stew

if he was in the freezer one more day."

Murray said, "I thought he already did."

Everyone laughed, though I was unsure if that was humor or not. I had never killed an animal, and it surprised me when I saw the pitiful, strangled martin, stiff with death. But I was a city boy and new in camp, so I kept my sentiments to myself.

Dave pulled a plastic bag into the room from the snow bank. "This must have been like the last of the brood left over from the trappers, eh?"

Sam nodded. "I thought we trapped them all. Let's see." Sam spoke good "residential school" English, but God knows what amount of personal humiliation he endured from the priests. He extended a meaty, brown hand, took the bag when Dave passed it to him, and looked inside. He grunted, reached in, and grabbed the martin by pinching both its dead eyes between his thumb and index finger. When he pulled out the bloody carcass, frozen blood gobs, from when Dave had clobbered it, clung to the fur on its head

Sam said, "If you grab it by the head, you can break it off and ruin the pelt." He held the martin up, so we could all observe Dave's trophy. I was sickened at the thought of its eyes bulging under the pressure of Sam's fingers. The room became silent. I felt more than a little queasy when Sam pulled a knife out to skin it.

Dave said, "Uh, can you skin it here without making a mess?" Sam, holding with the knife, looked at Dave. "It's just, now," said Dave, "I don't feel so much like I want the pelt. I was gonna tan it and clean it up and give it to my ol' lady, as a present from the Arctic, but now I think I changed my mind. Do you want it?"

Sam nodded. He said, "This is worth three dollars at the Slave Lake store. It is better to skin it when it is half frozen." Then he went ahead and skinned it in less than a minute. Sam wrapped the pelt in the plastic bag. During the process, hardly any blood splattered onto the cardboard of the empty beer case Murray kicked over to Sam before things became especially gory. We looked at the skinned skeleton.

Michael said, "They look like a huge squirrel."

I was weirded out by this dead animal on the floor. The moment had become awkward, though it was probably completely normal to John and Silent Sam.

Murray said, "Better get rid of it if the cook already has his eye on it."

We laughed, the spell was broken, and then we were quiet again. Sam was in control. John said nothing that might interfere with his elder. Sam said, "Throw this outside and it will be gone by tomorrow." Dave opened his window again and threw the carcass out, then shut it. We waited for the hordes of predators to come along and clean up the carcass, but nothing so dramatic happened; in fact, nothing at all happened.

My first night in camp had suddenly become anti-climactic. The weather was picking up to a howling blizzard, and it was getting late. It had been a long enough travel day, the beer was finished, I was in debt to the company up to my eyeballs, the food was gross, and we had chased off bullies, strummed and sung songs, and skinned a martin. My bed was probably going to be slightly less comfortable than sleeping on bedrock, but I still looked forward to it. I took the opportunity during the lull in the festivities to bow out.

Michael came back to our room a half hour later. He was out almost immediately and snoring like an honest man. I had a bleeding nose, a gusher, from the crackling dry Arctic air combined with the hot air blowing into our room through the un-grated portal over the door. I was trying to pass out with a single sheet over me. I tossed around in futile attempts to fall asleep in our dry sauna. I was jealous of Michael's snoring.

My discomfort continued late into the night, and I suffered fitful bouts of anxiety. I listened for hours to the wind picking up, slamming hard into the side of the building, then abating. When I finally fell asleep, it was past three a.m. I dreamt a disturbing nightmare: I fought off ferocious wolverines with a crescent wrench; watched Michael fend them off with his knife until they turned on the re-animated, skinned martin, and tore it apart in a frenetic orgy; blood splatter sprayed across my face; the walls of the bunkhouse ran red while the beasts and Sam, huge, accusing martin eyes stuck on the ends of his fingers, drew Aboriginal designs in a pool of gore across a canvas of ice. I startled myself awake every few minutes until the alarm clock finally went off.

The first few sleeps in camp were always fitful.

12. Jack and M-M-Mike

By the time the kitchen opened the next morning, heralding the official arrival of a new day, the wind steadied at north, fifteen mph. It was still dark outside and looked cold, cold, cold.

At breakfast, Dave reported the martin carcass was gone. He said, "It's –53 Fahrenheit, not counting the wind chill." If we don't count it, I thought, why do we mention it? Dave's weather synopsis explained why everyone wore winter snowsuits all the time.

"Dave, is there still a possibility of exiting a bunkhouse and tripping over a wolverine?"

"Hey, are you psychic? In January, Jimmy hired Sam and his trap-line partner. The other guy already left camp to sell the pelts. They had to trap out the animals because on Christmas day, one of the guys was heading for breakfast when a wolverine confronted him on the boardwalk. Back then, wolverine tracks were everywhere, that's nothin' new, but until then, no one had seen one close-up. The guy nearly crapped his drawers and ran for the nearest bunkhouse door. The wolverine chased him."

There had also been at least one family of Arctic foxes, two wolverines, martins, and a million mice and lemmings that ran around under the snow and bunkhouses. Within a couple of weeks, Sam and his partner had cleaned most of them out, except for the lemmings and mice. Sam stayed on as temporary surface labour. He found John a job, but with Michael and me in camp now, Sam and John were redundant and their time left in camp was short.

Dave said, "They only got the one wolverine, though. There is still at least one more around. The surface crew didn't get the garbage out every day, so the animals came in to rummage. The wolverines were sleeping in the shed off the back of the kitchen until last month."

Famished, I joined the line of men filing past the chef. I made the mistake of ordering my eggs over easy. "Royt, it's the royalty 'as arroyved, innit Liz?" said the contentious Cockney. Liz, who bulged in practically every place she should not have and displayed cleavage reminiscent of the business end of a milking cow, tittered from inside the pantry where her build confirmed she spent most of her workday.

I refused Les's bait, which he probably would have boiled or burnt beyond recognition anyway.

"Oh look, Liz, 'e's not so chipper in the morning then, is 'e?"

"No," I said, growling, "'e isn't."

Murray pushed me aside with his tray to place his order, "Two boiled eggs, hard-boiled." Then Dave ordered, "Two boiled eggs, hard-boiled." Then Eddie ordered, "Two boiled heggs, 'ard boil." I began to process the message. When it was his turn, Michael ordered French toast, evoking a round of sarcastic, chirpy mirth from Les. Lizzy looked away, shaking her head, and returned to whatever it was in the pantry that was in such desperate need of her attention.

Our chef said, "Sorry, lad, but there are many still be'ind you," and there were at least forty men in the line, "an' Oy don't 'ave the toyme to prepare foyne French cookery for you. Will that be 'two, over easy' then?"

"That's okay, I guess." Michael slid his tray along to wait in line beside me. The boiled egg crew was busy making themselves stacks of toast at the two toasters. I watched the cook take orders and crack eggs onto the griddle. When he lifted my two eggs with the spatula, they were still goopy. He slopped them onto my plate, handed it to me, and then engaged the next man. The slime Les offered me turned my stomach. An egg-sucking gila monster would have thought twice about slurping at this plate. I scooped tepid, greasy pan fries on the plate and three strips of over-cooked oven bacon. Both the orange and apple juice cans were empty when I tried to pour a glass. I made two pieces of white toast, and then went to eat with the boys. My toast was still warm so I ate it before the margarine congealed. The coffee was brackish and weak.

"What's wrong with this water, anyway?" I asked.

Eddie said, "Dey pump it up from da lake."

"And where do they pump the sewage?"

"Dey pump it down to da lake."

"So, if it ain't breakfast or dinner, what is this guy's specialty, anyway?"

"Stew," said Dave, Murray, and Eddie in unison.

For the next few minutes, I watched Michael, who watched me, eat cold potatoes, gnaw through tough-as-wind-dried-Caribou-hide bacon strips, and wash it down with the brown dishwater they called coffee in this depressing outpost. When I took my plate up to add it to the piles already stacked on the counter, my eggs were still untouched. They swirled around inside the potato moat I built so I could eat the rest of the food on my plate. I had missed three meals the day before and was determined to find a way around our Les-than-acceptable chef and his dizzy Lizzy. I did take note that Dave and Eddie ate their toast after they slathered it with strawberry jam. Murray spread Marmite on his and seemed content with that.

Fifteen minutes later, I left the kitchen alone. To minimize the burning effect of the cold, and avoid chance wolverine encounters, I ran between the buildings. After pulling on my snowsuit and lacing up my new boots, I walked up and down the hallway to test my footwear. Each step I took, my feet slid forward in their boots to rub against the steel toe, so I doubled up my socks. By the time I was ready for work, I was soaked in sweat from the effort. Michael came in to dress for work. He lit a smoke and filled the room with an acrid pall; I vowed, again, to never start smoking.

"How are your boots, Michael?"

He looked up, disappointment crossed his face. "They are tight. Hey, in that suit you look like a little kid." He laughed at me, but we both looked implausible in our new gear. I put on my orange hardhat and oversize gloves and left the room. Michael followed me.

When I stepped outside, the wind tore into my face like a flat file rasp. Overhead lamps still cast a dull amber glow onto the snow. It would be hours before the sun would appear over the horizon. The long stairway down to the works yard intimidated me. My clown boots were tough to manage in the ice that had built up on each step.

We were about to present ourselves to our foreman, Jack Sabe. We descended into the amber, shadowy world of overhead lighting, as yet unblessed, said Murray, "… with the light of Dawn's crack."

The shadowy vagaries of the garages and abandoned storage warehouses made the air feel even colder and the site more deteriorated. We were unsure about where to go, so we opened doors and peered inside each building until I spotted smoke blowing sideways from a short chimney pipe. Errol and the pudgy goon Mike were inside, hogging space around a propane stove.

Michael and I found a space to wait out the uneasy truce. My first impression of the shop was that it smelled like engine oil, and that it epitomized the ramshackle appearance of Port Radium, which,

95

so far, had the character of industrial entropy. A film of fine, black grime coated every surface. The bare, low-wattage bulb glowing above the door produced only a feeble light because of the black dust settled on it. The month-old Edmonton newspaper I lifted off the filthy coffee table was gritty. The chair seats were clean, but the rungs were black with the same powder.

Eddie was sitting behind the desk in the office. He shuffled papers and probably wanted us out of his shop. Friends or not, we had invaded his lair, and, after months in any camp, a person can become sensitive over things like "morning space."

A tall gangly man came in; I recalled his abrasive, mirthless laugh at our reception at the plane. If he had been in the cook shack, I hadn't seen or noticed him. He invaded the quiet room with a noise thinly veiled as jocularity, reminiscent of insecure high-school sophomores trying to attain clique membership and "cool" status. He ranted about "moose meat and pemmican" to John Mantla and Sam. It was their unfortunate timing to follow the mouthpiece through the door.

I had an aversion to the man. Phony people irritate me and I dismiss them as ignoramuses and certainly anyone who provides his own laugh track meets the requirements of my disdain. He said to me, "Virgin meat. Well, how do you like the weather so far? I'm Frank."

John and Sam retired to a bench against a pile of used tires, melting into the background, freed from Frank's brashness.

"Weather's fine, but the wind is relentless," I said. He missed my hint.

"Stick around awhile and you'll see a real Arctic gale," he laughed. His amusement was as hollow as single-hand clapping. "Yup, surface crew gets the worst. The mechanics and miners hide in the shops and scurry underground while we brave the elements. Right, Eddie?" Eddie kept reading. The loudmouth laughed again. "Say," he directed his attention back to me, "you're wearing a new snowsuit. You're lucky. They haven't had any in camp for a couple of months. You must know someone."

I replied that I doubted my interview with JT constituted anyone's idea of *knowing someone*, then busied myself making a Sanka.

Frank turned a one-eighty to confront Michael. "What's your name?" he asked, following the enquiry with another loud laugh.

Michael responded as I expected to the socially inept oaf who stood before him, "Who are you?"

"You're a Frenchy, eh? Well, *salut*. I'm Frank."

"Fuckin' loudmouth Frank," said Errol.

"Hey, c'mon, don't be like that. I'm only trying to be friendly."

My God, this guy is awkward.

The door opened and a hefty man in his fifties walked through, bludgeoning the last of whatever ambience Mouthy Frank had already wrung out of the crew. The older man's face was weather worn, and he packed the sagging paunch and jowls of a heavy drinker and heavy smoker. His thick grey mustache flourished beneath a vibrant red nose. His white scuffed hard hat was resplendent in grime and was perched high on his head, like a pumpkin on a fencepost. Beneath a press-on outline of a polar bear, the logo read: Echo Bay Mines

He slammed the door to capture his audience. Immediately, the door opened again and another older man came in. He was short, stocky, thick-necked, and clean-shaven. He held his hard hat in one hand, exposing a shiny bald skull that expanded backward as far as his coronal suture. A quick look of annoyance appeared then vanished from his red face. Innocuous as a church mouse, he closed the door and then walked straight into the office. Eddie never looked up. The latecomer took off his gloves, put on his brain bucket, and then kicked Eddie out of his chair.

Though he never looked back, the first man yelled an apology, "Sorry Mike. Never saw you behind me."

Mike said, "O-o-okay, J-J-Jack, b-b-but y-y-y-you almost t-t-took m-m-my n-n-nose off." Mike had a bad stutter.. Either that, or he was in the final stages of hypothermia. Young Don walked through the door last, smiling, and happy-go-lucky.

Jack put a quick end to that attitude. "We start at seven-thirty here. You're late."

Don was standing at the door as if his boots had been nailed to the floor. "Sorry, Jack, it won't happen again."

• • •

I already knew that Jan was Jack's niece, so Jan and Donny's jobs were a family affair. Dave had filled in the blanks on the plane. Mike and Jack were partners who specialized in "fixing" floundering mining operations in the North, top guns hired to turn failing mining operations profitable, cut corners, rid the operation of "bad apples," set production schedules and keep to them, interpolate spreadsheets and vague sets of boardroom notions into higher production, build a team, and instill pride in us working fodder.

Dave told us JT had hired Jack and Mike in January, "because of their reputations," but specifically, to bring the original Eldorado mine back into profitable production. Even though it was a 'hot" hole, there was silver down there, and JT wanted it. JT rejected Jimmy's recommendation they close the mine because it lost too much money, that it cost the family enterprise. But no one believed JT could let that silver lie there dormant and frozen in rock beneath the Arctic snow, so he'd found an alternative, Jack and Mike.

Mike's contribution to the recovery of the fortunes of the mine had become legend. Priority one, which Mike decided to undertake his second day in camp, and which was the day he acquired his camp nickname, was to remove a failed water pump from the Eldorado mine. To accomplish this, Mike used the fifty-ton D9 cat, which currently occupied over half the same mechanic's shop where the surface crew marshaled for work. It was the largest piece of mobile machinery at the mine site and was invaluable to operations. They used the cat to move heavy machinery, grade the summer airstrip, maintain the roads, and tow sled loads of tailings and the worst of the chemical waste to the lake dump.

Mike was an innovator, so he decided to take a short cut. He drove the D9 brute down the ramp and onto the lake ice in order to shorten the preposterously cold nighttime drive to the Eldorado mine adit. Mike rumbled over the dark ice created by the putrid volumes of power plant effluent poured continuously into the lake.

At the same time Mike was walking the cat across the lake, Jack was in his quarters popping the cap on his second bottle of whiskey. The phone rang. He answered a call from the agitated power plant mechanic. "You better get down here. Some idiot drove the cat onto the ice. I think he's in trouble out there."

Jack knew exactly who *the idiot* was. Jack jumped in his pickup with his bottle, but without a second thought about drunk driving, and raced down the narrow, icy incline toward the power plant and the lake. Observers waiting for burgers at the crowded community hall remarked with wonder how the snow banks kept his truck on the road. At the bottom of the dangerous hill, Jack launched onto the lake at the east end of LaBine bay, via the Echo Bay mine ramp. He performed two 360-degree donuts, but managed to carry on speeding toward the accident scene. In the pale amber light, Jack approached a flatbed delivery truck, a pickup, and the forklift parked around a new hole in the ice, a hole big enough to accommodate a three-bedroom rancher or a D9 cat. What looked like a white cork bobbed in the center of the hole. When Jack was out of his truck, he saw the cork was Mike's hardhat.

"Get him the fuck out of there," Jack hollered, though his command was redundant; the rescuers were already reeling Mike in. He flopped, jabbered, and floundered on the ice like a wounded seal until Jack bundled him into his truck and drove to the warm mechanic's garage.

Both men drank gulps from Jack's whiskey bottle. In front of the rest of the rescue crew, Jack asked, "Mike. What the fuck happened here?"

Mike stuttered back, "D-d-d-d-d..."

That would have gone on for a while, so Jack guessed, "The D9 cat?"

Mike nodded. "I-I-I-I-I..."

Jack guessed at the obvious, "Ice?"

Mike was struggling, but nodded before he took another drink from the bottle. "B-b-b-b-b-b..."

Jack winced. "Are you telling me the cat broke through the ice and is on the bottom of the lake? Jesus fucking Christ! I oughta throw you back in ... Gimme that bottle."

After another stiff belt, Jack launched into a fit of unbridled rage, which was, actually, the only skill for which he was infamous throughout the territories. Fueled by the whiskey and the sheer embarrassment of such a monumental blunder their first week on a new job, Jack gave full vent to a vitriolic rant and tore up one side of Mike and down the other. His fifteen minutes of wrath made several return trips over the same abused territory.

Mike was defiant, and stuttered back his defense, "F-f-f-f-f-f-..."

"Don't try to talk to me like that, you stuttering m-m-motherfucker."

A nickname was born.

M-M-Mike went silent. His dunking was worse because of his long-time partner's humiliating scolding. However, the fact remained, the D9, and Jack and M-M-Mike's reputations as well as their hopes of ever finding another job, had sunk possible hundreds of feet to the bottom of Great Bear Lake. Mike's hypothermic blood boiled.

M-M-Mike exploded with anger. "B-b-b …"

"Bullshit is it? If that's all you have to say, you can stand here arguing, but I won't. Consider yourself fired. I'll see you're on the plane in the morning."

"G-g-g-g-g-g…"

"Good riddance to you, too."

Mike passed out drunk in the powerhouse that night. He had it the easiest of the two.

Jack stormed out to his pickup and banged off snow banks at dangerous speeds until he returned to the bunkhouse he shared with Jimmy, Schläger, M-M-Mike, and the other managers. The rest of Jack's long night was an endurance test.

"Moronic and useless, no, worse than useless," was Jimmy's summation of Jack and Mike's performance. Jimmy's drunken tirade, witnessed by Bill, Ernie, Stalin, and Carl was ramping down by two thirty a.m. Jack tried to quit several times, if only to dodge Jimmy's liberal shower of abuse, but to no avail. "The fuck you're quitting … You and that stammering fuckup who just closed this mine and put everybody out of work are going to fix this. You've lost the right to quit." Jack said nothing; he tried to leave the room. "Where do you think you're going? You owe me, you and that sidekick of yours."

"I don't owe you fuck all …"

"You son-of-a-bitch. Both you two stay here and work your debts off. Do you hear me? Get that cat back and operational, or I'll take a shotgun to you both myself. You start the recovery today. Your choice." Jimmy also pointed out the additional matter of their penury. "You owe me for your flights in and out, your company store debt, not to mention the booze and smokes bills you two already have at the curling rink."

The Cigar Lip reputation for wringing pennies out of pockets exposed itself. Without any wiggle room, Jack and M-M-Mike remained in camp.

That morning, Dawn cracked the dark, morning lock after nine a.m., but Jack had already seen the light. By six, Eddie, who was in early due to the loss of the D9, listened in as Jack talked to M-M-Mike, who shivered inside a couple of greasy pairs of coveralls in the mechanic's office. M-M-Mike was nursing his hangover and recovering from his hypothermia.

Jack finished his hasty, assuaging monologue. "After all," Jack said, "we're partners." M-M-Mike agreed, returning a stuttered apology. Finally, the two old friends shook hands.

They devised a plan to raise the cat. Over the next twenty-four hours, during another horrendous January blizzard, they wrestled one of the huge mine winches out of the Echo Bay mine, then trucked it across the ice to "M-M-Mike's fishin' hole." They fabricated a triple-pulley tripod system that provided enough lifting capacity to raise the fifty-ton Caterpillar D9 off the bottom of the lake. In effect, they went fishing for the machine.

"Through sheer, blind whiskey-soused luck, son-of-a-bitch if they didn't hook onto it on one of the few places where the lift would not tear the purchase off the cat," Dave commented.

At –55F, minus the ignored wind chill, over forty-eight hours of dark Arctic nights and through that howling blizzard, they resurrected the cat from what surely, without divine intervention, was going to be the watery grave of the gunslingin' legacy of Jack Sabe and his troubleshootin' partner, M-M-Mike.

When Michael and I arrived in Port Radium, M-M-Mike was still rebuilding the cat, bolt by rusty bolt. He disassembled each mechanical and hydraulic component, sent it out of camp by truck to Yellowknife or Edmonton, and then trucked the refurbished parts back into camp, where he reassembled the items. The timeline for completion of the exorbitantly expensive job was four to six months. The estimate for the rebuild ran in excess of $300,000, plus M-M-Mike's time and the begrudged labour of several heavy-duty mechanics.

Jimmy cut corners to make the camp budget work. One of those corners was in the kitchen. To eclipse another expense, Jimmy took over as General Manager of the mine operations, interviewing short-timers and firing anyone who refused to "re-up." This allowed Echo Bay to bill them for their flights; free labor was synonymous with free enterprise to Jimmy. JT and his kid knew how to save a dollar and keep it in their own pockets.

Dave said, "If I know Jimmy, after repairing the cat, Jack and M-M-Mike will leave camp without so much as a sou when he runs them off."

13. Cement

Jack stabbed at us with an index finger. "You and you. You got cement." Michael and I had cement, whatever that meant. "The rest of you take bars and picks and clear the ice off the tracks in the Eldorado service tunnel. Sean knows what to do." *Sean who?*

Jack sent us off to places I had no idea existed, but which had something to do with cement and the mystery man, Sean. Frank, Sam, Don, and John filed out of the shop. Michael and I scrambled behind them, rustling in our new winter clothes.

When we stepped again into the bitter cold of the Arctic pre-sunrise morning, we agreed our boss' shoulder was slightly colder. A forklift idled noisily in the road, spewing a cloud of noxious diesel exhaust while the driver waited inside the enclosed cab. I had the sense that beneath his muffles and padding, behind his ski-goggles, and inside his hood, his game was different from waiting for us. Resolute and mute inside what looked to be a comfortable, heated, cubicle, he pointed at Michael and me. He jerked his thumb backwards. No wrinkle of a smile creased the stoic face beneath his thin, blond beard.

"I think we go there," surmised Michael.

To my surprise, we were enjoying the benefit of a blue-grey dawn leaking into our day from the east. We followed the forklift through the industrial gauntlet of warehouses and shops to the Quonset huts and the long balustrade of barrels on Silver Point.

"This should be interesting," I said. My teeth already hurt from the cold. "We work outside while the other guys chip ice in a tunnel, the lucky stiffs." I turned into the cold and felt under-appreciated. I walked like Charlie Chaplin in my clown boots, laughing with Michael, who hobbled beside me like he was foot-bound.

When we arrived at the flat on Silver Point, we caught up to the forklift driver. He waited for us in front of one of the green huts with a pallet of cement bags on his forks. He had broken the pallet out of a frozen snow bank covering many more like it. The pallet crunched in the snow when he lowered it. We were in the lee of the wind below the crest of the ridge. On the plane, Dave had told me we were at the spot where the company dumped "a zillion tons" of radioactive ore tailings into the lake from the conveyor belt. Of course, as ghastly a crime as this was, it paled when compared to the fact that Michael and I walked on some of the 170,000 tons of concentrated, radioactive tailings dumped right in the camp, within spitting distance of the Eldorado ventilation shafts.

But we jumped right in, like many before us, clown boots and bound feet notwithstanding, with no protective breathing apparatus or clothing, no choice, and certainly no information regarding the risks of contamination through breathing the deadly dust. I dragged the Quonset hut door open; the grime on the hinges and the buildup of snow on the jams bound the door.

"Jesus, Michael, all that silver," I said, clapping the black grime off my mitts, puffing up a small cloud of dust, "you'd think they'd put a couple of bucks into cleaning this place up a little. The war ended in '45, right?"

Jack's order, "You got cement," translated into a chore of humping frozen, eighty-pound bags from the pallets into the hut. Michael's face was the color of a ripe pomegranate, and I assumed I looked the same. I squinted at the orange glare forming on the top of the ridge across LaBine bay. Those long fingers of hopeful, orange rays would fail to reach us down here for hours.

Before he sped away, the operator opened the door of the cab an inch. Over the roar of his heater, he yelled, "Welcome to Silver Point." His instructions helped us nail down the intellectual part of the job: "Don't break any bags. Pile the cement in the hut. Make neat rows. Right to the roof." He slammed the cab door, and then backed off a few feet to observe us.

Michael observed, "That must be Sean. I guess everyone here is an asshole except us."

I tended to agree. We looked at each other in the subdued shadows of Silver Point and burst out laughing, and then turned to the task. We had to move the twelve bags of cement stacked in three layers on the pallet, still covered by a thick cap of snow. Sean tore off at warp speed to retrieve another pallet.

I grabbed a corner of one of the top bags with both hands. It remained frozen in place, so I reefed on it with a little more heart to break it free. I moved the bag around, brushed away the snow, and then picked it up. The effort caused me to exhale with a short, involuntary grunt. I was out of work shape, but was able to Chaplin twenty feet in my clown boots to the Quonset hut. The last ten feet to the door was a narrow path stomped flat through the deep snow berm. The low, small door of the hut required both a step up and a simultaneous bending maneuver to duck beneath the upper jam. I shifted the bag of cement as I stepped inside with a tossing motion, then pulled off a sort of catch, utilizing my forward momentum when I stepped over the high doorsill and fully into the dim interior. Inside, I could stand tall again. The move was tricky wearing clown boots.

The light filtered in from the door was enough to make out, twenty-five feet farther inside, a tier of cement bags piled halfway to the rounded ceiling. Cement from bags that had broken some time in the past covered the floor. I clopped across the dusty floor of the hut, raising a clogging cloud. Michael was right behind me. I placed my bag on the pile. Michael did the same. Neither bag lay flat. We studied the bags; "80 lbs" was perfectly legible on each bag. I picked up my bag and dropped it harder onto the tier. It broke its frozen shape, but the bag held and it lay flat. Michael followed suit. We hustled outside again; the forklift was back already.

Sean had returned with a second pallet. "I guess he's in a hurry," I said. Wasting no time, Michael and I each broke another bag away from the first pallet and humped our loads into the hut, then hot-stepped it back to repeat the sequence. Three pallets later, in order to stack the bags right to the ceiling, the stacking procedure required we drop the bag to the floor to flatten it, then lift it again, make a final shift and half-press lift as well.

Within a half hour, I had taken off my toque despite the obnoxious cement dust cloud in the hut. The cold was a relief. A couple of completed rows later, I unzipped my parka and the zipper on my snowsuit to halfway down my chest.

Michael and I made a game of the job: if we hustled through the bags, we could make it hard for Sean to keep up with us. Our goal was to be waiting over an empty pallet every time he returned with another full one. Sean kept the pallets coming for two and half hours; our stack of empties was impressive. At ten thirty, Sean waited with empty forks, faked slitting his throat, and pointed to the shop area before he drove off. We had emptied eighteen pallets, filling almost all the empty space in the hut. My forearms and hands felt a bit sore, and I had put my lower back through a workout, but neither of us was feeling debilitated. If this was Jack's idea of hard labor punishment, it had failed. Michael agreed. "They want to see if we are tough." Michael and I followed Sean's vapor trail toward the rising orange sun. I looked forward to a cup of hot Sanka and the friendly camaraderie shared by those of us roughing it in camp.

I calculated the tonnage we hand-bombed that morning at over seventeen tons of cement, which was over eight tons each — before coffee time. Michael and I agreed ours was a good start to the first shift. Jack was somewhere else when we returned to the shop, and Sean had vanished, so we fixed up a coffee and watched M-M-Mike work on the cat. Forty minutes later Jack came in. He was mellower now, and said, "You guys moved that cement already?"

Ignoring the muscle seizures that had begun to rack my body, I said, "Yeah. The guy on the forklift was tired, I guess; he quit on us. You want us to do the rest, Jack?"

He looked at me and discerned at least a modicum of smart-ass, then said, "You always got something to say, eh? No. You guys stay here and sweep up until after lunch." I was relieved Jack didn't call my bluff, but to maintain my bravado, I pretended mock disappointment. When he left, we sat around for the half-hour that remained of our first morning.

At lunchtime, we tramped up the "stairway to heaven," through the bunkhouses, and across the ridge to the cook shack. We sat down to bowls of yellow-green stew. *Chicken, at one time, maybe?* I ignored the stew, and slathered margarine and jam on toast, then gorged that down. The hot coffee was weak, but better than Sanka and milk powder, so I had a quick cup or three. At first, I was going to avoid the stew, but Frank explained that the more you take and throw out the sooner it disappears. The theory had a major flaw, however, because the supply never ran out. Les was a stew impresario, a magician with leftovers and a ladle.

After lunch, the surface crew reassembled in Eddie's shop. Jack showed up before Frank could run his mouth. Jack said, "More ice. Everyone over to Echo Bay mine shaft." His leadership and enthusiasm failed to energize us for smashing ice in rock tunnels.

However, we squeezed into the only two-crew cab pickups, then followed Jack through the gloomy ground fog to the Echo Bay silver adit. Frank explained this was the primary silver warren at the Port Radium site, situated at the east shore of LaBine Bay. This mine featured a wooden structure built over the entrance. Two smaller storage sheds leaned against the main, windowless shed. The heated, larger shed was the mine dry room, where the miners changed into their work clothes. It was also the office and where the dynamite and blasting caps were stored.

Michael and I followed the others to the door of the office shack, but Jack stopped us. "You don't go in there; only miners, the bosses, and the geologist go in there. You're going here ..." He shuffled us across the black snow to a door in one of the dismal storage sheds. Like every other building in Port Radium, it was rough-built and deteriorated. This one looked like a miniature of the first Rogers Pass avalanche sheds. When Jack opened the squeaking door, we found an assortment of digging tools inside: shovels, picks, peaveys, and steel pry bars.

"Grab your shovels and picks. You're gonna crack some ice."

I selected a peavey, the heaviest tool I could find. I thought it might be easier to make headway wielding something heavy. Also, it made me appear an earnest "ice man." Once armed, we soldiered over to the mine entrance. Mouthy Frank whistled the dwarf tune *Heigh-Ho* as we entered the tunnel. Jack flipped a switch on a beam and a string of overhead bare bulbs illuminated the tunnel. "Fancy," I said. "Do they have TV, too?" The lighting painted crazy reptilian-skin shadows along the irregular walls, but it was pleasant and warm in the tunnel, at least 10F. I took my mitts off and stuffed them in my pockets, but the frozen wooden handle of the peavey forced me to put them on again.

Fifty feet in, where the light string ended, we stopped at the opening to a branch tunnel. It looked like it might run off to our left. However, this puzzle would remain unresolved because a wall of ice blocked the entry.

"Take this out," Jack said.

"Where do we put the ice, Jack?" asked Frank. "In our pockets?"

"Always the lip. Go get an ore car and load it up and push it as far as the tracks go that way." Jack pointed to yet another tunnel mouth farther down the original tunnel. The tracks in our tunnel linked with the light gauge tracks coming out of that tunnel. "Dump it down the 'winze'; that's a hole in the floor for you new guys. They're all over the place, so don't fall in. I'll send Sean with the bus when it's quitting time. The miners will drive the trucks back." He left us to it.

After Jack left, I said, "It's been *quittin' time* since I got on the plane." Instead of a laugh, there was solemn agreement from everyone.

Errol and Mike left to find an ore car. Frank shared his opinion of the job: he complained about its impossibility, postulated on the insurmountable effort required to crack Arctic ice, extrapolated on the unfeasible expectations we might fill even a single car. He lamented the danger of the dumping procedure and groaned about the obvious lack of respect with which management treated the entire surface crew by forcing us to work underground. In return, we gave him crap for using words too big for even his mouth, then started to hack away at the ice.

Frank was right, though I would throw myself down a winze before I ever acknowledged it, the ice was as impermeable as Italian granite. We poured our hearts into it, but the tough-as-diamonds surface yielded little to our steel assault. Our Arctic version of a Louisiana prison gang scything weeds in a ditch kept at it, and soon ice chips flew up into our faces and we scratched the diamond-hard surface. Frank, our shovel man, tried to assume the position of straw boss, so we heaped verbal abuse on him, then ganged up on him and filled his boots with our ice chips. Half an hour later, Errol and Mike returned, pushing an ore cart along the tracks. When they stopped, Frank shoveled a few shards into the ore cart. This project was going to take time.

We talked between ourselves throughout the afternoon, getting to know each other better, except for "Silent" Sam, who was always stoical, but he could lean into a prying bar. Within minutes, my gloves and hat had come off. I opened my snowsuit to the belt. All of us were sweating, except Errol, who refused to work; he remained silent, smoking, out of the picture, "quit" written all over his face. His bubble had burst and no one except big Mike had much time for him. Frank and Big Mike were our shovel men, so occasionally one of them scraped a thin layer of ice shards up from around our feet and flicked them into the ore car. We kept at it for three more hours. We filled two and a half cars, hacking frozen chunks from the practically impenetrable wall of ice.

At one point Frank said, "This ice can't be frozen water.

Mammoth piss, maybe, but water, no." His solitary laugh echoed awkwardly in the tunnel.

I said, "You must have been an only child."

When Sean and the bus returned, his goggles were propped over his forehead. In the gloomy light, I saw now he was roughly my age and thin. Frank told me his family name was Sigurdsson, so he was of Scandinavian descent. His fuzzy beard covered only half his chicken pox scars. Sean's eyes appeared strained behind his John Lennon granny glasses, which perched on his ski-slope nose above a turned-down slash of a mouth. I decided he was arrogant, but not formidable. His aloof demeanor irritated me, but I could handle that.

I said, "Hey Sean, we're working here. Careful, the concept might rub off on you."

He ignored me. "Day's done. If you want a ride, the bus is outside. Put the tools back first. Errol, you have to return the ore car to the train. I'm leaving in five minutes; I still have a delivery to make. Anyone misses the bus can walk." He left.

The acute drop in temperature between inside and outside the mine caused me to gasp. The sweat on my forehead froze during the few steps to the tool shed and the idling bus. Before the bus ride ended, I felt blisters on my hands where I thought I had calluses. The tendons in my hands and muscles in my arms were weak and sore. I should have kept my gloves on; my hands would start to cramp within fifteen minutes. By then, I expected to be in a hot shower, anticipating a great meal of steak, fries, and gravy, the kind of comforting food you want after hours of grinding labour in the strength-sapping elements.

For show, before Mike had a chance to sit, and because he was the last to arrive in the bus, Sean sped us away. Big Mike flopped into Errol's lap; Errol pushed him off and onto the floor in a mound of snowsuits and cursing. *Welcome to the live Gong Show.* Frank, Don, Michael, and I laughed at the two idiots. John and Sam saw all of it, but remained quiet. Eventually Errol's cursing and our catcalling and laughing stopped.

Looking outside, and even in the dark sky, I saw the weather had taken an ominous turn for the worst; a monstrous system of low, thick snow clouds mushroomed in a stall over camp, and above us grey layers swirled in an inverted cauldron, stirred by conflicting wind currents.

Errol said, "We're takin' a hit tonight, boys."

Maybe so, but my plan was to be well fed and in dreamland before that atmospheric bomb dropped on us. To my chagrin, my first day was far from finished.

14. The Convoy, the Stash, and Chicken Arms

At -55F, we were under siege. Looking out our bunkhouse window, I pined for the tropical climes of Edmonton in February. The unabated, vengeful hurricane from the north screamed angry menace at us as it whipped snow off the ground, mixed it with the falling snow, formed it into swirls of ice crystals, and then slammed the shards at our window.

I pitied the animals that had to endure the storm, the beasts unable to shield themselves from the wind or burrow into the snow and survive beneath the worst of it. For millennia, through the interminable dark months of winter, an endless barrage of killing blizzards stole the strength of wintering caribou. Throughout the worst of the storms, the bulls held fast, turned against the onslaught to create a sheltering circle for the cows. They, in turn, protect their calves, never letting them lie down inside the life-preserving windbreak. Magnificent bulls have frozen to death saving their mates and the next generation. What tenacity keeps the species alive despite Nature's fury?

Man's exploitation of Nature, however, and his waste, threaten to obscure the legacy of thousands of magnificent generations of which today's vanishing, bedraggled herds are the last. It is painful to know that hundreds of species vanish from the world forever each year, and yet we continue.

Amber lights illuminated the nighttime chaos. Driven snow whipped over our heads, creating a maelstrom armed with razor-sharp edges. Prolonged exposure could strip exposed skin to the bone. The wind chill had to be below -65F, however, as Dave said, "No one bothers to measure wind chill in Port Radium."

Being stupid and desperate enough to hire on as surface crew at the Arctic Circle in winter, I knew I might have to brave the elements occasionally. Still, these exotic conditions slapped even the seasoned veterans. Like them, I kept my snowsuit on to travel back and forth to the cook shack.

At dinner, talk of the weather overshadowed my disappointment with the stew. Dave also informed us of Jack's reprieve; we were finished, for now, our futile attempt to drive a hole through six feet of ice in the tunnel; the night shift miners were going to blow the plug with powder. "We'll clean it up," Dave said, "like rabid badgers." To a man, our crew was willing to sublet the job to the professionals.

We were emptying a semi-trailer truck, and I cursed to damnation the hail of ice shards stinging my eyes. Though we worked in the lee of the ridge and out of the brute force of the gale, there was no way to see, and at the same time bend or twist to avoid the swirling assault. Every light standard in the works yard swayed in the gale, but one light danced the craziest, clanging like the last call to board Charon's barge to Hades. Our shadows flitted across the snow, darting like elongated phantoms across the amber-tinged walls of the storage sheds.

We were working in the gale because Murphy's Law dictated the inevitable knock on our door would occur at the most inopportune moment. Half an hour after dinner, just thirty minutes earlier, a loud, obtrusive thump had wakened me out of a sound sleep. Sean stood at our door.

Until then, I was able to endure my aching muscles silently. I fooled myself into pretending I was not horribly sore. However, the moment Sean arrived, my pretense blew away with the blizzard.

After supper, I had stretched out on my bunk, fake-reading the words in my book. I was listless and drowsy from the excessive heat, and despite the torture of my mattress and Michael flicking his pig-sticker open and closed and smoking Gitanes like he owned a tobacco plantation, I conked out. Until my eyelids closed, Michael had been explaining the correct technique to employ when killing and skinning a Harp seal.

"Trucks are in," Sean said. "You gotta unload the freezer car. Now. It's mandatory for surface crew." He left to press Frank, John, Sam, Don, Errol, and Mike into the gang.

I said, "I sure as hell don't want this overtime."

"It looks like you got a nice nap."

"What nap?" I snapped back, annoyed at Sean for waking me. I stood up, unable to suppress a monster yawn, pulling on my snowsuit again. "I was reading."

"Is that a BC trick? Read with your eyes closed. Anyways, we have to unload the trucks."

"How are your feet?" After work, I'd watched Michael

remove his under-sized boots. The blood had dried on the toes of his socks.

Michael shrugged, then pulled on a new pair of socks he'd purchased with credit at the company store. "Not too bad, not too good."

When the rest of the crew tramped past our room in single file, we joined the chain gang. I clown-hopped down the long set of icy, snow-covered stairs ahead of Michael, who limped behind me. Through the blizzard, I saw a semi-trailer truck in the marshaling yard, parked in front of a doublewide Quonset hut. Neither Michael nor I had been inside this building.

The conditions were extreme and disorienting, dark side of the moon stuff. Thankfully, the full force of the north wind raked over the exposed buildings at the top of the ridge, which protected us from the storm raging overhead, although we still had to work through an unending, swirling blur of ice crystals and snowflakes. From the sound of it, the wind speed was increasing by the minute.

When Sean unlocked the padlock on the shed door, he confirmed the temperature and that the wind pushed it down to "Minus dead if you're caught in it."

The back half of the trailer was already empty. We still had to unload the truck's freezer locker and hump the cargo into the storage hut. Sean said, "Only Jimmy, Jack, and the cook have these keys."

I watched Sean use his own duplicate key to open the freezer-shed door. "How'd you get a key?" I asked.

"What key? Don't mess around in here and don't get any ideas. Right?"

I looked inside the well-lit room and realized this was where Ali Babba lived when he was in town. Ideas of grand theft passed between us when I caught Michael's keen eye. The shed walls were airtight. The heated interior was the size of a double-wide house trailer. Out of the wind, it was dry and already half-stocked with cases of goodies, piled from the cement floor to the eight-foot, rounded ceiling. Sean left to unlock the freezer car.

"There has to be a way to get in here, Michael. And now we know there is more in this camp to eat than fucking stew." A quick inventory of cases of shrimp, oysters, crab, rows of jars and cans of condiments pissed me off. I peered inside one of four unlocked freezers lined up against a sidewall, and found whole Sockeye salmon, halibut roasts, and lobsters. Inside another freezer, I saw racks of pork ribs, Baron's of Beef, and in another, an entire freezer full of porterhouse steaks and pork chops. We were too far north for there to be fresh vegetables or fruit squirreled away here. At the back of the hut, there was another mysterious door secured with a padlock.

Frank noticed my interest. "They store the bonspiel liquor in there."

"How come we never see this food?"

"This is for the sugar shack; this is what the mine managers eat. That's why they hardly ever eat in the cook shack. Sean delivers the fresh fruit and vegetables from the plane to the sugar shack."

Michael and I looked at each other, both of us scheming.

Sean came inside to yell at us, "The sooner you start the sooner you get out of this weather."

For that minute, I forgot how weak and sore I was; I felt like a little boy again, discovering presents and nametags beneath the Christmas tree before my parents came downstairs.

But we had a job to do. Big Mike and Errol had climbed into the freezer unit and piled boxes at the door. I wanted to know how much we had to unload, so I also climbed into the freezer compartment. We had four hours of work; if we hustled, it could be three. Curiously, it was far warmer in the freezer than it was outside, which explained Errol and Big Mike volunteering to work inside the icebox. The simple exercise of climbing into the truck re-acquainted me with the strain in my back and shoulders. Both my arms were like cooked spaghetti noodles, and my sore hands ached when I flexed in my mitts. When I lifted a box from the freezer deck to pack it inside the shed, I had to engage my whole body to roll a thirty-pound case of crab onto my complaining shoulders. Soon, each load was a fifty-foot test of will to make it to the shed, but I kept the pace for an hour and a half.

We took a break to warm up in the freezer car. I was soaked with sweat under my snowsuit, so it was unwise to stand around outside; sweat kills in the Arctic. Sitting on a stack of frozen chicken breasts, I announced to no one in particular, "Don't know how much more I have in me tonight, boys. I'm already pretty useless here."

Nobody was inspired to comment. After they smoked the break out, we resumed unloading the rest of the shipment. Except for Errol and Mike, who walked away into the night claiming this over-time job was "bullshit." Frank and Don took over emptying the freezer car. They both brought me lighter loads, but my body had shut down during the break, as if I were a distance runner who'd hit a wall in a marathon. There was no quit in me, but I had no choice; I was done.

My last effort was pitiful. I accepted the challenge of a frozen, twenty-five pound butterball Turkey. I patted it, rubbed the label clean of frost to confirm the weight, and said, "Okay, bird, it's you or me." The intervening Fates decided this turkey would unfairly employ gravity to purloin my honor. I rolled the turkey into my arms, locked my hands together with the last of my strength, pulled the frozen bird up to my chin, turned, took a step, and the damn turkey slid between my arms, broke free of my hands, and dropped to the frozen snow. Now a featherless insult, the bird mocked me. I was embarrassed. The gauntlet thrown, the frozen bird was the challenge. If I was to be a member of this surface crew in Port Radium, I had to pick it up and pack it to a freezer in the shed. Through sheer grit, I thought, my will can overcome utter exhaustion. For inspiration, in my mind, I sang *Why Can't We Be Friends* and was determined I would conquer trivial gravity. Beneath an amber light, I saw a vision of myself resurrecting the bird and my pride and transporting both into the freezer shed. I dropped to my knees and rolled the turkey into my lap, locked my fingers around the fowl, and prepared to stand up tall on depleted legs. I stood up, but to my chagrin I was without the turkey. My arms had slid around my capable adversary again. I doubted I had the strength to wrestle as much a rattle away from a toddler, so, on my hands and knees, I pushed the turkey across the snow to the door of the shed. I tried the same lift again. No go, same result. I was a three-time loser. My life had come down to a face-off between the butterball and me, at –55F, in a howling blizzard at the Arctic Circle. I lost.

Played right out, defeated, and kneeling on the snow, I blocked the door to the shed. Strangely, nobody razzed me when stepping around me, bringing boxes, bags, and turkeys into the shed. I humbled myself before the frozen bird for the last time. I stood up, walked back to the freezer car, and announced, "I'm done. Sorry, boys, but I have nothing left. If I can't pack a turkey, I'm going back to the bunkhouse. I'm not sitting around here in this cold."

Don said, "No sweat, we're almost done here, anyway."

I began my lonely walk of shame through the blizzard to the bunkhouse, up the poorly lit plank stairs, which, for the moment, felt like gallows steps. Thirty minutes later, Michael came in from the storm. I told him I had never been so useless.

"It don't matter. But that Sean is sure an asshole."

"Why? What did he say?"

"Never mind. I told him to fuck off anyways." He lit a smoke, looking at me with raised eyebrows and laughed. I joined him. I was so drained everything was funny. "*Tabernacle*," he said. "We moved a lot of cement today. They should be happy with us."

I knew there would be more to it than that, but for now, I didn't give a crap. We talked about the booze locker and the high-end grub that sure as hell was missing from our cook shack. From behind a cloud of cigarette smoke, Michael said, "I think I will join that curling club. They got the girls, the food, and the booze."

He spoke to me from far away, down the dark end of a lengthening tunnel, where the echoes of his precise insight rang true. I passed into sweet, heavy sleep, serenaded by Michael, who clicked his knife open and closed. It was past two a.m.

15. Socks

I didn't toss around much in the dry heat. All too soon, the obnoxious clanging of Michael's alarm clock ushered in our second morning in Port Radium. A lengthy string of French invective followed the abrupt cessation of the alarm. I looked through our window and saw it had stopped snowing. The earth's celestial wobble would prevent the sun from appearing above the horizon for another few hours.

I had to climb out of my rack, but when I tried to move, I knew I was in trouble. My body was one persistent, aching cramp; my seized shoulders held my neck for ransom; it actually hurt to blink. I stirred like a fetid zombie digging out of a grave. My stomach muscles complained bitterly when I half-raised myself on one elbow to free my legs from the tangled sheet. "Hey Michael, I think we know what they fill these mattresses with now."

He mumbled back something like, "Cement, *tabernac.*"

I was sure a flesh-eating virus was attacking me, consuming my muscles like a bear tearing into a fallen elk. Michael rose fast, dressed, and left the room as if his hair was on fire. I cursed my disappointing body and its weakness. I was sure I had made it through worse before, but was unable to recall exactly when. As a pain gauge, I compared my first weeks on the CN wire gang as a sixteen-year-old and logging as a twenty-one year old. *This ranks close, but isn't that bad, is it?*

My own rule of thumb was, "If I cannot pull my work socks on, I will not go to work." I should have left them on the night before, but it was just too hot in that room. It's that simple: if every effort I can muster fails to provide what it takes me to pull on a pair of socks, then I refused to take that uselessness to a job and accept wages. I work for my money, and I would not take anyone's charity. If an employer doesn't understand that, my response was, "I was looking for a job when I found this one …" That flippant offer to quit on grounds of integrity worked in logging camps to stifle aggressive management, but I was in the Arctic and thousands of dollars in debt to JT.

I rolled and flopped around to work myself into an upright position. I was severely sore and embarrassed. Sitting on the edge of the bed, I maneuvered my body with a little less agility than Frankenstein, so I could use both hands to pull my sock drawer half-open. My right forearm cramped painfully with the effort. I rubbed out the cramp with my other hand, until that forearm cramped. *Jesus H. Christ.* I forced both arms straight and stretched the cramps out, discovering new pain in my hands and fingers. My neck cracked then it cramped. I felt a simultaneous and unnerving "pull" from the middle of my back. That pain became acute and trumped my stomach muscle cramp, of which I had suddenly become aware. *Goddamn cement.* After I'd stretched and massaged out most of the cramps, I was stable enough to re-focus on my socks.

Fed from a spring of optimism and vitality, the source of which I guessed might be my inexperience and youth, I thought, *This might be okay, after all.* I broke out a pair of socks. My fingers seized and the cramping threatened to return. I had to finish this feeble attempt before Michael returned, or I would never live this down. Desperate, I mustered my depleted stamina.. At the end of my dead arms, weak fingers pinched a single, wool work sock. Every fiber in my body, mind, and spirit wanted to pull that sock onto my foot, so I could dress, put on my boots, and join the crew pounding at whatever ice Jack had for us.

Try as I might, I was unable to bend. I almost rolled off the bed, emitting an involuntary yelp when I stopped myself. I tried again, and managed to hook two of my toes into one sock, but strained my lower back muscles, which dictated I release and sit up or succumb to months of traction. Again, I put my best effort into the reach for my toes, but lost the position even exhaling to lengthen my reach, to pull on my wool sock. Each of my next several attempts failed worse than the previous. Finally, I was out of gas.

Beaten first by a turkey and now a wool sock, it seemed the inanimate objects in the Arctic had turned the tide against me. A gust of wind slapped hard against the window with what seemed like an unnecessary victory salute. I rolled onto my bed, pulled a sheet over myself, and read my book.

Michael returned at 7:15 a.m. He said, "I thought you were having breakfast?"

"Not today. If I can't pull on my socks, then I don't work. That's my rule."

Missing the translation, he asked, "Your cock?"

"Sock! Not cock." I held up my wool Waterloo to dispel his confusion. "I'll go see the nurse and try to work this afternoon. Can you tell Jack for me?" Michael nodded, but looked doubtful. We both knew the unstated rule that new guys don't miss the second day of work because of soreness. I said, "Michael, I'm serious, I can't pull my socks on. I ain't goin' ... They can fire me if they have to."

"So, then we will see you at lunch. Have a nice sleep." He closed the door when he left, a kind gesture, but his final comment irked me.

Not even a slight orange slip of sunrise appeared outside the window when he left. I felt like a soldier in the trenches with foot rot, who cannot go over the top with his mates into the murderous machine-gun crossfire. At least in that situation, I could have thrown myself across the barbed wire so the others could run across my body to advance. I didn't sleep, I worried; I needed this job. Reading was out of the question and I was hungry, having missed another meal. It was already crucial to eat something every few hours. Without food, I would lose stamina and grit, two qualities required for this job, and both of which I was temporarily without.

When I was sure the bunkhouse was empty, I staggered to the showers. I stood in the hottest water I could stand on unsteady legs, bent over like an eighty-year-old. I twisted muscles and stretched tendons, then stretched my neck and back until I'd drained the tank. I could reach my knees with both hands and still tolerate the pain, so I toweled off and returned to my room. I'd pulled on my jeans and a shirt, but still no socks, before the cramps returned to cripple me again.

Ernie was banging away with a mop and steel bucket in the latrine. It became quiet, except for shuffleing footsteps approaching, and then there was a knock on the open door. Ernie asked, "You have the flu?"

I explained my sock ethics to Ernie. He listened, an un-lit, spit-soaked roll-yer-own hanging from his lower lip. He listened and stared, unconvinced, until I finished my soliloquy on footwear and the modern workplace.

"No. You do not have stiff arms, young fella. You," he stated, "have the flu. That's if you want to keep this job. And if you do, you go tell Jack or Bill you have the flu. It's already after nine and you most likely already got yourself fired."

Ernie told me Errol and Mike quit that morning. They would fly out before the sustained front of the next storm arrived, which was bearing down on us from across thousands of square miles of barrens. None of the surface crew would miss Errol and Mike, but I would miss watching them leave, laid up as I was, and would miss the final jeering session.

Ernie's pep talk ignited me. "You're right!" Only two days ago, I was penniless in Edmonton, bumming a place to crash. This job had to be the jump-start I needed for the rest of my life. I did need this job.

I rallied and slipped bare feet into my running shoes. Unable to reach the laces, I left them untied, but that was unlikely to cause any slit wrists along the runways of Canadian fashion. I grabbed my parka and started the long slow limp up the torturous flights of stairs. I groaned and creaked through deserted bunkhouses, shuffled through the darkness of the nightshift miner's bunkhouse where men slept behind painted windows and closed doors. Feeling like Igor in Dracula's castle, I dragged my bum legs up more stairs. I reached the last door to the outside and began the cold limp across the top of the ridge past the community hall until I entered the cook shack.

I bumped into Jan. She flashed her baby-doll eyes at me again. Gushing, she said, "Oh. It's you. Sorry, I have to work."

"I don't recall asking you to stop."

She turned away and whether she was glad, miffed, or disappointed, I cared little. I focused my attention on the twins.

Both were redheads, maybe nineteen, both had very, very green eyes. They giggled at me and then scooted into the pantry, where Liz ruled supreme. They were Playboy material under their blue and white checked shirts and skintight jeans. I was all eyes until Les interrupted me. "Royt. What 'ave we 'ere, Liz? The king of Canader, eye? Not at work todeye, is it then?"

I reined in my stampeding hormones. "Where's the nurse at, anyway?"

"Got the flu, have you? Well, I hear you're already booked on the next plane out of here … and if you have other plans, you better get to the building on top of the hill, then, shouldn't you? And I shouldn't waste a lot of time lollygagging around here, gaping at the girls like they was monkeys in a ruddy zoo."

"Thanks. Is there any coffee left, guv'nor?"

"Right. Well, that's cheeky then, innit Liz? Maybe there's some left. Ernie 'asn't been around yet for his pots."

Not understanding why Ernie had anything to do with my snagging a cup of non-Sanka coffee, I filled a Styrofoam cup with the dregs and fixed it with warm evaporated milk before I left.

Despite the temperature, I became aware of the sunshine, the new day, and the spectacular vista before me. At my feet, the tarpaper roofs of the many sheds sullied the grandeur, so I lifted my eyes past them. The lake extended beyond the curvature of the earth and merged with the universe in the blended spectrum of subtle hues of this incredible world. The infinite azure of the sky above the lake runway, which drew my eyes to the west, made me feel I could see into my future. So impressive was the limitless expanse of Great Bear Lake ice that the impact of the moment diminished the guilt I felt over these miserable scrapings. I felt my shameful mortality, standing at the center of this industrial, erupted pustule. I turned toward the east. The brilliant, huge orange-yellow morning sun dominated the truly cloudless sky. Though I was standing on radioactive tailings, I was overlooking most of the camp, to where the air was fresh and timeless, and I imagined Canada's soul rode on the currents.

I shook myself from my daydream and continued hobbling toward the First Aid building. My shadow had elongated to forty feet or more as I watched it take steps along a boardwalk then zip behind the building at the crest of the ridge. The red cross painted on the door gave me hope I would find the nurse and enjoy a little pharmaceutical relief, but the locked door disappointed me. *No nurse today?* There was neither a note nor any sign of recent footsteps through the deep snowdrift built up against the door. Disgusted, I threw down my coffee cup and left.

Judging from what Ernie said, I knew my next stop would be unpleasant … I had no note from a doctor to defend myself.

16. The Warning, the Ointment, the History

"Save it. You're on the next flight out," sneered Bill, unimpressed with my claim of having the flu.

I had just set a new personal record for getting myself fired. Bill had left the manager's office door cracked open. I knew Stalin could hear us, so I took the offensive. "Gonna cost you guys a bundle to fly me in and out, I guess? I have a tab at the store and the bar, too. Seems we're a little short-handed today for surface crew. Isn't there another convoy due in soon?"

Bill shuffled a stack of paper, interrupting our uncomfortable discussion. "None of that is your concern now. Be ready for the plane today. You have about an hour."

In his office, Stalin cleared his throat. Bill faltered, ever sensitive to the ol' hammer and sickle behind the manager's door. I left the office, unsure if I should pack or not, but I was relying on JT's pecuniary stinginess. After his politics, his religion, and his argument against communism, which was any politics left of his extreme and particular view of the world, I was sure JT measured a man's value in terms of how much it cost to feed him while he scraped uranium and tainted silver ore from his hole in the ground. Stalin might have occasion to consider the stupidity of flying me into camp and then right out again. That might be hard to explain to JT if word of these things ever reached him. But truly, personnel problems are micro issues, and I thought I could bet on this group not wanting that old bulldog JT crapping in their yard. Stalin cleared his throat again. Bill, the ass-kissing, bureaucratic running dog, was being summoned.

An hour later, Bill appeared at my bunkhouse door, where he huffed up and screwed his face into a menacing scowl. "There better not be a next time." He pulled his lips away from his teeth, displaying a history of failed dental care.

I could not restrain myself. "Too bad for you there's no dental plan at Port Radium."

Bill's face changed from intimidation to confusion, possibly his only states of consciousness. "No, there isn't … This is your last chance."

Ernie appeared approximately three seconds after Bill left. He was startled when I swung my guitar at his face. I was just able to stop myself before I mistakenly bashed out his dentures. I thought Bill had returned for another round. Ernie looked a little shaken. "How'd it go? You tell 'em you had the flu?"

I put the guitar down. "Sorry about that, Ern. Your idea worked like a charm. Thanks. Hey, what's the story with that Morlock office suck, anyway?"

"Bill? That's for show, but not so with a couple of these guys. One of 'em hails from the US Black Ops. Served with young Jimmy when he was an MP in Germany. That guy, Schläger, you watch out for him. He was effective in Europe, they say. The Army sent some of our guys to Germany to watch the Russians build the wall and not let the Americans start another war." I flashed back to 1961, when that same general, Lemay, wanted to nuke East Berlin all the way from Checkpoint Charlie to Moscow. "But Schläger, well, he's special. The Germans kicked Schläger out of their country. Now we got him 'cause JT called him up for duty. I'll warn you now, among other things he does around here, he's our security. Schläger manages the curling rink, too. The other managers act like they're hired thugs because they're afraid of Schläger. Why … you didn't cross Bill did you? That could be real trouble."

"Uh, no, but thanks for the timely warning. I'll be sure not to draw any more fire from management." I cursed myself for my interview with JT, my comments in the waiting room in Edmonton, the cook shack revolution, my insolence toward Jack, missing a day of work, and I had just insulted Bill's teeth. *Jesus, did I miss anyone?* "How many of these company boys are up here, anyway?"

"All of the management staff, a few guys in the mill, two of the miners, the pilots. And Schläger."

"Jack and Mike? Are they part of the Nazi entourage?"

"No, they're local drunks. They've been in the Arctic screwing up mines since forever." Ernie laughed at his summation and then left saying, "Better keep it simple for a while, eh?"

So, Stalin's doppelgänger and a squad of neo-Nazis run this camp. Well then, simple it is, unless it's already too late for me.

At 4:45 p.m., stomping footsteps coming up the stairs heralded the crew's return from the salt mines. Each of them, except Michael, yelled at me and assaulted my fine character and work ethic by calling me "jerk off," "pansy," and "wimp." I had it coming. By the time the last of the marching line receded further into the bunkhouse, Michael had already flopped onto his bed.

"I thought you were fired … they said so." He looked at me with drastically arched eyebrows and sunken brown eyes.

"Naw. I smoothed it over in the office. What'd you do today?"

"Cement, *tabernac*, and more ice. Boy, that Frank, he is an asshole. He cannot shut up."

I took this opportunity to recount my revelations regarding Bill and Schläger and my conversation with Ernie. Michael listened while he smoked a Gitane. "Anyway, maybe that Frank, he's all right, eh?"

After supper, which consisted of mopping up a bowl of stew with six pieces of bread, I tried the nursing station again. There was no one around, so I went to the store where Bill sold me pain relief ointment. I bought four tubes on credit. I'd never used this stuff before, but anything was better than nothing. I went to the bar after that and met up with Michael, Don, Jan, Dave, and John Mantla, who had to sneak in because of his heritage. Murray was working the nightshift and Eddie was too cheap, or smart, to pay the pub prices.

We drank a lot. It was one of those intense and magical pub nights when you realize you found a bunch of new friends and so you bond like family. I felt close to all of them. It might have been the grog, but these people were my only allies for the next four months. I accepted it as the best of luck that so many of us were normal sorts, slogging through our young lives, trying to build our bank accounts and follow our dreams. We bought off-sales, except Jan, whom we snuck into Dave's room, and sang songs and caroused until midnight. Even Frank joined us, but we made him stay at the door. Eddie dropped by followed by several stragglers. Murray came along after his shift ended, around eleven p.m., and we had a great hoedown.

It was midnight, and I was double done. Michael was droopy-eyed, too. About four seconds after we returned to our room, Michael passed out. I began to apply the ointment I'd bought earlier. The tube promised: "For over 60 years, this ointment has provided fast, effective and lasting pain relief from sore muscles by reaching deep into the sore muscles with restorative heat." That was exactly what I wanted, so I slathered on two full tubes, covering my shins, calves, knees and thighs, both my forearms and hands, and then greased up what I could reach of my shoulders, lower back, and then my stomach, chest, and neck. When I finished, I smelled like a pro wrestler's towel.

I was desperate for sleep. I noticed a slight tingle in my hands and forearms; my chest glistened in the light before I turned out my reading lamp. The tingle turned into a buzzing sensation. I told myself the tingles and the *deep heating action* would soothe my aching carcass. I hoped a deep sleep would regenerate my stamina for the next day. My drowsy, boozy euphoria and sense of contentment were a huge relief to me before I drifted off. Tomorrow, I vowed to myself, I would make amends for missing work.

By my reckoning, just seven minutes later, I sat up in bed, panting, and tore the sheet away; my skin felt like someone had flayed me with a rawhide whip, and now I was burning alive in excruciating pain. I did not want to wake Michael, so I endured my torment in martyred silence. My palms burned as if I held them over a blacksmith's furnace. I certainly had plenty of relaxed muscles with which to twist and turn. My condition dragged on over long hours, in un-abating, blazing torture. True to the testament on the tube, I suffered no more cramping each time I ran to the cold shower, where, for the first two hours, I sought relief, but the burning continued. Every half hour, I ran rivers of frigid water over my body, horrified by the angry red welts formed wherever I had applied the gunk. If I stood in the shower the burning abated, but I was too exhausted to stand there all night. Between the showers, I lay in my bed and hoped the burning would subside. However, the pain advanced like a fever the minute my skin dried. Exacerbated by the dry, hot room, the torturous intensity drove me back into the shower when I could no longer stand it.

By five a.m., the reaction had subsided enough to allow me to pass out for an hour. Michael woke up at the alarm. I started when I woke, thankful the acute burning had faded. I refused to miss work, no matter what.

"How come you got a wet sheet?" Michael yawned as he sat on the edge of his bed. During one of my last showers, I took my bed sheet with me, soaked it in cold water, and returned with it so I could wrap my legs and arms to stop them from chafing. This allowed me to rest a little longer between showers because it minimized the effects of the demon ointment.

"I had a bad night. My muscles were still sore."

Michael was unmoved with my explanation. He performed his waking ritual, stinking up the room smoking Gitanes in bed and assaulting my lungs with second-hand cigarette smoke. Finally, he dressed and went for breakfast.

When he was gone, I searched myself for open lesions. Any movement of bedding against my skin felt like coarse-grain sandpaper was tearing at me, but I could endure that. I stifled any mention of my discomfort to Michael because that would be sure to elicit a barrage of sarcastic comments, and I had already brought enough of that kind of attention to myself. I chanted my working-poor mantra: *suffer in silence, everybody's got shit, no one wants to hear yours, get on with it, there's men and women waiting at the gate for your job, if you can't hack it.*

After I'd assured myself I had no open wounds, I followed Michael. I was more limber but worn out from my long night of showers. In my dopiness, I made the mistake, again, of ordering two eggs over easy. I watched Les splatter half-cooked eggs onto my plate. I made a point of scraping them off into a plastic garbage pail in front of him. I took slices of cold bacon, scooped lukewarm pan fries and onions onto my plate, then made four pieces of toast before the turkeys gobbling behind me in the toaster lineup forced me to move on. I joined our table and suffered good-natured jibes about being a Port Radium vacationer.

When we marshaled for work, there was an awkward moment when Jack came in to assign us our workload. Everyone was watching, so he made a big show of dispensing grief. "You didn't work yesterday. Why?"

"Sore. I'm okay now, though."

"Sore? So what?" he yelled.

My reaction was to tell him that he'd "best stand the fuck off." This coast logger was about ready to launch a full-on strike because after a second long night, my blood was about to boil over. "Look, Jack," I tried to explain, "this ain't my first rodeo. If I can't make it to work, there's a reason." I was defiant, but short of insubordinate. You have to leave the boss a little latitude to do the right thing.

Jack relented; he had made his point. "Miss another day and you're fired. You got ice; you go with these guys, back to the hopper and finish the job. John, Sam, you two can do mine deliveries with Sean today. When you finish, you got ice."

I followed the others out to our convoy of trucks that were new twenty years ago. Because it was so damn cold, it took Eddie almost an hour to start them all, ours being the last. Don, Michael, Frank, and I crowded onto the front bench seat like dirty marshmallows in a rusty sardine can. After we freed the frozen tires from the frozen snow, Frank drove us to the crushing mill at the top of the ridge, close to the entrance to the Eldorado mine.

We were supposed to break up the accumulated ice inside the hopper shed because the trucks couldn't back in to load up on tailings. We milled around, waiting for Sean to bring us a jackhammer. The conveyor belt rollers above us were jammed with dust, the walls were coated with dust, every crack in the siding was filled with the stuff, and the girders securing the hopper had inches of the fine material piled on every surface. Something about the place gave me the creeps. I told Michael how I felt, and he agreed, "Like there's a ghost here."

Though we were sheltered from the direct wind, our breath formed ice crystals in the dust we raised, further confounding our labored breathing. Frank said we were breaking down what Murray called the "Port Radium glacier." Twenty inches of ice had built up below the giant hopper that loomed over us. "Since it opened," said Frank, "the crusher and the mine have generated over 900,000 tons of radioactive uranium tailings and 800,000 tons of industrial chemical waste. This conveyor used to run right to the lake, but in '52 there was a conveyor fire. Since then, the company has used trucks to dump tailings in the lake. The mine has been dumping the heavy metal effluent, the arsenic, and stuff, into McDonough Lake for decades. That lake leaches into Great Bear Lake."

"Can't be that big a deal, though. This isn't such a big operation," I said.

"Big enough!" said Frank. "This mine has produced 37 million ounces of silver, 10.5 million pounds of copper, and almost 13.7 million pounds of uranium oxide."

"Well," I said, "we better get a move on or we'll be about 99.9 percent fired."

Throughout the morning, Mouthy Frank, who had graduated from a technical school in Guelph, Ontario, filled us in on the history of Port Radium. "Pitchblende mined here was transported through Yellowknife, to Fort McMurray, then by rail to Uranium City and Port Hope, Ontario, where subdivisions were constructed on the waste from the extraction process." When Frank talked about a technical field he had studied, he sounded almost normal. However, in social situations, he blurted out stupid stuff, then tried to cover it up until he fell awkwardly and flat on his face. Sean made one early cameo appearance during the morning, but failed to bring us the compressor and jackhammer. Instead, he brought us John Mantla and then sat in the pickup and gawked at us. We ignored him, so he left.

Frank told us he'd read the numbers during the research he'd done before coming into camp. "Throughout the life of the mine," said Frank, "but especially during the late spring and summers, the dumping process continued. Heavy equipment breaks up the frozen ore and tailings accumulated over the winter. Every day, all day, the cat feeds the belt to the hopper and fills the trucks. After processing the crush for as much of the uranium, silver, or copper, they truck the deadly tailings to any one of our dumping sites."

"How do you mean *as much of the uranium*? Don't they get it all?"

"U-235 is formed as part of a decaying process, so they extract only the existing uranium at that moment. They miss a lot of it; which continues to appear in the tailings for thousands of years, giving off radon all the time. And that's not even taking into consideration the other deadly poisons along the decay chain that appear after U-235."

That was news to all of us.

"For a decade after the mine opened, they dumped 170,000 tons of radioactive tailings practically into the laps of the men working at the mine. Hundreds of truckloads are beneath our bunkhouses, and the rest they used for road cap in camp and along Silver Point. Then they filled the Murphy and Radium dumpsites, across from the cook shack. There's three radon vents right there, too. We're breathing mine dust right now! They say over another 1.5 million tons of radioactive and toxic waste went into either the Murphy site or McDonough Lake, but lots of the tailings went into Great Bear Lake off Silver Point. Only a few yards offshore, the lake drops off to a depth of over four hundred feet."

"They recovered some of the tailings from the lake in the '50s, but the rest is still down there, and now they're afraid to disturb it. Same thing in Port Hope, right by Toronto— they stopped remediation projects because it stirred up more radon than they could remove, so they told the homeowners to avoid digging in their gardens and yards. Here in Port Radium, I've seen pictures of the pile beside the ramp we drive down to get to the lake runway. There was a mountain of radioactive tailings, a hundred feet from the bunkhouses. After the fire, they built this hopper. I guess it saved them money to fill every natural depression in camp."

Over thirty years, McDonough lake received so much broken or discarded equipment, radioactive tailings, and human garbage around camp, we called the expansive water-body Garbage Lake.

"How old is this mine, Professor?" I asked.

"Eldorado mine started operating in 1932, then closed for three years in 1938. It's funny, all the uranium they took out of here, they tossed in the lake as useless or too expensive to process. Besides, they wanted the silver and copper. There was a glut of Belgian Congo uranium on the market — that was the only other source in the world, until the Australians discovered theirs in the late '40s and early '50s. Our government re-opened this mine in 1941. The Nazis controlled the Belgian Congo and seized the uranium stockpiled in Europe. Eldorado uranium was far more potent, anyway, and we supplied the Allied war effort. After the war, the Canadian government retained co-ownership with Eldorado and produced the enriched U-235 for the US military until 1960. This shit fueled the Cold War and lined the pockets of all the other owners with US greenbacks."

"But during the war, the Nazis almost had an atomic bomb, didn't they?"

"Naw, they gave up on the atomic bomb by 1943."

We pounded, scraped, and cursed at the ice while we listened to Frank. "Echo Bay Mines bought the lease from the Canadian government, who had already turned Uranium City and Port Hope into nuclear waste disasters. I grew up in Port Hope, so I find this interesting. The new managers here, the company we work for, produced copper and silver ore from 1960 to now, flying under the international environmental standards radar. Dumping waste is essentially ungoverned because the mining end of the industry is pretty much self-regulating, and we never fine the owners."

Frank went on to tell us that according to unnamed bureaucratic sources the mighty pens in the Department of Mines withheld information about the dangerous and deadly effects of radon at the site by suppressing the facts. They stopped measuring the levels of the exposure to radon that killed workers, which sometimes took twenty years, but lung cancer got many of them.

"In fact," Frank said, "no one tests this site for radon or radiation anymore, either. Why bother, if the mine is a silver and copper mine, right? Government Health Administrators blamed the extremely high rate of on-going cancer deaths of miners and uranium mineworkers on tobacco. Before the '70s, our government supported Big Tobacco. In 1954, Big Tobacco issued the infamous Frank Statement advertisement, claiming smoking was unrelated to lung cancer. The statement appeared in over 400 newspapers and targeted 43,000,000 people in the US, but when it was convenient, the government blamed the miner's lung cancer on smoking."

I said, "Maybe the company didn't know what radon could do to a man."

Frank said, "They had to know, or they should have cared enough to find out. There was lots of scientific and medical literature warning of the consequences of radon exposure. In 1947, after so many miners who worked here as essential services during the war died, scientists from Montreal measured the radon in Eldorado at a thousand times above the world safety level. Considering the number of dead and dying miners and native transporters who've died since then, yeah, it's a crime keeping this mine open."

While we chipped away at the glacier, John Mantla told us that across the lake from Port Radium was a Dené settlement. Donny-boy chimed in to tell us Alexander Mackenzie came through in 1780, and, imperialist and British company-man that he was, he renamed the settlement Fort Franklin. Mackenzie, and those few who followed his footsteps, anglicized the map and claimed the land for the Hudson Bay Company. He traded for the natives' assets, and exchanged parish priests and subservience to the Church of England for pelts highly valued in Europe.

John said, "At first, the mine employed many Dené men to transport the ore. Many returned sick to the village, where they died from cancer. The Dené had no word for the disease before Eldorado. We call Franklin River the 'Village of Widows.'"

Frank told us he'd researched how, since 1940, pension-protecting Canadian politicians bowed before the US Atomic Energy Commission, to fuel their military juggernaut. Canadian politicians ordered shrinking-violet bureaucrats to suppress the alarming warnings regarding radon poisoning. Sadly, it was easy for our government to find contrary opinions from well-paid "experts" willing to attribute so many native and miner cancer deaths to smoking tobacco, rather than exposure to the deadly ore and dust. Even the US National Cancer Institute was unable to change the minds of the Canadian politicians. The net result of the suppressed documentation was that people died while the mine remained in production since WWII with few safety improvements. The lease-holders made money and the Canadian government balanced the books.

After lunch, Sean brought us the jackhammer and compressor. I wrestled with the hose while Michael tried to figure out how to start the compressor. The jackhammer lay on the tire-worn ruts on the roadway ice. For the moment, no one volunteered to pick it up.

I wondered aloud, "How'd water get here to make this ice, anyway? This is a lot of ice, isn't it?"

Frank answered, "There are hoses that come up from the mine and another from the lake to wash the trucks. I guess one burst."

I asked, "Why would they wash the trucks in this stinkin' hole?"

"They don't actually wash the trucks; they use the water to blast the ore grime off the brake shoes. It saves on maintenance. The ore dust is murder on the pads."

"Well," I said, "JT's gotta protect those brake pads."

Michael, the mechanical genius, watched Frank push the green button that started the compressor. A plume of black diesel exhaust choked off our conversation. No one jumped in, so I grabbed the jackhammer and lifted it up. It weighed eighty pounds, and at that moment, I decided tow work with it until we finished the job. I connected the air hose to the hammer, steadied myself on the ice, strained first against the weight, then against the hose, and finally against the vibration when I squeezed the trigger on the handle. At first, the explosion of noise and strong vibration surprised me. My hands were so weak, I couldn't hold the damn thing in balance. But I fought off cramping arms again, unwilling to sublet the job to anyone else. That afternoon we broke up three hundred square feet of thick ice. The guys behind me removed slabs and large chunks of black and yellow ice. We had the area cleared away and accessible again by four p.m. When we arrived back at the shop, Jack took me aside. He said, "You did good on the jackhammer. No more time off, okay?"

"Not till the fishing gets better, Jack."

Jack called it a day, so we parked the vehicles, plugged in the engine block heaters, then climbed the stairs to our bunkhouse. There was no convoy or plane expected, so we had the night off.

I made it through supper, which included a slab of "UBM," otherwise known as unidentified boiled meat. Speculation was rampant it was either the dried up remains of a Woolly Mammoth dredged up from the mine, or the remains of a caribou carcass the wolverine left behind. Side dishes of lumpy instant potatoes and over-boiled, unpeeled, lukewarm carrots with tough skins garnished our repast. I wolfed down slices of bread. A rumor circulated there was no beer night, but the girls would open the hamburger hut by seven. Though my eyelids felt glued shut and I walked like a zombie, I had to see the twins for the first time. After all, these other guys were slouches, and I simply wanted more of those two green-eyed daughters of Scotland.

The last thing Michael said at dinner was, "Al, I got sore arms. Do you have any of that ointment left?"

"Sure, but I'm warning you, don't use too much. What's left of it is on our lamp table. Go for it."

17. Burgers and Howling Timber Wolves

The interior of the community hall was 110 feet long by 60 feet wide, but the usable floor-space was much smaller. The tired linoleum flooring dulled the senses and the monotonous, off-white walls made it impossible, or uninteresting, to discern when winter's nine-month vice grips clamped down on or released Port Radium. A huge, dark green ceiling fan, its blades still, hung from the vaulted ceiling fifteen feet above the pool table. Tall windows, crosshatched into small panes, broke the uniformity of the walls. On close inspection, I saw they were painted shut and had probably been so for decades, during the winter, to keep the cold out, during the few months of non-winter, the insects.

A raised stage dominated the west wall. Employed as a storage area for stacks of dusty, wooden folding tables and rows of gray metal chairs, it was hard to imagine any performance that might have increased camp morale. Beside the stage, the single door opened to the bunkhouse boardwalk, and opposite the stage, double doors opened toward the cook shack. On one of those doors, someone had screwed a painted, though fading, atomic symbol with pool ball electrons orbiting on silver strands. The caption read: Port Radium — the hottest place on the planet. Until my chance meeting with Corey, I thought the slogan a weak expression of irony related to the weather. Opposite the windows overlooking the power plant and the lake, the kitchen and the short cafeteria-style counter filled the other wall, where Genna and Morag, Jan, and Ernie sold burgers after supper. A barroom pool table dominated the center of the hall. The enduring, abused, and faded blue felt was badly in need of repair or replacement. Still, out of sheer boredom, there was a lineup to play. Whenever anyone entered or left the community hall, the resultant door slam reverberated throughout the gymnasium.

When Michael and I walked in, the wind slammed the door wide open. I had to use two hands to close it behind us. I realized I smelled burning onions, and the aroma was a heavenly change from Les's bubbling pots of gruel, which were slightly less appealing as food than a Yellowstone sulphur pool. As was customary, everyone stopped what they were gossiping about to stare googley-eyed at the latest arrivals — as if we had returned from a moonwalk. When they

133

were satisfied we were not space aliens, they resumed as one their particular diversion from reality.

The piercing voice of hurtin' Hank Williams, tortured by his lover's cheating heart, poured out from a scratchy record player beside Sean. His hair was gooey with Brylcreem and dragged straight down over each ear from a center part, a mere wick away from *The Little Rascals'* Alphalpha. Sean, in his way, was stepping out. He sat on a stool quietly observant and sipping coffee. I nodded at him, but received only a cold stare in return. *Fuckin' hick*. Dave and Don also sat at the counter having coffee. Michael and I joined them.

Dave said, "If you're up for high cuisine, you should order now. They get busy fast, and you have to wait your turn. Some of the guys only eat here, for obvious reasons, so they order big."

I was fixated on the twins, dressed identically in faded, skintight jeans. It was my considered opinion it would take a journeyman bricklayer armed with a cake spatula to slide credit cards into a rear pocket of those jeans. Under-sized, white V-neck T-shirts sculpted an alluring view of twin cleavage, over which they both wore tight, pink-checkered shirts, tied in an exaggerated loose knot above the waist. They had both rolled their sleeves halfway to the elbow. The cutest pink paisley scarves held their hair back, reminiscent of WWII factory bomb-girl posters. When they flashed their darting eyes from behind those long, Scottish bangs, I was in love, twice.

I introduced myself by way of ordering a burger. Jan ran over to serve me, hip-checking one of the twins out of the way.

"Hi, Jan. Who you working with there?"

Jan looked disappointed, which was weird because I knew she had no interest in me, and it was mutual. We were friends, and that was it. However, for Donny, it was another bad sign. *Don, are you getting this yet?* Jan's flirting with me was a hollow gesture. I knew, at best, I rated only as a rebound or a decoy; she had already conscripted someone else for romance duty. I ignored Jan's pleading eyes.

I spoke to the closest of the identical twins. "What's your name?"

"My name is Genna. That's my twin sister, Morag."

Morag raised her eyes from the sizzling patties on the griddle. She blushed when she looked at me. Morag had a pretty smile. *Oh yeah, something's happening here.* "Sorry," I apologized, "I don't see the resemblance. I'm Al. You two are supposed to be totally identical twins?"

They both laughed, and Genna said, "Morag is the funny one."

Morag came out from beside the grill, and they both appraised me. Morag yelled, "Three cheeseburgers up." She kept her eyes on me.

"Well, pleased to meet you, too, Genna and Morag. So, what is there to do around here, after you finish your shift, anyway?" They both tittered at that, and four shining, green eyes locked on mine challenged me to keep my gaze steady.

"Maybe I'll drop by the sugar shack, and we can play some crib or something."

Their smiles faded. Genna said, "Don't even think about that. No boys allowed, ever. You'll get us fired if you even try to come in and they find out."

"Really? No boys allowed at the sugar shack?"

Under her breath, Morag said, "Only wolverines and bad boys try to get in." She followed with a wink and a wiggle.

"Well, I'm no wolverine ..."

"Hey, meathead, if you're not ordering anything, get the hell out of the line," Deputy Frank yelled, apparently bored by my banter with the women. He was fourth in the line that had formed behind me without my noticing.

"Forget the burger." The deputy's snarl and fierce look suggested he was about to serve me up a knuckle sandwich. "Can I just have the ketchup and a couple napkins instead, please?" I had to pretend I held up the line for some reason other than banter.

I sat beside Dave and Don. Michael placed his order. Don watched Jan. He denied the obvious, allowing in only the hurt. Jan was trying to send Don the message, so she found a way to let every guy she served know she was available. The last to figure it out, if he ever did, Donny had a front row seat to the performance of Jan's rejection.

Ten minutes later, the deputy walked by with three hamburgers and a hell of a pile of fries, took my ketchup bottle, and said, "My food better not be cold or I'm coming to see you."

I looked at Dave, who shrugged and threw his eyes to the ceiling.

"Sorry, Frank," I said. "Just saying 'hello' to the girls."

Frank snarled at me and left to sit alone near the pool table. Eddie changed Hank over to a scratchy version of Neil Young. Two and a half songs later, one of the older miners walked over and put on a Dolly Parton album; no one challenged him on taste. The endless pool game carried on.

"Hey," Dave said, "I'm writing more words to 'Arctic Momma.' Let's collaborate on the words ... I want to finish it here and take it with me when I leave."

"Hell yes, I'm into that. Soon as the cafe closes, let's do it."

The door banged open again and two smarmy men walked in wearing immaculately clean street clothes beneath unzipped, green parkas. The room remained quiet as the newcomers walked across the floor to the kitchen, until Dolly launched into her syrupy, "I Will Always Love You." The pool game stopped. The two men chatted with Genna and Morag; they were all familiar with each other.

"Dave, who are those *Bobbsey Twins*?"

"The skinny kid rattled on reds is the camp geologist, Corey. The other one is Schläger. He flew in today. They're planning the bonspiel. He considers himself a big man on campus. He parades around like a cop, but he ain't no cop."

Schläger stared through me to nod at Sean, but Sean ignored the greeting.

I remembered the skinny guy from today's plane, but only in passing. The other one, Schläger, I didn't like. "Funny," I said, "I never saw him. He must have slipped by us on the ice. I guess it can happen."

Whenever the plane arrives, the surface crew leaps into action and hauls luggage and light deliveries around camp. There was a beer order on the plane today, a couple of hundred cases, so Sean stared at us as we unloaded it, because if he didn't, we'd have snagged a couple of cases from the shipment. Otherwise, Sean is supposed to meet all the passengers with the bus, except new surface crew, then whistle them out of our immediate company. Which is what happened today with Corey and the beer, but Schläger, like a bad smell, must have drifted up the stairs through camp.

Schläger was my height, fit, blond, and broad-shouldered. He stared around the room like a security dog, except he had dead eyes, no smile, and Mick Jagger lips. An arrogant man, if I ever saw one.

He and Corey left together just minutes later, after an awkward sheet of ice silence formed between the twins and Schläger. When the door closed, both Morag and Genna did a poor job of hiding the sour looks on their faces. The pool game resumed, and Dolly sang "9 to 5."

I said, "Oh yeah, the bonspiel. When is that, anyway?"

"Early May," said Dave. "Lots of money changes hands over lots of drinks and hookers that weekend. Only way they can keep this mine open. Ain't that right, Sean?" As usual, Sean's response was a minimal shrug. "And I don't give a shit," said Dave, "how they do it, either. As far as I'm concerned, they can pay off whoever they need to until I can get back to a real life in Sudbury."

"So when are you leaving? And why do they have to pay anyone off?"

"When does anyone break formation? When it's my time. I'll take you down the mine one day when we're not working, and you can see the underground for yourself. You'll get a better picture then of why there are payoffs. I can't believe you've never been underground."

"Most Canadians haven't been underground, Dave. I don't go for working in holes when I can be in the wide open spaces enjoying the easy, relaxing life of a logger." We both laughed. "But for sure, I'd like to see that ..."

"Okay, you're on. Maybe we'll scare the crap out of a few crows, too." I looked at him, failing to understand. "Wait for it ... you'll see soon enough."

At 9:00 p.m. exactly, the girls rolled the metal blind down after sending us off with a big wink and smile. As a group, we groaned over our loss. Sean sat alone the entire time. Don was going to wait to escort Jan back to the sugar shack. I suddenly clued in to who Jan's new mystery man might be ... *I'll never understand women.*

I joined Dave, Michael, and John Mantla, who had arrived late, and we all went over to Dave's room. My eyes were burning for sleep and I was dead on my feet, but Dave wanted me to hear his new lyrics. It haunted me when I heard him sing his words to the tune of "Country Roads."

Always frozen, Arctic Circle,
Cobalt momma, on a sea of tundra.

Hard-rock miners, digging for their gold,
Homesick for his family, on the Great Bear ice floes.

Then the chorus …
Silver bird, take me home, to the arms of the one I love.
When it's my time, I'll say my goodbye,
to my friends, for ever more,
Arctic friends, for ever more.

Then the break went something like …
I hear the howling of the timber wolves at midnight.
The lonely sound reminds me of my life far away.
Each day I do my job, I miss the love, held in my arms
like it was yesterday, now far away.

We cheered. Besides banging on my guitar as rhythm, I had no idea what else I could contribute.

It was time for me to turn in. Michael stayed to chat for a while longer, but for me, another long day in camp with no sleep was one too many. Lying in my bunk, even my fantasies of the twins could not keep me awake. Real or not, I attributed each look I thought I caught from Morag as a tease or, at least, an invitation. Small things can sustain or upset you in isolation, but I didn't really expect much would happen. Three blinks later, I fell asleep.

Disappointingly, my hopes for a sound sleep my fourth night in camp became a replay of my previous restless nights. When Michael's French-Canadian mumbling woke me up, the room reeked of ointment. My room partner, the applicator from Quebec, spent the night getting up and showering, and then tossing in the sack.

At six a.m., the alarm put a stop to my hopeless attempts for unbroken sleep. "Why in Christ were you up all night, disturbing my sleep?"

Unraveling from a soaked sheet, Michael looked at me with sunken, death-head eyes, and said, "That ointment really burns."

"How much did you put on?"

"All of it."

I cracked up. "I warned you! Why'd you use so much?"

"*Tabernac*," he said, displaying a nasty red welt rising along the full length of one arm. "I had a sore muscle." Michael made us both laugh.

18. Battlefield Promotions

I settled into a camp regimen throughout the next month. The days melded together. Long hours of routine numbed the mind, as did the continual battle against the cold, the hypnotic and curious adjustment to short daylight hours and long nights, the poor quality of our food, the grudging banter with Les, the continual assault on my savings wasted as company credit, my sad mattress, the planes that brought no one interesting into camp, and the bi-weekly arrival of convoys. My daily goal deteriorated to trying to exist on the job like an automaton. It was a challenge to find something fresh to bring to socializing with the same men I worked with. My other goal was to avoid becoming an alcoholic.

I came to know everyone better, of course. Mouthy Frank was a harmless, if constant, background soundtrack. John Mantla and I became kinship-type friends. When Dave worked the night shift, John hung out with Michael and me. John had an inner peace, born, I thought, of the ability to tap a simple core of place; the Arctic was his home. On the other hand, maybe he was born with the personality to handle the irresolvable conflicts that might affect his life. He was, after all, a native man working in Port Radium. We passed slow evenings; Michael smoked and paged through old biker magazines and eavesdropped as John answered my incessant questions about what it was like to grow up in the Arctic.

It was almost a relief from the boredom when a late convoy arrived at camp and we had to rally for the overtime. Other nights, I tried to teach Eddie how to play the notes to *Ya Gotta Move*. It was a slow go, but where was any one of us going? Murray was always funny and upbeat; Dave was already the older brother I never had, and Don and Jan lingered through their breakup. Michael and I had something about each of us that allowed us to trust the other. It might have been that, in my eyes, he could do nothing so wrong that I would not back him to the ends of the earth, which was close to where we actually were. I knew he would do the same for me, and that was enough.

On the job, Jack showed signs he trusted me a little more each day. He gave me a break when he offered me the bus driver job. My new responsibility freed Sean, still as aloof as ever, for other chores. I was responsible for ensuring the crew met the plane and the convoys and organizing the simple chores: the regular food deliveries to the kitchen, the light deliveries to the mines, and dumping the cook shack garbage on the ice at Garbage Lake.

"You have to make sure the bottles get to the leeching plant, every morning; they can't run out. Got it?" Jack referred to the constant supply of one-hundred-pound steel bottles of pressurized acetylene delivered by the convoys. The camp used acetylene to generate heat and light in the mill and both mines. We delivered bottles to Eldorado, too. Frank said they had re-fired a "completely antiquated and illegal" lighting system that burned explosive oxy-acetylene. "It's retarded," said Frank. "They outlawed those heaters right after the war."

Another of my "vital" duties was to supervise the placement of the thirty or so soccer-ball shaped oil pots on the ends and sides of our lake runway for flight arrivals. The real trick, and it could be tricky getting that runway set up after dark during one of our many winter gales, was lighting the wicks in the gusting wind that whipped across the lake. Those markers were still the only visual guide for the pilots. Ever since the tower light had burned out on the abandoned RCMP building, there had been no other markers for the pilots to hone in on at night.

Ernie said, "That light can stay out if Jimmy thinks I'm climbing that rickety-runged bastard-of-a-ladder. He can break his own damn neck."

We watched Michael try one day. He ignored Frank's warning, "Michael, don't do it; that tower is unsafe."

We were all tired of the valid complaints from the pilots, who whined to us bi-weekly about the danger of landing a plane on the ice in the often-horrendous weather, or incredibly bright, reflecting sunlight, or in the dark. So, Michael was inspired to replace the bulb, no matter the condition of the ladder or it's rusty rungs.

"Gimme that bulb. I will show you how we do this in Port Radium."

From the peak of the snow-covered roof, our forewarned, great white leader climbed twenty feet up the tower until two rungs broke simultaneously and the replacement bulb and its installer arrived back at the roof after a rapid, unscheduled descent. Shaken, his face white as a ghost, Michael clambered down from the roof.

"Fuck those pilot."
Indeed, great leader, indeed.
I was still amazed the pilots were even willing to try night landings, but it was common practice in Port Radium. How many pilots bottomed out in Arctic whiteouts, during the day, after inaccurately estimating their altitude above a lake surface? Blowing snow across a lake simply obliterates depth perception, so if it was before dark, Jack made us wait in the trucks and the bus at the lake landing strip to provide the visual aid to the pilots. It's a fact, in those empty, ker-zillion square miles of frozen, blowing snow, Echo Bay Air depended on the unrelenting, unqualified expertise of the Port Radium surface crew to land safely. Sean always re-fueled the plane before it made the return trip to Yellowknife. He did that under pilot supervision, the job being technical, and all. It is another Great Bear Lake fact that without the flaming diesel pots, a successful night landing was about as probable as Bob Hope and a half-dozen Playboy bunnies dropping by.

The 1951 half-ton flatbed dinosaur-of-a-truck I used for deliveries featured a wooden deck and side rails re-purposed from cement pallets. To my chagrin, and Eddie's too, I ground away what was left of the truck's clutch during my first week of steady driving. The truck was in the shop until Eddie fixed it, so, during the interim, Jack assigned me to drive the fifteen-passenger school bus to make my deliveries. Every morning, except Sunday, Sean drove the miners to the mine by seven a.m., then I used the bus all day. Then Sean took the bus to meet the miners every afternoon at three and bring them back to the bunkhouses. The night-shift men drove themselves around because enough pickups were available after day-shift hours.

The day of my promotion, Don, Michael, Frank, and I were at Silver Point, loading the bus with pressurized acetylene bottles stored on a lowbed trailer. Jack had called me over to join him while he mulled over his inverted merit list, possibly because he trusted me more than the others, but it was more than likely this casual one-way conversation was his idea of an interview. He applied his unique style to the dilemma, arranging the crew hierarchy based on ethnicity and nepotism.

Jack mumbled through his dismissals: Michael forfeited any consideration because he was a French-Canadian; Frank was a possible candidate, but his education held him back because he used phrases like, "cyanidation process and sodium sulfide solution processed with concentrated acid, alkaline, or peroxide solutions to leach out the uranium." In Port Radium, any loose or specific references to science, or uttering multi-syllabic words in mixed company, by which I mean management and labor, caused others to suspect a schooled brain, and, ergo, identified the speaker as a threat. John and Sam were off the A-list on two counts: they were Native men, and because they could only drive dogsleds, and in that order. Don was both a candidate and ineligible because he was "family." I had suffered enough times the indignity of being the last pick to a side in schoolyard sports and competitive spelling bees to understand how Jack's process might conclude. I boosted my position to the top of the now-empty candidate list when I pointed out that showing favoritism toward Don would make Jack a nepotist, playing on the probability he would be suspicious of the sound of the word. I was right. Jack was stuck with me. Eventually, he asked, "You can drive the bus, can't you?"

"I can drive, all right!" I hoped my enthusiasm demonstrated that I was the right man for the job. I would do or say almost anything to be out of the damn cold. In truth, I had never acquired a driver's license, because, until that moment, I'd never needed to do much more than move pickup trucks around on logging road spurs, hundreds of miles from the nearest traffic controls.

Loud, rattling chains interrupted my promotion interview. We watched Mouthy Frank unhook the last chain securing twenty pressurized, rusty gas bottles. The potential for disaster tangentially increased when eight of the un-certified metal bottles tumbled and clanged onto the flatdeck and rolled around pinging into each other like so many highly explosive bowling pins. Recognizing the danger, Jack threw himself flat on the ice, yelling a creative string of obscenities at Frank for being first, an idiot, and secondly, a careless idiot "trying to kill us all." Thankfully, we narrowly avoided the explosive outcome as none of the bottles rolled off the tilted deck of the low bed trailer. And neither did Frank crush his own leg. I waited for Jack to collect himself and stand up again.

Frank, an educated and sensitive soul, took Jack's criticism to heart, and, pouting like the student he was, kicked one of the heavy metal bottles hard enough to set it rolling again. We all stood mute and unbelieving as it reached the edge of the flatdeck where, before

143

anyone dared to intervene, it rolled off the deck. It landed hard enough on the frozen ground to break off the valve assembly. The bottle launched as the tremendous roar of escaping gas filled the tranquil Arctic landscape. We stood dumbfounded as we watched the bottle careen off the rear wheels of the trailer, prang into a less than symmetrical trajectory, and describe a low, horizontal flight path articulated over the snow berm, beyond the lakeshore, and halfway down the runway.

All but one of us stood stunned in the resultant vacuum of silence. After he raised himself from the ice for the second time, Jack's tirade was memorable. However, he stopped short of firing Frank, even though he had put us in imminent danger. In the Arctic, quality help is hard to find and harder to keep, so Frank kept his job. Jack's new lithium prescription, which we knew had arrived on a plane two weeks earlier, allowed him to regain his aplomb before he ordered Frank, Michael, and Don to find and retrieve the bottle because, "we pay a deposit on those Goddamn things. After that, you all got cement."

Jack recovered his authority, if not his dignity, and turned to menace me. "Why the hell are you yelling? I'm right here. And what the fuck does that mean, *all right?*"

The thought of the warm bus had made me hopeful, so I toned my reaction to Jack way down. "Yeah, Jack, I can drive the bus."

"Okay, then you drive the miners to work in the morning. You keep the keys. And Michael can drive the truck until he fucks that up."

Jack left before any more mishaps occurred. That was my interview and subsequent field promotion, and it meant no more stairs for this driver and fewer for my crew. Michael, by default, became the de facto truck driver. He was ecstatic when they returned from the runway with the bottle and I told him about his promotion.

Causing no small amount of mirth at my expense amongst the crew, however, I soon generated several serious complaints from the testy miners. It took me most of the following week to find most of the gears in the four-wheel drive bus and make my way through them in appropriate sequence. By that time, I had to report my concerns about the tenuous longevity of the bus clutch to Eddie. It took a while before I convinced Eddie the cause for the failure was "bad parts."

At the end of the week, an alarmingly red-faced Jack cornered me. "It wasn't *bad parts* until you started driving it." I thought it might be imprudent of me to point out he overstated the obvious. When Jack left, I suggested to Eddie he had finished his last private guitar lesson if he continued the rhetoric around the shop. The lessons continued.

At the end of each shift, I parked at the sugar shack and plugged the bus block heater into an electric outlet to keep the engine from freezing solid overnight. At the start of each shift, which was an hour earlier than everyone else, I warmed up the frigid bus, but only after I'd walked across almost the entire mining site to where I'd left it parked. I earned an hour of over-time every day for sitting outside the sugar shack in the dark at -30F or colder, daydreaming about warm beds and warmer, wet kisses. More difficult still was braving Les's chirpy observations at breakfast. I determined, through process and elimination, if I ordered two eggs "over and broken" I would receive what I ordered. Les's large dollop of unsolicited commentary came free of charge as a side order.

Every morning that scrawny little Cockney serial killer of perfectly good food started in with, "Royt, rubber eggs, innit Liz? Blimey, these Can-eye-djuns eat worse than the Oyrish." Many times, I considered revealing why I ordered my food desecrated, but I knew it might raise the ugly specter of his culinary incompetence. I was afraid to wonder, if he cooked like this with confidence, what he would have delivered if publicly humiliated. Really, though, we had become familiar, so I couldn't hurt his feelings. In camp, go along to get along. In the kitchen at Port Radium, that included weathering Les's banter and the routine mangling of even the simplest, bland dish. On my new schedule, I was usually on my way out of the kitchen while passing the surface crew filing in for breakfast. We insulted each other good-naturedly, and then caught up later at the shop for deliveries after I drove the miners to work.

I enjoyed the days more, bouncing with John and Michael over the lake ice or bucking through the camp potholes. Sometimes Frank or Don would jump in too, leaving Silent Sam to ride shotgun with Sean. We took our time picking material from various warehouses, and then making deliveries around camp. I met more of the men who worked in the mill and power plant, although the miners, except Dave, always kept to themselves.

I often managed to divert my helpers to other duties before most kitchen deliveries. This strategy allowed me to take full advantage of one-on-two time with the twins. As we grew more familiar, though, I found I flirted more with Morag. I still had aspirations that I could melt her defensive icebergs, hoping one day soon that I might extend my Aleutian Chain to Morag's Alaskan inlet and become a midnight visitor to the Port Radium convent.

After my first weeks of driving, I kept the crew out of Jack's hair and his firing range. I made sure we spent most of our workday looking busy and being elsewhere. That changed if Jack was pissed off at one of us or if JT's kid or Stalin raked Jack over the coals when one of us screwed up. When that happened, we spent the rest of the day on ice or cement detail after a loud, lengthy redressing. Jack was a pro at violent raging, venting his wrath on us if M-M-Mike was unavailable to take the brunt. I guess where Jack came from, if you were angry, you beat the ox to death and then cried about it when it was time to plow the fields.

19. Jimmy, Schläger, and Old Scores

A few days after Jimmy fired and re-hired me, things began moving faster in Port Radium; *de-volving* might more accurately turn the phrase. I had seen the potential for the decay since my arrival in camp, vented in gossipy snippets of rumors and dribs and occasional drabs and even gobs of character-gutting innuendo. Over coffee one night, Ernie related a Port Radium fable to me. I can't pass on the favor using Ernie's specific words, but he certainly knew the personal histories of Cigar Lips and his only son. If I'm guilty of paraphrasing or expanding on Ernie's narrative, I hope at least, to capture his tone and accurately reveal the gist of his tale.

• • •

Jimmy was always the sort of under-performer who relied on the failure of others to inflate his own ego. He sat at his expansive desk, rocking in his black Naugahyde captain's chair, presiding over the rooftops of the shambles of buildings at the mining site. Through frosted, double-paned windows, he contemplated the success of his latest conquest. Between the index finger and thumb of one hand, he pinched Mary-Ellen's photograph, while in the fingers of the other, he toyed with a cubic zirconium ring. Jimmy wanted her and was unsatisfied with only the torrid nights they shared during his brief Edmonton sojourns. As far as he was concerned, Mary-Ellen was wasting her time in the Edmonton office, working for his father. Jimmy planned to propose to Mary-Ellen the first night of the bonspiel and free her from living under his father's thumb, a position Jimmy knew all too well. The imitation gem sparkled in the sunlight, producing counterfeit rainbow swatches that danced on the walls. He was delighted and rehearsed his carefully crafted proposal, which he hoped would dazzle her, but if not, well, the ring was returnable.

Jimmy sighed and surrendered to one of his two vulnerabilities, indulging his obsession with Mary-Ellen's temptations. He pined for her, more so with each day he remained in camp. She had ceased relations with him months before, and since that day she was always in his thoughts. He recalled their precious yet fleeting hours, usually on weekend nights, those luscious lips, that wonderful cleavage, her bucking hips; he wanted to win her back like Genghis Khan took Samarkand and to possess her like the Khan ruled over

147

the Silk Road. Money and sex comprised Jimmy's concept of intimacy, and though he was woefully unaware of the fact, his shallow understanding of love was exactly the same as Mary-Ellen's.

Jimmy set the ring back in the black felt case and swapped it for a small vial of black ore, which was always in his top drawer. As was his habit when thinking, he rolled the vial around in his fingers. What was obvious to most of the world was something Jimmy could trip over on the community hall floor and still fail to comprehend: Mary-Ellen was a prostitute, or, as Ernie postulated, "a fucking hooker. She's good at it and has made her rounds through this company a few times." According to Ernie, she met Jimmy first and then opted for JT, the man with the money. The real hook she set into Jimmy was her irresistible persona of virginal-but-naughty vulnerability. That was her intangible, developed with the diligence of a woodpecker working on a rotting tree trunk. As a young professional, she doled herself out to her sugar daddy but with an eye to economies of scale. She made herself available only within an exclusive vertical market, and that *market* was JT. As a measurable, if expensive, commodity, she learned how to encourage his lust for her young and spectacular body as if it were an investment asset that returned profit. Though the ship had sailed on her best years, she ignored the inevitable downward spiral of her diminishing physical appearance. Mary-Ellen seemed destined to prosper, regardless of what it cost JT. Her backstory would always be about what she could take from him; the more she took, the more she wanted and the more she despised him for it. She disdained those who thought highly of her as plain stupid. She was a simple girl making her way through a man's world, and the second JT's money ran out, so would she, just like she had with his son.

Jimmy's second vulnerability was his vision of the near future, in which he saw himself as the owner and the mine operating under his control. This point of view was a direct product of his rearing. JT had always correctly assessed his only child as stupid, lazy, and ineffectual, but blamed the outcome on a different cause than did Jimmy. During his son's formative years, JT heaped on those young shoulders truckloads of punishing, humiliating criticism. As a father, JT never considered his efforts might backfire, or that trying to make the boy more than he could ever be might actually make him much less than what his genes were capable of developing. The result was their bitter distance and total inability to span the emotional rift.

JT was also no slouch when it came to shifting blame to others, so, while she was still alive and even posthumously, JT was comfortable citing the boy's mother as responsible for ruining Jimmy. Quite without conscience, JT created a venomous enemy in his own camp; an enemy who associated his father's demise with the opportunity to purge his lifetime burden of failure. So, at just seventeen years, Jimmy swapped the bullying and bickering in the familial home for the abuses inside the iron grasp of the military, where he developed the insensitivity and the aggression required to solve his problems. In fact, JT supported his son's decision, however, JT never imagined that Jimmy would join the Army and end up becoming an MP, busting the heads of drunks and shaking down transvestites in Europe. JT wanted his son to discover his inner serial killer by murdering "gooks" in Vietnam. It just worked out another way.

At boot camp, Jimmy hated his father more for giving him no other option in life than to enlist, but he was out and free from his father's influence and that was good enough. In uniform, Jimmy learned how to devalue dignity, and in particular, the dignity of others. It was in the army, Ernie guessed, that Jimmy decided to bump the old man off.

JT had approved of Schläger the day he turned up in Edmonton and soon ordered Jimmy to hire him to maintain a security presence. "Get that man on the payroll. We need to beef up our grit in camp," JT had said. Of all JT's demands to which Jimmy took offence, the top of the heap was JT's "Schläger" directive. Producing yet another of a long lifetime of belittling insults, JT blew off Jimmy's efforts. Hiring Schläger was the final straw for Jimmy; he was determined his patricide fantasy was going to become a reality.

Jimmy protested, but only in the unwieldy role of devil's advocate. "We might be able to use someone like Schläger, but you don't know him like I do."

"You?" said JT, incredulous. "Schläger's not afraid to pull out the truncheon while you're whittling in your jeans. The man has spunk and determination. So, let me make myself perfectly clear; hire Schläger. And I mean today."

What JT did not know was that Jimmy had an old and painful score to settle with Schläger and saw this hire as his way to kill two birds with a single stone.

The source of the animosity between Jimmy and Schläger began in the military, the night of Jimmy's overseas hazing. The day after his arrival at the base in Lahr, Germany, powerful hands grabbed, blindfolded, and kidnapped the new recruit for a long night in front of the drunken battalion, a night that included bondage, paddling, and humiliation. Late in the festivities, Jimmy passed out from his cocktail of valium and vodka. However, his blindfold removed before he lost consciousness, he saw the terrible, evil vision of a masked and ghoulish figure standing over him, holding in one hand the studded, black paddle and in the other, the leather leash of a huge, obviously male, slathering Doberman Pinscher.

Chained to the floor by a neck harness, Jimmy woke naked and horrified the next morning in the abandoned beer hall, his camouflage cargo pants tangled around his ankles. After calling for help for half an hour, the camp vicar responded to Jimmy's hoarse cries. At first, the vicar was sympathetic. He released Jimmy from his chains, procured a blanket, and helped him to his quarters. There, the vicar evaluated the situation again, and admonished Jimmy, "We are all God's children, my son, but, really, I cannot condone homosexual spanking. God help you," mumbled the scandalized vicar. "It was never like this before Berlin …"

In the shower, Jimmy suffered excruciating pain from the many welts on his buttocks. He had disturbing multiple dog bites on the back of his shoulders and deep, long scratches down his back and legs, as if several voracious timber wolves had attacked him. The fact his sergeant had arranged for Jimmy's bunk to be within barking distance of the camp kennels assured that the man would never attain respite.

The instigator of Jimmy's suffering was a bi-pedal sadistic predator: Sergeant Schläger. Before he transferred to Lahr to serve in the Canadian forces, he had enlisted in the US military. This sociopath had spent time in the garrison in Berlin, infamous for the underground nightlife frequented by men searching out garish transvestite prostitutes. Alcohol fueled and ignited Schläger's peculiar, violent tendencies. The sergeant's addled imagination made Jimmy's initiation unforgettable and crossed the hazing line into the dark realm of bestiality. Since that night, Jimmy's hatred for Schläger and his irrational fear of Doberman Pinschers boiled under his already thin, damaged skin.

"Jimmy was never right after that night," said Ernie. Those lingering, hateful memories were the repudiated origins of his night terrors. The condition followed him home after his premature discharge, effective within months of his hazing incident. The army discharged him because of his misdiagnosed "combat fatigue," which might have been more successfully treated as cynophobia. Adding insult to his misdiagnosed PTSD, after he returned to Canada, the Canadian Forces sent Jimmy a letter thanking him for his service to his country. In the same letter and as quick as you can say "chest full of valor medals," they disqualified his condition as non-conforming and cancelled his veteran medical coverage. They refused Jimmy any veteran benefits because he ended his term prematurely and was officially uninjured. In those days, Canada barred her war veterans from having mental or emotional issues, thus the government dodged any responsibility to provide the ruined young Canadian much-needed extended psychological treatment.

Jimmy attached himself to his father's contacts, wealthy and important people who were enthusiastic about John Birch politics, expressed in influential circles and only behind closed doors. Jimmy wrote articles vehemently supporting the ROTC murderers on the Kent State campus, denounced "Hanoi" Jane Fonda, and anti-nuke, anti-war demonstrators as dog-loving, communist homosexuals. He would fistfight anyone who suggested it was someone other than Oswald alone who had murdered JFK, and he supported all of the CIA propaganda and Vietnam war lies. Weekend nights, he spent his leisure hours bonding with bullies, hanging out in alleys, queer-baiting and battering gay men.

Meanwhile, still in Lahr, Schläger had firmly established his own violent, sadistic reputation while stationed with the Canadians. Busting the enlisted for unsubstantiated disorderly conduct, Schläger was always the MP farthest out on the edge of sanity and violence. Well-founded rumors whispered on the base charged that Schläger extended his duties to include off-hours assaults and robbery of sex-trade workers. Schläger's European tour ended after a weekend when he assaulted, some say "almost murdered," the base commander's lover. The convened tribunal, however, downplayed the incident as an unfortunate accident. Schläger was accurate enough in his assessment of that one particular transsexual: she was a cross-dressing he, but

Schläger was unaware she was his commander's paramour, whose routine was to step out on weekends, whoring around with other officers on the base.

Schläger's vitriolic and violent blunder exposed the social under-belly of the Armed Forces elite. When the scandal broke, the tribunal court-martialed Schläger and sent him home to Canada in disgrace. To avoid his own court martial, the base commander accepted a demotion to captain. The transsexual victim made a full recovery, changed lovers, and co-habited with the presiding judge advocate, who himself had re-upped twice in post-war Berlin before accepting the position in Lahr.

Far from being ostracized and imprisoned on his return, Schläger switched sides again and advantaged his notoriety as an "up and comer." Though hammer-fisted and clearly psychologically damaged, Schläger fit the type the CIA profiled as a perfect field agent recruit: amoral, ex-military, dull-witted, sociopathic, and a ruthless racist with a neo-Christian background. Schläger traded in his skinhead ways to perform as required on several in-country missions until his sexual propensities emerged again in San Francisco. The victim remained in a coma for several months, unable to identify his assailant. When he finally died, the Americans sent Schläger, the second-time loser who was officially "in hiatus," back to Canada. With open arms, Canada has always been willing to accept America's worst. Treating hardened criminals like refugees and performing only trifling background checks, Canada flung out the "welcome mat" to anyone at our borders with a half-baked story and in need of asylum. In fact, a one-way bus ticket and expired prison identification was always considered one piece of personal information too many for the Canadian Immigration Service.

Schläger was living at the Canadian Armed Forces base at Cold Lake, within driving distance of Edmonton and close to his former corporal. After a quick and unofficial investigation, Schläger had found Jimmy in business in Edmonton with his father. Schläger needed a job, and if Jimmy was reluctant to help him out, Schläger could always remind Jimmy of the video tape he had of Jimmy's hazing. Soon after his arrival in Cold Lake, Schläger's weekends coincided with increased incidents of bashed-in skulls, multiple-stitch wounds, and gay men in the area left for dead. Schläger's past was catching up with him, and so he began hanging around the head office in Edmonton, befriending JT and volunteering for odd jobs. Jimmy was afraid of Schläger, and rightly so, but he also saw in Schläger some potential to "get the job done," especially when legalities proved a persistent deterrent. Jimmy told Ernie JT's plan to utilize Schläger in the corporation "served the old bugger right."

Though most of Jimmy's old unit was gone now, discharged, imprisoned, or dead, he reminisced with surprising pride how his men had responded with vigor to the orders of their sergeant and corporal, none other than Jimmy himself. The willingness of the squad to gang up on a drunk went some distance to re-inventing Jimmy; he owed the memory of those soldiers something. Now the best, or worst, of them, Schläger, had followed Jimmy to his promised land of ice, radiation, and silver. Jimmy had promoted himself as a visionary-developer and an adventurer-mogul in the Canadian Arctic, a leader and explorer, undaunted by the extreme challenges of location and uninterested in the environment, if still somewhat anally retentive around dogs.

Jimmy thought Schläger might be helpful securing his legacy. When Jimmy made the phone call offering Schläger the correct amount of money for the security position, he tossed in a bonus for Schläger's silent loyalty. The scene at Cold Lake had heated up for Schläger; he needed to be elsewhere. Jimmy's promise to Schläger of "a little extra-curricular work" sounded right up his alley. Schläger agreed to the terms, filed his resignation request, and walked away from the military.

The near future held a promise of excitement for Jimmy, too. If things came off as planned, he would complete his coup the weekend of the bonspiel. It was the perfect stage; Jimmy would have the money, his revenge, the silver, the power, and the woman of his dreams on her knees in front of him.

With Schläger in the picture, Jimmy saw no possibility of failure. Four would take off in the plane, but only two would return. Many times, Jimmy watched the film clip roll in his mind: Schläger unpacks the freight by disembarking JT from 5,000 feet off the ground. Then, crack, a single bullet to the back of Schläger's head, a stiff boot in the rear, and arrivederci Schläger. Jimmy would take care of the pilot later; the idiot would never see a dime of the bribe. *He'd be dead from cancer by the summer. Same as that little snot geologist Corey … The meek do inherit the earth, six square feet of it.*

Mulling these thoughts, rolling the deadly vial of uranium ore concentrate in his fingers, Jimmy also sealed his eventual fate into the bargain.

20. The Here and Now

I made a snap decision during my first solo nightshift in the kitchen. I searched through the fridge until I found all the leftovers I thought destined for Les's stew pot. Careful to check that Petunia was sleeping somewhere away from the garbage pile in the shed, I dragged the hated mush across the road and dumped it at the Murphy radioactive tailings dump. This practice became standard procedure for me at the start of every shift. After finishing that chore, I turned to the pressing problem of feeding the nightshift crew. But before I had time to dig in, I heard a light knock on the back door of the kitchen. When I opened the door, I saw it was Morag.

• • •

He's opened the door, it's too late. I should run away, but that damn wolverine might be around here somewhere. "Hi." *Jesus, I sound like a schoolgirl. Why are you standing there, idiot, invite me in!*

"Oh, it's the funny one. Hi, Morag, out for a stroll?"

"Shut up, it's freezing out here." *Did I really just push him out of my way?* "Close that door, quickly, there's wolverines out there." *Good, he's closed the door. God, what am I doing here?* "I was ... I was looking for coffee for the morning. We're out of coffee." *That's lame.*

"Yeah, coffee we have plenty of. I have some hot and fresh if you'd like a cup, or, do you have to get back right away."

Well, that's nice. "I just need coffee." *Did he mean that?* "Grounds, I mean, to take back to the sugar shack."

"Okay, I'll tell you what, it's my break and I'm going to grab a cup myself. If you have time and want to join me, I'll be playing solitaire at the closest table."

He's staring, no, just looking. He's nice. "Well, I'm expected back, so I can't stay." *Liar. What are you afraid of? Genna, why did you send me over here, why why why?* "I'll just get what I need and be on my way." *Damn it. Why am I behaving like this?*

"There's hot water for tea, too, if you'd prefer. And I think there are biscuits in Liz's office."

"Liz's office? Where's that?"

"The pantry."

Oh God, that's funny. "You call the pantry Liz's office?"

155

"Cruel, I know, but it's so out there, I couldn't resist. She's got a great heart."

Interesting boy. "If I got fat, would you say the same about me?" *He has stopped to look at me. His eyes are far from unkind, shy, but intelligent, soft brown, even.*

"I don't think so. Why don't you stay? I could use a little company."

• • •

I walked Morag back to the sugar shack after her second cup of tea. "Oh, damn," I said. "You forgot your coffee."

"That's okay. I don't think we're right out. Thanks for the tea." Morag was about to climb the steps to the porch, then turned and kissed me on the cheek. At the top of the stairs, she turned again, and said, "You're sweet for walking me home." When her door closed and I returned to the kitchen, I was sure Morag's kiss warmed the sting on my cheek from the -42F bite from the wind.

I was excited Morag stayed for a second cup of tea and the kiss, but now I was pressed for time. I began my foray for something to feed the night shift in earnest but produced only an unopened case of hamburger patties. I brought dozens of those out and was able to thaw them in time for the men coming off shift. I sliced up tomatoes, made deep fried home fries, heated cans of beef gravy, cut fresh carrots, and made a monster bowl of salad from what produce I could find still fresh enough for human consumption. I found and put out half a dozen wrinkled apples, dried oranges, and cans of two kinds of grapefruit juice. I put out whole wheat bread for toast, and made two carafes of coffee for the miners to take back to their rooms in their thermoses. There were always Pekoe tea bags out, but I found a stash of Earl Grey Black Tea and put that out, too. As an afterthought, I removed half a dozen bags and kept them for Morag, just in case she came back again. I diced and pan-fried potatoes for anyone who might want breakfast, starting sausages and bacon at 1:45 a.m. By the time the men arrived, the kitchen smelled like a cook shack.

Each man saw I was trying and complimented me on my efforts. Some ate burgers, some breakfast, and everyone ate well enough. The hot, fresh, simple meal went over well; for the first night, I was as satisfied as they were. They ate everything I put out, or took it away, or I disposed of it across the road. Nothing remained after their dinner hour. I vowed never to encourage Les and his leftover stew. I thought that maybe I could include a desert the next night. My goal was to do better for them each successive shift.

After the last two men left at three a.m., my routine was to perform a quick wipe down of counters and tables, and then begin my breakfast prep. Every day, I had forty pounds of bacon to strip and slice, and a hundred pounds of potatoes and forty pounds of carrots to peel by hand. The first night, I finished the carrots just before the earliest of the breakfast diners arrived. It takes time to peel that many vegetables.

I learned about scale after the bulk of my first ever throng went through my breakfast lineup; the latecomers arrived to find my trays empty. I had run out of fresh bacon and sausages. I made it up to them by cooking omelets. I offered Michael French toast, but first he had to take back his comment that all male kitchen staff were *you hoo*. By the end of the week, I had it figured just how much to prep for what the guys would eat. My interaction with the cooking staff, or any of my friends for that matter, diminished to "Hi-Bye" before I trundled off for interrupted and fitful daytime sleep.

It didn't come easy, but I began to feel more comfortable in the kitchen. I picked up the rhythm of the shift by the end of my second week, discovering that after I cleaned up the night shift lunch table, I could write for an hour or so, then peel half the spuds by midnight. After that, I prepped for the late meal, fed everyone, and then peeled the rest of the veggies and sliced the bacon after the men left. This meant I had ample time to set up for breakfast and that kept me moving during the last long hours before six a.m.

I made a discovery during my first night's foraging. Les had hung a multi-page order sheet on a nail in the stock room, where he did his paperwork. The next morning over a quick coffee, I asked Les about it. "That's the manifest for the kitchen," he said. "If you see some'in' on the list you need, put a check mark besoyde it. If we don't 'ave it already in camp, then the list is filled in town, the trucks bring it into camp, and the surface crew delivers. It magically appears 'ere."

I believed, in his mind, he had just authorized me to order up an extra can of tomato sauce or more napkins, but I had a different idea. I flipped through the pages and pointed to an item. He said, "Everything except the Scotch, that is, you cheeky git."

So, Les gave me the key to Pandora's Box, and it wasn't long before I became wildly creative with my ordering. Taking advantage of the administration blockheads and their preoccupation with the bonspiel, I added a dozen new items to every order. The surface crew delivered cases of crab, Sockeye salmon, tuna, and smoked oysters, more steaks, prime rib roasts, chicken, turkey, ham, smoked meats, pâté by the pound, cases of fruit, pallets of fresh veggies and salad makings, sauces, jams, and condiments, including more Marmite for Murray. No doubt, JT popped a forehead vein when he saw the invoices, but I hoped he assumed it was for the bonspiel. At the end of my second week, I served the night crew two whole-baked Sockeye salmon with fresh lemons and butter sauce, mashed potatoes, corn, carrots, green beans and fresh salad.

However, I was creating a monster. The miners ate more each night, and the breakfast crew ate more, too, a lot more. Where I thought I was feeding everyone that first week, it seemed like double the men showed up in the mornings for my second week. Everyone stacked his plate. I became so busy I had to double my breakfast prep and the number of eggs I had to cook. My Frankenstein was a growing boy!

By the end of my second week in the kitchen, Morag and I had used up the Earl Grey tea and were well into the Pekoe. When Genna joined us, we played three-handed crib and when Michael joined us three, which became a regular game, we played Whist. I already knew Morag was wicked-good at Hearts and loved thrashing me, but I could hold my own at Cribbage. It was almost as if we had nightly dates now, and she occupied most of my idle time and thoughts. I found out that when she was deep in thought or wanted to say something to make me listen, she talked with a charming, throaty Brogue.

At the end of my third week, I could handle eight mixed egg orders going at a time. While frying bacon to order, my sausages and pan fries sizzled, too. I babied my fried, lightly peppered tomato slices and onion rings, which I added to the breakfast menu, and which were always cooking on the side. I made porridge, too, and heated up pork and beans. I could break two eggs at once in either hand. The men in the lineup cheered me on when I flipped four eggs over easy without breaking a yoke. Besides being smooth and fast, the trick, I discovered, was putting the grill on a hotter setting. Men ordered with a hearty "Good morning," and a smile rather than a doubtful, angry accusation. Though it had become a grueling job of long hours, I looked forward to cooking for them. My specialty became making omelets, and I made a lot of them, with grated cheddar or American cheese. I never used packaged cheese slices. But still, Morag beat me all the time at Hearts.

The only person who I knew was still angry with me after the second week was Ernie. He hated me for one thing: my porridge pot. Regardless of how I cooked the porridge, the bottom of the pot burned black and thick every night. I felt bad for Ernie, but the best I could do was to leave it soaking in the sink every morning. He grumbled at me but in the end, he tolerated this low moment in his day, scraping out the burnt-on residue. He leaned hard into the job, but because the men were happier with better food, he stifled most of his griping. What I cooked was the same basic food, simply prepared with a twist of variety by someone interested in doing the job right.

My third week as night shift-breakfast cook, Dave told me that the men considered breakfast their main meal in Port Radium, followed by burgers much later at night.

"Oy cut the dinner budget," Les said, the same week, "due to the drastic reduction in moy volume and 'ave accommodated the increase in supplies for yer starvin' noyght shift and yer new rush at breakfast."

That was both a compliment and a burden. It meant the men were happy, but I fed most of the camp by myself. Les was also happy, relaxed, and refreshed because of my efforts, and by shuffling the budgets a bit, it meant there was no increase in the overall kitchen expenses he had to explain. He had it "made in the shade" while I worked for him.

It was exhausting work, and the hours were long, but I would be damned before I'd let any memories of me as a cook ever sound like, "Over and broken? That's a Can-aye-jun dish then, innit then, Liz?"

21. The Kitchen Turnstile

I moved.

My new room was on the north side of all the bunkhouses and was quieter during the day — for a week. My new room had been occupied by the indiscreet, young, gay fellow, Phillip, who had shown me the guitar riff to Neil Young's, *The Needle and the Damage Done*. Phillip had worked in the kitchen as a minion on Les's shift, and had always been the pub bartender.

The Arctic days were starting to lengthen, and because of the light, sleeping during the day was impossible. I asked Michael to bring me a gallon of paint and a brush so I could paint over the window glass.

When he brought the paint, I checked the label. "Really, man, lead-based paint?"

"It's all they have here. Besides, it will shield you from the radiation, won't it?"

"I guess I can't be killed twice. Thanks."

When a new bunkhouse project began, power saws revved and hammers slammed outside my window throughout the day. Michael told me the project was supposed to run though the summer, well past the end of our contracts.

Around my fourth week in the kitchen, Les and Liz departed for another camp where they would undermine the gastro-intestinal health of those workers for years to come. Our replacement chef was a short, pot-bellied, brown-skinned Tunisian man, a "specialty" chef. He had a habit of moistening and then sucking on his pursed lips during a conversation, rolling his eyes, and shifting his shoulders when he talked. He minced and pranced around the kitchen, bitching at the women, and shadowing young Phillip.

His second night in camp (Morag had already left for the night), the new chef "just happened to be in the neighborhood," so he dropped by to visit me after midnight. He called me away from my potatoes, saying there was something in the fridge he wanted to show me. In that uncomfortably close space, he took a fig from a gallon jar and sucked on it like it was Saturday night in the Gandy Dancer parking lot. Batting his eyes at me, he said, "It's so good. Do you want to try?"

I guess I was feeling a bit of the Arctic blues, because I raised my potato paring knife between us, and, with an attitude somewhat icier than the Freon in the freezer's cooling system, said, "That kind of fruit would give me hives. Not interested."

Embarrassed, and maybe a little intimidated, he fled past me and ran out of the cook shack with his small, fat hands up by his shoulders, wailing like a banshee. Phillip quit and left the next day. The chef flew out of camp two days later. Ernie told me Jimmy refused to accept the Tunisian's complaints. Running to Jimmy with an ultimatum had been a mistake; the chef insisted Jimmy fire me, or he would quit.

"Why?" Jimmy asked, suddenly fascinated by the fingernails on his left hand.

The Tunisian whined, "He threatened me." I had made sure that all my friends knew about the come on scene in the fridge. I guess the story made it to Jimmy's lofty office, but I had a reputation to protect, too.

Jimmy said, "He can cook; the men like his cooking. Maybe he doesn't want an ass-bandit for a boss, especially one that comes on to him in the fridge after midnight. Frankly, I don't want that either. You're fired, he stays."

That was that. The managers lost their specialty chef for the bonspiel. I stayed on as night shift and breakfast cook, and I inherited Phillip's room two days later. That little realignment occurred three weeks before the bonspiel.

Morag visited me and I wanted to share something with her that was valuable and even impossible in Port Radium: privacy. We took tea and oranges to my new room and she stayed for an hour, but this night, there was very little talking. We were good friends and wanted more. Morag spun me around and pulled my mouth down to her. After that, I was as intoxicated as I had ever been and soared on a magical, sensual carpet across a sexual universe that promised more with every touch. Hot hands moved, guided by instinct, and our mouths met at a wonderful, writhing combination of lust, fantasy, and flesh. We completed a camp mosaic that was devoid of so many amenities because our moments of love-making, like they should be, were ecstatic, intense, lingering, and comforting.

Alfred Cool

Another new cook tried out. "Bald" Ed was okay. I tried to
help break him in; the poor bastard was without credentials other
than having been the sandwich guy at a lunch stand at the Edmonton
International Airport. Ed was a warm body willing to work any shift,
probably unaware he was up for termination the minute they could
Shanghai someone into camp who could produce a $20 meal from a
$2 slab of flank steak. Murray told me the lunch counter improved,
but still, stew made its way back onto the dinner menu. I made
money betting Bald Ed would quit before the bonspiel.

The revolving door in the kitchen kept rotating. It was
challenging, working nights and keeping up without a program.

22. Dogs

It was mid-April and still very cold during the night. At Sunday breakfast, John asked me if I wanted to meet his father. I misunderstood John, thinking his dad was on his way into camp, that he was arriving on a plane. It seemed inconceivable to me he might brave the dangerous ice road at thirty-five below zero.

"What flight's he taking?" I asked.

"Not a flight. Dogs."

"Dogs?"

"He came here on a dog sled."

"He's here? Really? From Rae Lakes to here by dog sled? A hundred and fifty miles? That's amazing. Is he staying in the guest bunkhouse?"

If I didn't know him better, I might have thought John's shrug was sarcastic. "No. He brings a tent with him."

"He's camping? Do people do that? What about the dogs? Don't they get cold?" I was a dog lover.

"They sleep outside all winter. What's the difference where they sleep?"

Because of our conversations, I knew Rae Lakes was part of the Gamèti nation and their territory was due south of Port Radium. The village is northwest of Yellowknife and southeast of Déline (Fort Franklin) NWT, equidistant from both villages. Over the weeks, John taught me about his ancestors; how they travelled to Déline to trade with the Dené and Alexander Mackenzie when he was in town. Mackenzie navigated that great river for the Hudson's Bay Company in the 1780s. John talked about the explorer like he was a neighbor who might drop by any time.

"So when do I meet your dad? He'll come in to eat, won't he?"

"They won't let him eat in the cook shack; besides, he brought his own moose."

"He brought a moose in with him, on a dog sled, at -35F, across a hundred and fifty miles of frozen barrens?" It had snowed heavily the past three nights. The grader was going day and night, clearing our roads of the heavy snowfall. Management wasn't even thinking about the summer runway yet, besides, the D9 was still in

163

the garage.

"Of course. He hunts all winter. We all do. Summer, too. He needed to eat and feed the dogs. Do you want to meet him?"

Sunday, mid-morning, John gathered me up from my room. I was excited to meet his father. My head wasn't straight. I was thinking April in Vancouver: Japanese Cherry Tree blossoms and daffodils, and failed to dress for the Arctic April. We were only going down to the ice, so I wore my parka and camp shoes. I didn't put on snow pants and neither did I bring my mitts. It was relatively warm out, -5F, and we weren't going far.

The camp was set up on the far shore of LaBine Bay, across from the power plant, on a knobby outcropping that extends like a uvula into the throat of the bay. When we walked into the camp, I saw John's father had pitched his tent in the natural lee of a ridge, which protected him from the worst of the wind. The obvious signs of his camp were a square, sixteen-foot canvas wall tent and a dog sled tipped on its side. Wood smoke drifted out of the tin chimney, a pleasant change from the bitter power plant effluent I had grown used to. John called out and then poked his head inside the tent. He waved me inside.

After wading through a foot of the previous night's snowfall in camp shoes, the ambient heat inside the tent was immediately pleasant. My first impression was how clean John's father kept his living quarters. The carpet layers on the floor were overlaid on the frozen snow so there were no gaps; his bed was raised on light, strong plastic milk carton carriers; he had standing headroom; a small airtight stove in the middle of the space cranked out enough heat to melt water, or in this case, slow-cook an aromatic moose stew, and there was a makeshift kitchen where a two-foot slab of moose tenderloin hung over a collection pot. But John's dad was elsewhere.

We left the tent. I looked at the sled flipped on its side and wondered why there were no dogs around. I asked, "Did he take the dogs for a walk or something?"

John laughed at me, then clapped his hands and yelled, "Ho."

White mounds of snow erupted when seven Canadian Eskimo dogs stood up, shaking snow off their bodies, inspecting us, tails wagging. I reached out to the nearest dog, feeling sorry for its having to survive outside. John stopped me, taking hold of my arm. "What are you doing?"

"I want to pat the dog."

"You don't pat these dogs; they're not pets. You don't go near them, either. Just me. They bite. And it hurts." I considered where misdirected affection and dog bites intersected in my life, agreeing it best they never did. "These dogs are mean in the winter," John said. "But are way worse when they're fat and lazy in the summer. They would tear each other apart if I let them get close enough. That's why we stake them like this, so they can't bite each other. But when they run, they don't fight, they run together."

The Canadian Eskimo dog is a big dog. Beefy, even brutish in a bulky way, but they are powerful runners. These dogs were hefty shouldered beneath raggedy, long, reddish-brown or white and black thick winter coats. These were not show Huskies or long-legged Malamutes. Their legs were muscular, medium length; these were working dogs with deep chests and wide, thick paws. Their rumps were stockier than a Malamute or a Husky. Long, bushy tails wrap over their faces for protection from the bitter cold and blowing snow. Their heads were huge, shaped half like a Rottweiler and half like a wolf. When one looks at you, it wants food or water, and, if disappointed, it looks through you. When the pack of them looked me over, I felt outnumbered.

"What do they eat?"

"Moose now, but mostly fish."

"How do they find water when everything is frozen?"

"They eat a lot of snow. Do you want to go for a lake run?"

"Hell yeah! A dogsled ride on Great Bear Lake? Where do I sign up?"

John laughed at my enthusiasm then told me to wait beside the sled. He flipped the sled onto its four metal runners to free it from the frozen snow. The sled was ten feet long, tip to runner. The tube construction frame was ultra-light when it was empty. I asked John about the strips of tanned moose hide reinforcing every joint. "Makes it stronger. Hold them for a minute ... stand on the anchor." I stood with both feet on the hook driven into the snow to hold harnessed dogs. Above the runners, the bottom of the sled was made of light sheet metal. He slipped into the tent and returned with enough hides and blankets to form a wind-proof, narrow pocket in the sled.

John had often told me how important his own twenty-four

dogs were to him. I knew his younger brother cared for his pack while John was in Port Radium. As if I might mention I needed a new set of tires for my car, he said, "I have to cull five or six when I return to Rae Lakes." John told me he fished for Arctic char for hours every day during the summer to feed his dogs. "They're mean when they don't work. They have to be afraid of me, always."

"Why don't you just buy a snowmobile?"

"I might, but we can't get gas delivered to Rae Lakes; it costs too much. Besides, if the snowmobile breaks down, no one can fix it. I want to take a mechanics course."

John flipped the sled onto its side again and then went to bring over the first dog.

A tall, red-orange mongrel, one blue and one light grey eye, was already standing, but it cowered when John approached. He took the dog by the back of its neck and pulled it halfway across his leg, then he lifted it so his thigh supported the dog's shoulders. Its front paws off the snow and its tail stiff, John held the rubber ring around its neck in a confident grasp then he released the dog from the chain that anchored it to the frozen snow. The dog beside the dog John had selected snapped its jaws, but John held tight and avoided the fight that surely would have developed when he spun the dog in his two-handed grasp out of harm's way. He frog-marched the dog to the sled and set it in the elongated harness where he slipped a second ring over his head. The dog shook itself out then sat down and took a long, wide yawn … none the worse for wear despite John's brusque handling.

While this was going on, the other dogs howled, yipped, and whined. Six more tails flew high, they were ready to run. John repeated the maneuver five more times, arranging the dogs so they were staggered along a 20-foot harness, like bangles attached to a bracelet. He told me this setup gave the dogs more freedom of movement, so they could pull the sled through smaller gaps in the ice ridges.

The dogs were excited, but showed no aggression toward each other once placed in the harness. The last dog John brought over, the lead, wagged its tail with what looked like affection, adding his yips to the excitement. John displayed no signs of affection or special affinity with this lead dog; when he marched it over to the lead ring in the harness, John was all business and never dropped his guard. When I thought about it, a dog bite at Rae Lakes could be a serious injury, and maybe deadly out on the tundra.

"Why don't they fight when they're in the harness?" My feet had turned cold, but I didn't want to say anything; I wanted to go, too.

"They want to run. Keep holding the handles tight. Don't let them get away. Keep standing on the anchor hook." I did as instructed. I felt the occasional strong pull as the dogs shifted forward in the harness. I noticed the lead dog had lain down as if he wasn't going anywhere.

John disappeared into the tent again. When he reappeared, he carried his father's sleeping bag. This was no ordinary sleeping bag; it was an eider down "mummy" bag, made to fit inside another eider down shell. The outer shell John brought out next was six inches thick with goose down. The double-bag system provided protection and warmth to at least -25F. I considered, once, buying a bag like this for winter camping in the BC Coast Mountains, but the bags were excessively hot, constricting, and bulky to pack. The manufacturers made these bags for use in the Arctic. I was a little insulted when John said, "Get inside for the ride."

I felt demoted, but a ride is a ride. I regained some of my pride by flopping in the sled in a sitting position. I draped the outer shell over my feet and legs. The material smelled of tobacco smoke but not sweat. The dogs raised a fever pitch ruckus after John yelled something like "Key-eye," and then we were off.

What a thrill! With a tremendous surge, we flew over the fresh snow, down the incline and onto the lake ice, where even the fresh snow was crusty from the wind. Seven long bushy tails wagged in the air, they snapped at each other until their tongues started to wag, and then they ran, and pulled, and ran some more ...

"Where are we going?" I yelled over my shoulder as the lead dog took us toward the mouth of LaBine Bay.

"The lake. We can go over to the fishing camp around the point at Cameron Bay. It's about six miles away."

The sun was bright after our days of snowfall, and the light breeze was at our backs. It was a fantastic, timeless, limitless day. The dogs picked up their second wind as we exited onto the Great Bear Lake ice sheet at the farthest end of our runway. We had passed Silver Point and approached Cobalt Island on our right.

Before we made the long sweeping turn south, John stopped the sled. "Look," he said. He pointed at the small straight between Cobalt Island and the rocky shore west of camp, where the Murphy tailings leached into the lake.

At first, I couldn't see why we had stopped, but when I stared harder through my tears and into the cold breeze, I saw a black patch on the ice. "What is that?"

"A wolverine. If I had my gun, that's a $175 pelt at the trader's."

"What's it *doing*?"

"Don't know, but I bet that's Petunia." He was thoughtful. "She's still hanging around camp. They don't usually do that after they've been hunted." We lost sight of her when she disappeared behind an ice ridge, as if it sensed we were watching it. I wondered if she was hooked on my nightly supply of stew fixin's.

"I guess you need a scope on the gun to make that shot?"

"No. Indians don't use scopes. Every gun has a natural shot. Our best hunters say it is better to aim with an open sight because scopes freeze up. Better to learn how to shoot natural, then get closer."

"Do you want to go over there and see her?"

"Not without my rifle." John hollered at the patient lead dog. The others looked eager to carry on. At John's command, the leader took us farther out onto the lake ice.

The day became surrealistic. The ice was wind-blown and clean, except where the many ice ridges had allowed snow berms to form. Whenever the lead dog approached a three-foot, raggedy ice ridge, he picked the spot where we could make it through. He seemed to have a plan and kept the sled's momentum working in our favor. Except for the big direction changes, John gave him the freedom to lead, and that dog never missed once.

Nothing stopped this dog team, not bare ice, snow berms, or jagged ice ridges. And if the lead dog strayed a little too far off our general course, John re-directed him to veer left or right with single commands; it was amazing to witness. Tuned to each other, the individuals solved each negotiation problem singularly, but still pulled as a unit. It was obvious how much an asset a string of powerful dogs and a smart musher could be in this unyielding environment.

John spiked the sled to anchor the team to the frozen snow

when we arrived at the fishing camp. The dogs peed, licked at the snow and then curled up into fur balls.

Screwed down sheets of plywood covered every window and door on the lodge. We explored for a while, but there wasn't much to see. We might as well have arrived at an outpost on an alien planet; the straight edges of the fabricated buildings felt so out of place on the rugged shores of the lake surrounded by those spectacular barrens. The buildings, like those at Port Radium, formed a drab, square, and inappropriate outrage on the landscape. After circumnavigating the main building once, we decided to head back. My feet had turned into two blocks of ice after I post-holed through the snow, but we were still in high spirits and I was having a ball.

When John started the dogs running again, everything changed.

Rounding the Cameron Bay headland, which was only a half-mile away from the fish camp, our bearing was northeast. When we were southbound, neither of us paid much attention to the light breeze at our backs, but now the Arctic revealed her punishing bite. A raw wind flows across Great Bear Lake like a river, and we had to make headway upriver. My face felt pinched, as if in a vise; the glare off the ice blinded me, though the sun, like a bad omen, had begun to wane in the western sky.

The dogs ran differently from how they had run on our way out. Though they continued to pull hard and in unison, each dog dropped its head and ran with its tongue out to lick quick slathers of snow. Navigating into that wind, it was only minutes before my eyes started to swell shut.

John ordered the lead dog to stop, and said, "You get in both bags. You have the wrong shoes." I heard the disappointment in his voice, and I felt worse because he was right. I had no choice, so I slipped into the outer shell. Out of the wind, my eyes watered. When I blinked, my eyes were grainy under the lids, and I was worried about frostbite. If anything at all happened to make our situation worse, we might have found ourselves in serious trouble. I snuck a quick look at John and saw his face had turned dark red from the wind and cold. Our joy ride had changed into something else.

"What about you? Are you going to be okay?"

"Let's go, eye-e-key-a," he yelled. Holding the sled handles, John ran behind us until the dogs acquired the momentum, and then he hopped onto the thin runners with a final shove. Immediately, he scrunched down on the runners behind me to block some of the wind.

I saw nothing but a bleary mosaic of smudges and my scalp burned in an odd and painful way. "I'm sorry, John, I have to take cover." I buried my head inside the outer shell, worried sick about our predicament. *What if John slipped off the runners? Would the dogs just take off? What about frostbite?* There was nothing I could do to help, except not make it worse. I felt useless. We had no choice but to make the run back, our situation was that harsh and that simple. There was no waiting around for rescue, no one knew where we were.

For the next hour, the faithful, amazing dogs ran. Whenever I peeked out at John crouched on the runners, he was struggling to use the bulk of the sled as a wind break. He had pulled his inadequate collar up and folded his fingers into his jacket to fight the dangerous wind. He looked horrible. *Cold* was not the word for it: his face was beet red and his eyes were slits, but he was stoic and determined despite the severe pain he had to be feeling. He popped his head up from his crouch, took bearings on our progress, shouted the occasional course correction, then scrunched down again and gritted his teeth.

"Are you okay?" I asked, knowing he absorbed more punishment than I could ever withstand.

He lied to me. "Oh, sure. This isn't so bad. When my brother and I were little, we used to play tricks on our elders by running naked up the main street of Rae Lake on Christmas morning."

"Some trick," I said, and then shivered at the thought of being naked in this torment.

When we swung east toward LaBine Bay, we were finally behind the protection of the Cobalt Island headland. The intensity of the wind became bearable enough for John to stand on the runners. I gained immense confidence from that although my feet were still like two blocks of ice. I popped my head and shoulders out of the down sleeping bag. Minutes later, we pulled into LaBine Bay.

My heart sank with shame when I saw the industrial waste that described Modern Man's fingerprint at Port Radium. Rusting barrels and fuel tanks, dilapidated storage sheds, and the polluting chimneys of the power plant and mills disgusted me. Even the yellow glow of lights from the windows of bunkhouses that dominated the ridges sickened me. How long would this cancerous wound continue to expectorate in this timeless land? And what was produced from all this greed? Only a vile poison and war.

The dogs pulled us through the last of the lingering twilight, past the mine buildings, and up to the snow camp. I tried to stand up on my own, but my legs were stiff from the cold and my ankles were inflexible. I needed John's help to climb out of the sled. I had no idea how that tough-as-a-bucket-of-railroad-spikes young man lived through that run. With my arm over his shoulders, I said, "John Mantla, that was one of the most impressive displays of guts I've ever seen."

He looked at me as if I was a little crazy; he still had work to do. "I was riding," he said then pointed at the dogs. "They did all the pulling. You should go in the tent."

The sky was black with storm clouds and it had begun to snow again. "I can help with the dogs."

John rejected my lame attempt to rally in the name of teamwork. He steered me toward the tent, but I saw he strained to move. The dogs growled and snapped at each other again. "No, you take care of yourself. I'll take care of the dogs. This has to happen a certain way, and I have to go fast or they fight."

I would be just another problem if I insisted, so I went into the tent. I thought the camp comfortable before the ride, but it had become a moose stew, hot, palatial patch of heaven. My nose erupted and my eyes watered as if I were crying my heart out. I wiped my face on my parka sleeves. I was out of the exposure to the wind, so my eyesight returned. I took my shoes off and placed them near the stove. I sat on the bed and massaged my feet and toes; my heels were like ice. When I felt the pain, I knew the circulation had returned, so I put my thawed shoes back on and stuck my head outside the tent.

I watched John with the dogs. He already had them all re-chained to the ground. They stood and watched John's every move as each tail wagged. He went to a nearby snow bank, dug up the lid of a plastic container and pulled out steaks of frozen moose meat. The steaks were not big, perhaps only a pound each. In quick succession, John dropped a slab in front of every dog but gave a second frozen chunk to his lead dog. John brought the sleeping bag back into the tent. I watched the ravenous dogs snarl down the meat, then lick the snow for any frozen, bloody bits that might have fallen from their jowls.

John seemed to move with less pain, but still struggled if he tried to go too fast. He passed me the sleeping bag and then rebuilt his father's bunk, then found an empty cooked-ham container and dipped it into the two-gallon tin container beside the makeshift sink. John used a plastic tumbler that hung from the crossbeam and took a quick drink, and then he filled the smaller container with water. "Want some?" he said. I realized how dehydrated I was, so I gulped a tumbler full of water. Back outside, John delivered to each of the dogs a slurp of water from a separate plastic bowl for each dog. Taking too long feeding or watering one dog might start a gang war, and dogs could die because of injuries. I understood now, from personal experience, how that would be bad news if it happened 150 miles from home.

Once tethered, fed, and watered, each dog peed again and then curled up, laying their tails over their noses. Multi-colored sets of eyes, a normal condition known as "heterochromia," watched from behind protective, furry tails. Finally, John returned to the tent. His face still looked like a couple of guys armed with cheese graters had attacked him. The animals were cared for, so we looked to ourselves.

He shook out hands still stiff from the cold. "You want some stew?"

"God, yes." I was ravenous.

The meaty aroma mixed with the wood smoke from the pine recovered from Silver Point pallets. The stew was amazing; only the gods themselves could have sent the simmering moose, carrot, and onion stew down from their banquet hall. We polished off two salty bowls and four pieces of bread each, but left the simmering pot still half full. I promised to replenish the bread from the kitchen that day. In between mouthfuls, I asked, "Where is your father, anyway?"

"He's getting ready to leave tomorrow."

"Leave? Already? Why?"

"He came here to ask for jobs for the men in our village, but Jimmy won't hire Indians." John checked the stove for wood.

"Why not?"

"He doesn't like us, I guess. I'm going home, too. Sam is flying out to Yellowknife. We won't work for them." He broke a slat over his knee then put the pieces in the stove.

We washed our dishes then left the tent a short while later. Contented dogs slept beneath a growing blanket of snow. John's father failed to return, so I never met him, but I made sure to repay him for his hospitality in absentia when I gave John four loaves of bread that afternoon.

Sadly, after Jimmy hit them with this final, unforgivable racist slap, John Mantla and Silent Sam left camp the next day. I had another reason to loathe Port Radium, and I felt like a dirty Caucasian. I had no excuse to make it about me, but I was going to find a way to fight Jimmy and JT; a battlefield had been drawn up and I stood at the ready. I lost a true friend, and it felt worse being the one left behind. I would miss John. I also missed his royal send-off because of work, but I heard Dave's room roared until after two a.m. I'm not sure how I made it through that shift, coming off the lake in that shape and with only two hours sleep. I challenged the night shift to ask for anything they wanted for their dinner and they selected a Baron of Beef with Yorkshire pudding and thick gravy, and then I fed the demanding breakfast horde. The moose stew must have given me the stamina, but it did not remove the anger in my belly.

• • •

My days in Port Radium had bogged down into a series of disappointing episodes. I spoke with Michael every day, and we formed a plan. I already knew I would not make the term of my contract, and if that occurred, then I would go out in either glory or a hail of bullets. Our focus was on the bonspiel, just a few weekends away, and I vowed management would never forget me.

23. Zen Dynamite

The following Thursday morning, just before the breakfast rush was about to go into full frenzy, Dave came to visit. "I have Sunday off. I'm rotating from days to nights. There won't be anyone around on the switchover shift. You wanna do something?"

I had seen less of Dave lately because his cross-shifts and my long hours in the kitchen broke up the continuity of the old gang. Dave and I still managed to meet up to play tunes, but it was usually at my expense, and the price was loss of sleep and diminished sobriety. "Sure. What do you have in mind?"

"I'll get us some beers, and I can show you the mine. You've never been underground, right?"

I shook my head. "Just barely in the Echo Bay tunnel."

"Okay then, come and find me after you finish breakfast Sunday, and we'll go for a walkabout. And we have to finish the song before the weekend; we're playing at the community hall the night of the bonspiel. I promise I'll have beer."

It was a shock to me how fast Sunday came around again. The last of the throng had demolished the last pieces of toast and disappeared after an enthusiastic, "Thank you." I indulged Ernie who again filled me in on how much he hated my porridge pot, listened to Bald Ed threaten to quit, again, and then I staggered off to bed having garnered only the briefest of wan smiles from Morag. It was silent outside, hammers and chainsaws did not torment me on Sundays, and I fell into a deep, exhausted sleep.

At eleven a.m., Dave knocked on my door, kicked my door, opened my door, turned on my light, ignored my filthy barrage of verbal abuse, and said, "Thought you might like this coffee before we go crow huntin'."

• • •

If you think of mining, you might recall images of the "Chunnel" or the expansive Tokyo, Paris, or New York subway systems. Perhaps you have memories of impressive, high-tech displays of massive boring machines tunneling through megalithic formations, cutting the edges, literally, of tunnel engineering; of projects with bloated budgets paying more engineers, auditors, and lawyers than actual diggers; of clutches of safety inspectors scrutinizing every milestone,

175

always underfoot; investors, politicians, and promoters counting and re-counting each dime of the many billions spent throughout the lifespan of the mega-projects while staggering personal services and consulting fees piled up. Who could not recall the spectacle of the meeting of tunnels through the practicality of engineering and the alchemy of science and computers? Though even Michelangelo dared not link the fingers of God and Adam, technology assured us any two tunnels would converge in Sistine symmetry. In celebration, beneath the bright lights and framed by cameras, politicians and documentarians backslapped each other as the champagne flowed and technology prevailed.

Well, forget that. Port Radium was plebian and dangerous, and a greedy, cynical, and entrenched profit philosophy ruled.

Wealth has never transferred to the grower, miner, logger, or fisherman. However, the distributor does well. The distributor controls supply and therefore stresses those on either side of the demand-supply paradigm. Commodity prices are slaves to supply; the supply side of the "free" market bows to the distributors. Distributors control the elasticity of macroeconomics. Curiously, there is little profit in production, but much in distribution, marketing, and retailing. The foundation of our financial system crumbles as the direct result of seventy-five years of corporate welfare and governments that pander to the wealthy. Billions are funneled to the few who rely on taking advantage of impoverished populations overseas, in the form of cheap labor, which has replaced economies of scale as the primary source of profit. The disconnect is that it is the working poor and dwindling middle class who buy retail goods, not the chronically under-employed, or the same woefully underpaid, foreign workers, or the obscenely wealthy.

In Port Radium, "workplace safety" was an empty paraphrase that mimicked third world reality. "Don't get hurt" was the limit to JT's safety policy. We labored hundreds of miles and many air-hours away from the nearest hospital, for example, and yet there was no nurse or first aid attendant at this industrial mining site because it cut into profit. No one conducted fire drills, chemical trauma drills, choking or heart-attack training, basic blood flow, exsanguination, or burn training. Nothing. In Port Radium, you had better hope ointment was all you ever needed. In Port Radium, Dave Rhodes would have died if he'd had his accident on site.

The Hottest Place on Earth

Fostered in the dirty Thirties, the prevailing attitude from
management was still, "If you don't like the job or the camp, plenty
of others will take your job, so good riddance ... And don't forget to
leave your wages at the door on your way out." Safety of the men was
the first corner cut in 1932, as it was for all workers in all industries,
and the same corporate irresponsibility prevailed through World War
II. In 1943, the Canadian government became the mine owners; they
extended the culture of the Eldorado Mining Company never
addressing valid safety concerns for those who worked at the mine.

The war effort swung Eldorado into full production. The
goal was to accrue as much uranium oxide as quickly as possible for
the American military, under the false guise of the Allied effort to
beat the Nazis to the nuclear bomb. By 1943 confirmed intelligence
flowing in from the British assured the Allies that the Third Reich's
program was "stillborn." Every politician wants re-election, so the
chore for President Truman was to convince a public bloodthirsty for
revenge and desperate for an end to the war that he was the man to
force the Japanese Emperor to capitulate. The likes of Generals
Grove and Lemay influenced President Truman, a dull-witted,
shiftless man, who was amoral enough to usher in the age of nuclear
war despite the Emperor's several attempts to surrender.

Any but a fleeting concern the Canadian government might
have had regarding mine safety paled against the loss of so many
sacrificed in battle. The government had deemed mining, fishing,
logging, farming, and ranching as essential services, bowing at the
altar of war. The message was clear: if you're hurt, lads; there is no
help forthcoming.

It is reasonable to expect that after the war ended, and in light
of the prolific documentation warning of appalling amounts of
radon in the tailings, water, air, and mines thick with dust at Port
Radium, the Canadian government might have turned to address the
many safety deficiencies. Common sense and owner responsibility
required safety standards be implemented; after all, for fifteen years,
safety inspection reports were ignored. Nevertheless, the owners, by
proxy, required the leaseholders, JT and Jimmy, to act on only a single
of the most basic improvements. Many doctors, leading scientists,
Madame Curie herself, warned the world and the regulatory
commissions in Canada and the US about the cancers caused by men
inhaling the deadly radioactive dust particles. The Canadian

government finally acquiesced and installed a single fan in the Eldorado mine. Canadian safety standards for the mine, and indeed so many other mines and ore processing mills and plants in Canada, were grossly inadequate. And, like the vile tailings pollution, they remained ignored through the thirties to the eighties. Turning a blind eye and deaf ear was and is the status quo as Canadian politicians sell rights to Canadian resources to foreign, corporate carpetbaggers, happily unrestricted by Canadian environmental law, and ready to sue Canada under trade agreements favoring corporations whenever we ask them to clean up their pollution.

Port Radium workers, like so many others in Canada's uranium industry, fell ill or died. Family members left behind had to live with huge holes in their hearts and lives, and endure the lies spread by doctors and bureaucrats that tobacco was the culprit. "Scientists" looked for opportunities to step up, for the right price, of course, and declare the mines and processing plants safe. Worse still, the industrialists extended the cover-up of their predecessors and suppressed the research that proved so many Canadian workers had died or were dying from exposure to radon in the mines and processing mills. The trail to the Canadian uranium miner's graveyard is well worn.

• • •

Dave and I walked through camp, down the hill, past the turnoff to Garbage Lake, crunching over the radioactive road cap, looking forward to an extraordinary day. Our destination was the Echo Bay mineshaft. It was past mid-April and the temperature was 10F, so we were comfortable. A persistent rumor circulated in camp that spring would soon make her cameo appearance, though none of us old salts believed it. We each sipped a beer from the cases we carried. I looked forward to the tour of Dave's workplace. We walked up to the sheds outside the Echo Bay mineshaft. I was not surprised it was unlocked. Nobody worked Sundays, except the second cook and a skeleton crew in the kitchen, so security was nonexistent.

Inside the shed to which Jack, so long ago, had forbidden us access, Dave flicked on the overhead, bare light bulb. The dank smell of sweat permeated the heated room. The miners left their underground gear to dry here until the next shift. Dave picked from the shelf a hard hat with an attached battery-powered headlamp. He gave it to me after he tested it for a full charge. "You don't want to have to try to find your way back in the dark."

"No, I don't. How far in are we going, anyway?" I asked, after I'd donned the grimy, black rain jacket Dave also borrowed for me.

"Four hundred feet. I'll show you my jackleg."

"C'mon, Dave, can't we just be friends ..." He did not laugh at my lame joke.

"Light on." He reached above my hardhat brim and clicked a switch. "Follow me."

"Wait, my shoe lace." I lifted my clown boot up to tie the lace and placed it on a stack of cases. The labels read: DYNAMITE. "For Christ's sake, Dave. You guys store the dynamite right here? What happens if it blows?"

"It won't do that. You need one of these ...," Dave pulled from the shelf one of many boxes of blasting caps stored directly above the cases of dynamite and removed a blasting cap, "... which you place into one end of a stick of powder, which I will do at the appropriate moment, and then if you light the fuse, she'll blow. But the smallest shock can set a cap off, too."

I blanched.

Dave returned the box of caps to the shelf, but to my horror, I watched, in slow motion, as the box teetered and fell off. I turned to run, wide-eyed, flashing-back through slow-motion images of my life, when Dave reached out and caught the box.

"Gotcha." He laughed at me, quite pleased with himself.

After I'd regained my composure, I said, "You miners have a funny kind of a sense of humor. Anyone ever tell you that?"

"All the time. Sorry. I'm messing with you. Grab more beers. C'mon, we go this way."

"Hey, Corey told me this mine is hot, but not as bad as Eldorado. Is there a Geiger counter here?"

"Yeah, up ahead a ways, but no one pays any attention to it. It's been out of paper since I came back." Dave referred to the V-700 counter's ticker tape that was supposed to record every single radon proton that burnt through the men's lungs, leaving behind a scorched trail of cell destruction and cancer.

We stepped through a rickety wooden door. Its squeaky, rusty hinges complained about working on Sunday. Our two headlamps illuminated the blackness in the tunnel. It was warmer here. I followed on Dave's heels when the tunnel narrowed; I felt like I walked in my grandfather's footsteps. As a boy of seven, he worked in the coalmines near Cardiff. For five and a half days a week he was on his hands and knees, thousands of feet below the seabed, where he scooped coal between his legs. Eventually, he grew too big to fit into the tiny cracks at the ends of the veins, so they graduated him to a shovel and pick. He worked on his knees for years, which permanently curved his spine. Eventually, he contracted coal miner's lung. The company disowned him, so he and his family went on the dole, then emigrated to Canada. No wonder, like so many others, he became a middle-aged, abusive alcoholic. My underground reticence was genetic.

Dave scooted right along. I followed his headlamp and panned my light beam along the floor of the rough-walled tunnel, wary of each methodical footstep. I was determined to spot and avoid any winzes. I took a minute to look at the counter when I found it. Sure enough, it worked exactly as Corey described: the steady tick of the overloaded CD V-700 provided whoever passed the misleading assurance radiation levels were safe.

Forty feet ahead of me, Dave's headlamp drew an arc across the roof, then disappeared into the floor of the tunnel. "Dave, where the hell are you going?" I sped up to catch him and almost spilled over the edge of a hole. I peered into the abyss; a rock ramp sloped acutely downward at nearly the same angle as a playground slide.

Many feet down the shaft, Dave waited, looking up and over his shoulders at me. "This is how I get to work every day. Careful, it's icy and slippery. It's better to go down crab-style, so you can see where you're putting your feet. You stop yourself from falling by stemming your arms to the sides of the shaft. You might want to finish your beer before you start."

As recently as twenty minutes earlier, I'd trusted this man. Now, I had solid grounds, for the second time that morning, to have grave doubts about his mental stability. Port Radium was dangerous enough above ground; this was insanity. "You're telling me there is no elevator or ladders or boardwalks or anything for you guys to get to work?"

Dave stopped again, removed his hard hat, extended his arm, and tapped the top of the chute with the hat. "No head room for any of that. C'mon, it opens up about fifty feet below me."

"How do you bring the ore out?"

"We carry it to a dumb waiter that brings it to the surface, dump it into the cars that run on the tracks where you surface guys cleared the ice off the rails, then it gets loaded into the hopper. Trucks take the ore to the crushing mill. Careful near the top, it's icy."

I chugged the last of my beer before I followed Dave down and deeper. To accomplish this, I dropped into the recommended crab position and extended a leg down the hole. An icy glaze covered the rubble built up in the shaft. My foot slipped, so I stemmed my arms to the side to catch and then steady myself. I cursed that there was no rope to grab in case I slipped. During my descent, I knocked my hard hat off but snagged it before it skidded away. I pointed the headlamp down the shaft to see what I faced. By this time, Dave was far below me, and he moved even farther away and downward quickly.

"What the hell? This is crazy, crazy." It took me several more minutes to slip and slide down the shaft. Soon, the icy handholds at the top gave way to wet, dislodged scree that rattled ahead of me in the warmer, bottom half of the shaft.

Dave waited for me. When I stood up, Dave said, "Weird commute, eh?"

"You do that every day?" Sweat poured off me in the stifling, subterranean air.

"Twice, or more. Eldorado is way worse. It's pretty dangerous in that mine. C'mon, we're almost there."

Others had drilled and blasted these tunnels during the late sixties. I followed Dave through a black, forbidding doorway-sized shaft, then along an iris-shaped, narrow tunnel that we skittered through sideways. By the time we entered another maze of tunnels, some tight, others with low ceilings, I was lost. At one entry point ("a short cut" Dave called it) I crawled on my hands and knees to the next shaft. I had no idea how far we had travelled and felt claustrophobic.

When we were able to stand again, Dave stopped, turned to face me as calmly as if we were at the Stanley Park tennis courts, and said, "I gotta show you something." He turned off my headlamp, then he turned his off. Several bright spots floated in a random pattern in front of me. "Give it a minute." Soon enough, my eyes no longer perceived the phantom bulbs. *Black; really, really black.* "Now, listen." *Absolute, silence*, except for my shortened, anxiety-induced breaths. I had never experienced anything like this before. "Hold your breath, it's like Zen or something."

Deep in the west coast forests of Haida Gwaii, at the peak of Sir James Turner Mountain, on a lake in a remote, alpine Chilcotin valley, there was noise, sound, always, even if only the wind, but in that moment there was nothing.

"They say total silence doesn't exist on Earth any more, but they're wrong."

"Dave, this is so outrageous." *And spooky.* I waved my hand in front of my nose. *Nothing.* Panic tried to creep in on me; I thought of cave-ins that buried men alive. I reached for my light, but I could not find the switch. "How do you turn the light on?"

I felt a hand touch my headlamp. The cone of light filled the tunnel. Dave's smiling face appeared in front of me.

"Weird at first, isn't it? This is something that billions of people never get to experience. Absolute quiet and peace. It grows on you. To me, it's freedom. With a little practice, you can relax here and just 'be.' That's one reason I like it underground." I stifled a beer belch; I would not desecrate this Zen moment. "Don't look at my light. I'm turning it on. That's underground manners." I directed my cone of light away from his face. "C'mon, it's only another thirty yards or so."

We passed by a hole cut into the bottom half of the tunnel wall. I doubted it was big enough for a fat marmot to squeeze through. "What's that for?" I asked.

"My partner works there; that's his shortcut."

I considered the opening, which was only slightly larger than a forty-five gallon drum. "So where do the other six dwarves work, anyway?"

Dave laughed. "The vein continues in that direction for forty feet or so, far as we can tell. His space widens up again ten feet in. He can stand up in there."

Generous. I shivered through another claustrophobic reaction. Stand up or not, I considered what I had seen so far a downgrade from medieval working conditions. I offered Dave my opinion.

"It's okay, once you're used to it. In the past, they only followed the veins, to cut costs. That's why the tunnels are so weird." We eventually stopped in front of a rough, uneven rock face. "This is my office."

A skeletal, reptilian-like drill leaned against the working face. It was connected to air hoses, like umbilical cords that disappeared into the rock womb past the end of our light-cones. "What's that thing?"

"My jackleg. I drill with it, then blast, then pack the ore to the cars, then drill, blast and pack again. I have a very intellectual job."

I laughed with him. "So, where's the silver?" I expected to see the reflection of marbled seams or pointillated silver flakes across the face.

"It's trace, so you don't see it with the naked eye, even shining your lamp right at the face. Weird, eh? This mine is almost done. I'm going to fire this up for you. Wait here."

"Dave, are you sure you want to rile it? It looks pretty mean." Dave followed the hoses down a connecting tunnel, where he disappeared.

When Dave started the air compressor, the jackleg kicked once. Startled to life again, it hissed and clinked as the pressure pushed against the constricting valves of its pistol grip. The noise of the compressor was punishingly loud, especially after such perfect silence. Dave returned and lifted the brute tool with a grunt. He yelled, "Here, hold it for me for a minute, would you? I gotta put in some ear protection."

I took hold of the jackleg and the two-hundred-pound drill fell to the ground. "You're so funny." Dave laughed. "That thing is heavy," I said. "How many of you work with that at a time?"

"Only me, man. Here, I'll show you. It'll get a little loud."

He picked up the drill again, set the bit against the rockface and balanced it on its extended leg. The noise in the room became crazily unbearable when Dave closed his fist on the pistol grip. At first, he let the bit turn slowly and the drill clanged as it rotated at a single mark on the rock face. Once the bit started the hole, Dave leaned into it more and the noise level increased substantially. A fine, choking dust filled the room in seconds. I could taste the diesel exhaust from the generator, too. In the dusty cones of our headlamps, I watched water spray into and pour out from around the bit in the drill hole. The water helped suppress the dust, but the room was still thick with it. Dave leaned hard into the job and drove the drill bit into the wall.

With the power of the compressed air, the jackleg vibrated

and tried to jump the hole, but Dave had locked a wrestling grip on it and kept the bit on center. When the tip of the bit had made more than the starter hole, Dave leaned on the jackleg a little more and held it a little less. Though I put on the ear protection attached to the hardhat, the noise was still uncomfortable. Ten minutes later, Dave stopped the demonstration with the drill bit one-third buried in the rock face. He left the jackleg in that position. My claustrophobic anxiety was now replaced with concern I had permanent ear damage. Dave smiled and went to shut down the air compressor. My ears rang like the "Bells of Saint Mary's." Left on my own to inspect the wall and the jackleg in Dave's *office*, I squinted through the dust cloud to the face, where several more holes were already drilled. Several discarded drills, some broken, were left at the bottom of the face. I coughed. I was sure I had contracted black lung. "Ventilation fans are turned off, I suppose?"

"The only ventilation in this mine is up the hole we came down. No fans here, though there is supposed to be at least one for each adit." I looked at his face and knew the origin of his nickname, "Dusty."

"What about the dust and the fumes? You guys work in this all day?"

"Yeah, but we don't inhale. Besides, the V-700 says its safe."

"How many holes do you drill in a shift?"

"Twenty or thirty, depending on the size of the face and the hardness of the rock. Then I blow it up. Each of us cleans up his partner's mess. That's how we usually start our shift. We blow the powder at shift change so no one is underground. At least they got that right. Allows some time for the dust to settle before the next guy starts. Want another beer?"

"Always." We retraced our route topside. I barked both shins when I scrambled back up the chute, but refused to mention it to this gentle giant of a man. I was amazed he was able to work in those conditions and with that machine after he sustained such horrific injuries only two years before. I threw a disparaging glance at the lobotomized Geiger counter on our way out. We both washed our faces in the dry room sinks. I spat a grimy, dark gob into the sink.

Dave looked me over, and said, "Yup, black lung." He opened us a beer each. I watched Dave rummage around until he seemed satisfied with a dusty canvas ammunition bag he found in a corner.

"This will do fine."

"Fine for what?"

"Supplies."

I thought he meant the beer, which he did, but he also flipped open the lid on a case of dynamite. He filled the canvas bag with two dozen sticks. Next, he took a full box of twenty-four blasting caps off the shelf and put it in the same bag.

"How'd you get this unopened beer, and isn't that super dangerous, Dave?"

"Ernie has a stash. They never count the sticks or caps. They won't be missed."

"I gotta get to know Ernie better. What I was asking was won't that stuff go boom pretty easily? Should one guy carry both the detonators and the explosives?"

"Yeah, you do; Ernie has an incredible past. Never try this at home, and do as I say, not as I do; besides, if you're carrying the beer, I gotta carry something."

We left the mine with enough alcohol, powder, and caps to level the camp if we had been serious anarchists. Though I was open to exploring the concept, Dave had other plans. "Let's walk over to the tailing pond and find something to shoot at there."

I handed Dave another beer, then followed him like a third-generation Pavlovian puppy. *Shoot? This is starting to sound like fun.* I was never so happy to be back in the wind. Two pilgrims with no purpose, we progressed onto the frozen Arctic barrens with enough firepower to blow ourselves beyond any fleeting memory of our ever having walked this earth. Given the alternative, I was happy to leave that black hole behind us.

Eldorado is worse? How could that be?

The dull, dopey morning had yielded to uninspiring, leaden skies by the time we descended from the crest of the final rise, away from the road and over the ridge behind camp. A vast expanse of mercury, cyanide, and sulfuric acids stretched far into the distance of Garbage Lake, the poisoned Port Radium tailings pond, forever the repository of the heavy metal mine effluent dumped there for decades. Yellow-green swirls smeared in icy stasis, frozen into paisley patterns generated by the perennial north wind that blows across its surface. A disaster of staggering proportions, this chemical, radioactive cesspool is the footprint left behind by industrialists, our government, and the Cold War.

"Every time I see it, Dave, I hate those sons-of-bitches a little more." I stood above the shores of the ruination and I was horrified. This crime for profit was on a generational scale.

"It's bad, isn't it? Been like this a long time, too. We can cut up across the ridge, so we don't get too close to the shore. At the far end, this muck drains into the big lake after breakup. It's frozen now, but in the spring, with the snowmelt, it drains almost dry. Stinks up here, too. Every year, they refill it with the leaching plant waste. Only us fuckin' hippies ever ask how it's possible the glass is never full though they keep pouring. Too bad booze wasn't like that, eh?" He tapped me on the chest with the back of his hand to pull me back from my outrage.

"Indeed."

"You have to watch where you walk around here. We're over Eldorado and there are open-air ventilation shafts for the radon. Some are big enough to fall into and you could break a leg in the smaller fissures. When we come across one, we'll pass it upwind." Dave scouted the area until he found a ten-foot section of half-buried, discarded water pipe. We manhandled the rusting cylinder until he broke it out of the frozen snow.

"Here, dig here."

Dig, I did. We crumbled the mound into frozen earth and ice clods. We soon had one end of the pipe secured in the loose pile and back-filled frozen clumps around its base. The pipe pointed skyward, out toward the middle of Garbage Lake. Dave took a stick of dynamite, plugged a blasting cap into the skyward end, lit the fuse, and after flashing a confident smile at me, dropped the explosive charge down the barrel. As an afterthought, he placed a chunk of ice and dirt on the top of the pipe.

By expression of concern for my safety, Dave said, "You might want to step back a bit ..."

I two-stepped it to hide behind Dave and sipped on my beer. I waited with goofy anticipation, half-expecting to incur shrapnel wounds when she blew. The moment of explosion occurred, but produced only a muffled pung sound. I was disappointed when only a lazy plume of smoke drifted from the top of the pipe after the ice and dirt fell off. We looked at each other and laughed. When we moved in to survey the results, the pipe toppled over. On closer inspection, we found minor flaring at the explosion end, a shallow divot, and nothing at the shooting end.

Dave said, "Re-load. We'll double it up this time."

I was convinced beyond any doubt he was a stark raving lunatic, or bushed, and I relished every moment. I cracked two more beers while Dave rigged up a double shot. He scouted around for a load and found the broken end of a two-by-four left over from another epoch. I busied myself re-setting the base of the pipe on rock and back-filling it again. I held it steady while Dave lit the even-burning Thermalite fuse and slid the double charge into our cannon. He jammed the wooden shell into the top end, and then joined me ten feet away. A crow flew high above us, curious no doubt why we two idiots were out on the barrens. I pointed to it with my beer and Dave nodded, a wide smile on his face. This time there was a measurable reaction; the constricted double charge blasted the wood out of the cannon with a loud bang. The chunk passed within crowing distance of the bird, then arced out onto the green-yellow ice.

"Good shot, Sir Dave," I said, mimicking Ringo Starr in *The Magic Christian*. My obscure reference to the movie was lost on our powder man, who was intent on cramming more dynamite and fodder into the cannon. His enthusiasm was infectious.

We spent the next two hours blowing up as much stuff as we could find. The field gun lasted for several more rounds, but was eventually retired due to Dave's predilection to stuff it with larger charges each successive shot. We fired rocks, gravel, chunks of wood, and any chunks of metal we found. I will admit that I grew a little worried our salvos might draw unwanted attention from management. What we played at was loud, completely insane, and certainly criminal, but it was great fun. If management caught us, they would immediately fire us, but we would probably serve only a few years of jail time. If they found us and we had weed with us too, no doubt they would jail us, beat us senseless, and throw away the keys.

To minimize the possibility of incurring just such an outcome to an otherwise constructive afternoon, we kept on the move across the tundra. We walked a wide arc in the general direction of the lake, until we finally entered what I was suspicious might be the Murphy ravine, the same ravine Frank said was back-filled with radioactive waste. Until we descended the ravine, our vantage points from several tailings piles afforded us unique, panoramic views of Garbage Lake. We skirted up-wind of open radon vents; one was more than four feet across, that spewed clouds of dust that the north wind blew back into camp. We carried on across the snow-covered barrens and discharged our dynamite and caps, and drained the beer then blew up the bottles. We were intent on finding anything to blow sky high. We followed a general westerly bearing toward the shore road named after the compass point. In this area alone, poisonous Eldorado tailings filled a natural half-mile depression, where the ground literally exhaled radon as the tailings deteriorated through the eons-long decay chain of poisons.

We stopped. Dave said, "Look; here's one of the larger adits. Seriously, don't breathe the air."

He pointed out a rough fissure in the ground. It was three feet wide and half-hidden by sub-Arctic shrubs, which looked similar to the familiar juniper found at the tree line on BC mountains. The heat from the mine exhaust melted the deep snow pack that otherwise would have covered the opening. I couldn't imagine the volume of radon-infected dust that had poured from this portal since 1932. We carried on, beer in hand and blew up rocks, blasted holes in the ground, cracked ice, and made snow geysers.

Through the afternoon, I told Dave about my plans for the bonspiel weekend. I had been thinking about putting a little bit of civil disobedience into action. Dave warned me, "Sounds like fun. Just don't get caught doin' it."

One of the biggest bangs we created occurred when I threw a double charge off the cliff onto the ice between Cobalt Island and us. The reverberating echoes of the explosion bounced back and forth across the straight where John Mantla and I had seen Petunia.

When we'd swilled the last of our beer, our classic redneck afternoon felt like it had wound down. We walked toward camp along the gravel service road cut along the lakeshore. On our left, steep, red-brown cliffs loomed overhead. The government built the original crushing mill and leaching plant on the flat ground above us. By the sixties, the area and buildings were so hot, the company abandoned the area, built more processing buildings, and moved the waste transfer hoppers closer to camp.

We had two problems: our main priority now was to acquire

more beer; our second was how to dispose of the last of the munitions. We had more than a dozen sticks of powder and several caps left. Fifty yards farther along, the road turned east at LaBine Point, where we would be exposed to camp scrutiny. However, at that precise moment in time, Dave and I stood at the foot of a recess in the reddish, iron-ore rock face. A collection pool had formed at the bottom of the cliff, perhaps half the size of a community swimming pool.

Here was a possible solution to problem number two. The ice layer in the pool had sagged, like a huge, white sugar donut, hole intact, and was suspended two feet below the surface. We discussed the probability that a sober flinger-of-dynamite could conceivably toss the last of our supplies forty feet to the middle of the donut, where it might sink out of sight in the rusty-red water. Dave expressed his opinion that in the event this happened, and one of the caps was applied appropriately, we would experience a grand, explosive finale to our afternoon.

I pointed out that we were not Olympic discus champions. "Neither," I said, "is either of us sober."

By way of counter-point, Dave said, "We can't take this stuff back with us. We have to get rid of it now. One more corner and we're at Silver Point, and that's way too close to camp. Let's make it a big bang."

"Uh, how big, exactly?"

Dave rummaged in the sack. "Well, it'll go big, like bunker busting at Normandy."

"Let's not and say we did."

"C'mon, if we throw the bag into the center of that hole, it'll sink, and the water will deafen some of the noise, and it will go boom. I want to see the geyser."

It took me several minutes to talk my crazy friend out of the big ka-blooey. Finally, Dave agreed to let me toss the unarmed explosives into the watery hole and we would be done with it. "It's been a great day," I reminded him. "So why take the chance the bag might float, we might miss the throw, or we might vaporize ourselves?"

Dave acquiesced, so I fired the bag of unarmed dynamite into the center of the donut. To my surprise, it was an easy toss. When the bag sank, Dave matched my throw with the caps and remaining roll of fuse. It was over. We were done. To say we were half-cut and a little crazy would be a substantial understatement. However, we didn't care, because we were, in fact, in the full throes of both conditions. I was glad a pound of weed was about to arrive in camp this coming week; our crew needed to mellow out a little.

We walked with a new bounce in our steps and laughed about shooting at crows and putting half the lemmings in our corner of the Arctic on the run. Then, from around the corner, three idiots appeared: Stalin, Jimmy, and Schläger. Dave and I kept walking and laughing, completely clean of any implicating evidence and guilt-free. We nodded and said "Hi," but received in return only frigid stares. They kept their pace, just three good ol' boys out for a constitutional stroll on Sunday afternoon. They knew we knew and we knew they knew, but we were free, so "Fuck you."

That's when Dave told me he'd already told Stalin he was leaving Port Radium for good. He had given notice. That gutted me; I was about to lose another good friend.

"Aw, man. Really? You're leaving?"

"It's my time. You'll have your time, too. But I have to go now. I really miss my wife. We're going to have a baby."

"You crazy bugger. Congratulations. I'm sure going to miss you, Dave. Seriously, you will be an amazing father, and knowing you, I bet your lady will be a great mother. That's going to be one lucky baby. Are you staying for the bonspiel?"

"Nope. I might even leave tomorrow. You know how it is when you start thinking about leaving."

"Believe me, I know. You must be pretty excited to be gettin' out of this dump?" I hated the camp even more having just seen his working conditions, and I could not forget Dave saying, "Eldorado is really dangerous."

"Oh, man, like I can't say. We have to finish the song, so let's go ... We need more beer. Maybe we can talk Ernie out of some more of his stash, then play some tunes."

When we arrived in camp, our cabal congregated at Dave's room. They brought us much gossip about the furor around camp. As our explosive fun erupted behind camp throughout the afternoon, apparently Stalin and Jimmy had raged through the bunkhouses to take a head count. We listened in awe and joined in guessing what all of it meant.

We sang our hearts out for the rest of the afternoon, then, after a short nap, I went to work at nine p.m. I had another good reason to want out, and I was another day closer to my time.

24. Abandonment, Pot, and Cops

The week before Dave and I went on our Sunday tundra exploration, I had called my friend in Vancouver. "Brain? It's me. Over." I used my nickname for him — his name was Brian.

"Hey, how ya doin' way up there, anyway?"

"You have to say 'over.' Still cold. I need a pound of socks sent in here. Over."

"Right. I'll take care of it. When you escaping to the real world? When do I say 'over'?"

"You just did. Not for a couple of months yet. These calls cost a fortune. I'll track you down when I decide to split. Just tell me, is the beer cold and are the women still hot in Vancouver? Over."

"You bet. Watch for the parcel. Over."

Not too subtle, but I was still naive and young and thought the RCMP had lots to do fighting crime and protecting us innocents without worrying about *socks*. After all, it was 1975. Regardless, a pound of Mexican export was on its way. Hopefully it would help suppress my aching desire to arrange my departure before whatever was left of my sanity and tolerance expired. A bunch of us waited for it to arrive, and somehow, it became bigger news than I thought it would be; I should have known better – there's no "clandestine" in a camp.

Dave left Monday morning; it had been a quick decision. Being left behind felt like I had slipped climbing down the hole he had shown me and I had broken my neck in the fall. My great friend, soon to be a true family man, a generous kind soul, had left our world for the real world, escaping from one of the most isolated, darkest holes on earth. I was more affected than I should have been, but Dave was another friend gone forever. I knew I would never meet up with him again. We were at the plane that morning to say goodbye, after Michael came to wake me up. Murray, Eddie, Frank, Ernie, Don, we stood around stupidly until Dave shook our hands and then finally took a seat in the DC-3. It felt like we had loaded the standard plywood casket with our friend inside.

Monday and Tuesday should have been sad days of adjustment. One of the gang was gone; a new order would have to emerge. As these things go, the day Dave went out was also the day the weed came in. By Tuesday afternoon, we needed a good old-fashioned wake for our loss, so wake Dave we did. We pulled an all nighter, no holds barred. There must have been thirty people in Michael's room and his hallway trying to celebrate Dave's freedom. Don played guitar, and we sang Dave's song at least ten times. We made plans to phone Dave in Sudbury. We honored Dave and respected his passing, so we "partied hardy" in his name. I'm not sure how we would have handled it if he had actually died, but we would have relied on each other to get through that, too.

The next morning, a Wednesday and the beginning of my eleventh week in camp, six plain clothes RCMP from Yellowknife arrived by company airplane. They were hot on the trail of the weed.

Sean saw them first. He was a borderline insider with us now because he was tight with Jan, and in a convoluted twist of emotions, he was tight with Donny, too. He slipped away from the plane while the cops loaded their gear and themselves onto the bus. Michael drove them the long, slow way to the office. I understand he toured the tailings pond and took them out to the DEW line installation miles east of camp. While they enjoyed the extended tour to the scene of the crime, Sean came to my room and slapped me awake.

"Where's your pot? The cops are in camp. Quick."

The average sentence still handed out for possession of a single joint in Canada was four years in jail, so this was no joke. Quantity meant long jail sentences in nasty prisons where it was likely a pothead would share a penitentiary cell with thieves and murderers, or even worse, defrocked priests and fraudulent politicians.

"The closet. Under my laundry."

Sean spun around as I lay in the bed propped up on one elbow. He thrashed through my closet, until he found the baggy. "I'll put this in a safe place. You'll get it back when they leave. They're gonna toss the whole camp for sure." We had already split the pound up. The baggy was my share.

"You better take the seeds too — the Players Tobacco tin on the top shelf." Sean found the can in the closet. I said, "What about Michael? He's working. They'll nail him."

"Mouthy Frank and Don are already on it. Who else was part of this?"

"Lemme see ... Don, Michael, Eddie, Corey, and Murray, the guys, you know. Murray knows the guys at the mill who were in. I don't. Oh, Bill and Carl, too. And Ernie. And Jan and Morag and Genna."

Sean's eyes popped. "Jesus! Is anyone besides Jimmy not part of this? I gotta keep going. You're sure this is everything? Pipe? Papers?"

"Go. I'll get the rest." I stood up. His sense of alarm started me moving. I found everything else that had anything to do with weed, ran to the toilets, and flushed it all.

Ten minutes later the vengeful constabulary from Yellowknife burst in to "serve and protect" Mother Justice. They tossed my room. They found nothing, although they rooted around like starving swine after truffles. I lost count of how many times I swore at Schläger and Jimmy, who accompanied the cops. I had the distinct impression they looked for any reason to close the door and pound the crap out of me. When they came up empty, one cop slammed into me on his way out of my room before he said to Schläger, "We better get going fast. Looks like they're onto us."

I was angry, outraged, that the company had ordered up this shakedown two days after Dave left. They would never have done so with him in camp; they needed every miner they could muster. It was wrong to me, and when I'm angry I get even, and by even, I mean I win. The company's intention to do us harm was too brazen an overlord act for me to ignore. I vowed to get even with these jerks if it was the last thing I did in this camp.

Of course, we skunked the *thin blue line* and the rest of narc-squad. Ernie said they were pissed at Jimmy the raid was such a failure. I overheard the cops bitching to the pilots when they came for breakfast the next morning. The cops railed about Schläger and Stalin and how angry they were at the informant who'd wasted their time and budget. I was able to spit on their eggs and assault their bacon with cayenne pepper. After one bite, they spat the food back onto their plates and then joined the toast lineup, the Port Radium staple, firing nasty looks my way.

The creep who'd slammed me up against the wall came up to the counter, gagging, and red-faced. "We're not done with you yet ..."

"You'll be officer Starsky, or are you Hutch?"

"Fucking potheads. Better another dead addict than someone like you breathing my air."

I drooled a big gob of spit into my palm. "You enjoy your

meal, Officer?"

"You bastard."

"Nope. My father raised me. You ever go back to the sty to meet your parents?" He glared at me with bulging eyes, riled enough to come across the counter. I picked up a cast iron frying pan.

"The plane is leaving, Sergeant. Now." Stalin called off his running dog. The cop turned his food tray over onto the floor, then left the cook shack with the rest of the troop.

"I sure feel safe now. Thanks, Officers, it's been a slice." I yelled after them. The men waiting in line to order breakfast laughed.

25. Staff Meeting

Boredom and camp life are synonymous, but even in the drudgery of an isolated camp the mind does not shut down. I indulged a propensity to fictionalize my surroundings as exhaustion and stress pushed me toward the mental state of distraction. I found vent for my imaginings by caricaturizing what I saw around me. From this point forward, it is up to the empathetic reader to decide where fiction and non-fiction intersect, because that is precisely what happened. That, too, can be a symptom of extended isolation.

• • •

Jimmy loathed the thought of attending the necessary, final staff meeting before the bonspiel, but he would endure it anyway. The agenda consisted largely of quantifying the bribe disbursements to various government inspectors and auditors clearing the path for JT and Jimmy to realize their Wall Street ambitions. It was May Day, so Jimmy was in a foul mood. A knock on his office door interrupted his seething resentment; he returned Mary-Ellen's ring to his desk drawer. "Enter, for Christ's sake."

Bill said, "Jimmy, the men are here for the briefing."

Bill, Schläger, and Carl came in. Jimmy preferred Bill use military language at the staff meetings. Jimmy used jargon such as "executed takeovers," "skirmishes," and "subdued hostiles." He avoided "collaborating," which was a communist word, and the term "think tank" did not apply. Sadly, that concept, like so many others, was beyond his grasp. Jimmy was a "keep it simple, stupid" man.

Schläger established an advantageous observation post in a corner, near a window, where he remained vigilant. Jimmy said, "Bill, see if you can get that radio working. I want JT on the speaker no later than 0-900 hours."

Bill sat at the radio, which was the only wireless set in camp. He snapped the power switch and then fiddled with its knobs to dial in the correct frequency. Carl pulled up a chair near Bill. Ready to take notes, Carl sat turned toward Bill with his legs splayed.

Due to the limited range of the wireless set, they piggybacked on the decommissioned but still partially active DEW line installation just four miles east of camp. We drove by it on the road to the summer airstrip. Still pulling in radar data and transmitting a constant signal out again, this un-manned Cold War relic was a futuristic item during the heydays of Port Radium. The "dish" was a massive, flat construction of metal frame panels, seventy-five feet tall and one hundred feet wide. A grid of copper wire wound around a 7,500 square foot panel of plywood backing. A locked cement bunker sprouted like a goiter at its base. The US invaded Canada and built the installation to protect our flank before imagined invasions by the Russians or the Chinese could occur.

Michael once observed, "All they see there are those Canada goose."

Air Rescue also piggy-backed on the installation now, supposedly monitoring the skies for civilian aviation emergencies. By the late '60s, the Canadian government asked the US military to leave, or fabricate at least one finite, concrete foreign military threat. Over the decades, the US was unable to produce any such threat, so they left. No one cared much anymore about the antiquated DEW line. Still, hundreds of bored, junior and clandestine SAC personnel maintained the obsolete US military apparatus stretched across Canada's free north, even though the US had installed a system of spy satellites in sub-space. Transmissions across the insanely expensive DEW line had diminished to a trickle, and the system was reduced to intermittent use for military communications training and for the occasional convenience of far-northern residents. But still, line technicians recorded and deciphered every transmitted signal; in fact, the minute any transmission began, dozens of bored intelligence operators perked up, scribbling each syllable into official logs. Jimmy's call to JT's office in Edmonton was no exception.

They were several minutes early for the call. This was fine with Jimmy; *The sooner we start the sooner we end and the sooner the old fart is out of my hair.* The radio crackled and high frequency static zoomed around the room. Like a pack of dogs mesmerized in front of an RCA Victor player, they stopped to listen and cocked their heads while Bill refined the radio frequency.

JT's voice thundered, "For Christ's sake. I just had this suit cleaned. No, get up, get up. Get away from me. Pass me something to wipe this up. Jesus H. Christ! The Korean women had no problem with this sort of thing. Why are you such an amateur with such a simple request?"

Someone held the mic open in Edmonton.

There was a brief and pregnant pause. Mary-Ellen's voice was apologetic as she gagged, "I'm so sorry, JT. I was swallowing when it happened. Clumsy me, trying to work the mic at the same time. That will leave a stain ... Here, let me wipe that off your pants."

"Goddamnit, no! You've done enough. Get your hands off me and find my lighter. Where's your writing pad? I want you to take notes. And turn on that radio for the briefing. We're going live in a couple of minutes, and I have to talk to that idiot son of mine."

Bill inched the volume up a notch. Jimmy was mortified and humiliated at what he heard. Bill fought to suppress a laugh at Jimmy's expense. Carl was excited because the old man was boinking Mary-Ellen. They heard her grunt and then listened as her spiked heels walked across the room to the radio set. "Oh," she said, "it's already on. Let me see if they're live. Port Radium, do you copy? Over." She finally released the voice control button on the mic.

His heart torn from him, Jimmy was incensed at his father's betrayal. However, keeping within the staunchest of family traditions, he was prepared to hold only Mary-Ellen accountable for giving in to temptation. He jumped up from behind his desk and ran to the radio set, pushing Bill off his chair and into Carl's lap. Grabbing the microphone, Jimmy yelled, "You filthy slut." Carl began to protest his innocence, but Bill waved him silent. "And I loved you," Jimmy continued. "You perform oral sex on a stinking old man like my father, and you expect me to ask you to marry me? Over? You're damn right it's over."

"Jimmy?" asked Mary-Ellen, her voice syrupy with virginity, her innocence wounded. "Is that you, hon? All I did was spill some coffee on JT's lap. I'm a little clumsy, I guess. I'm just serving a cup of coffee. Why are you so angry? Over."

Jimmy's face turned to crimson as he realized his imagination had the best of him. The misconstrued moment put stupid grins on the faces of Bill and Carl, whose involuntary hand rubbed Bill's back. Schläger remained resolute, if aroused, by the sexual tension building in the room. Jimmy was never a "damage control" guy, so he threw the mic at Bill, who tried again to rise from Carl's lap. Frantic, Jimmy pushed Bill back down and waved his hands, mouthing, "Say something."

At first, Bill was dumbfounded and then he was inspired. Still in Carl's lap, Bill leaned forward, keyed the mike, and said, "Oh, that,

199

that wasn't Jimmy … he's not here yet." Bill was gaining momentum. "I was having a conversation with Carl here. The mic must have been on and we didn't notice it. Over"

Schläger, noticing Carl and Bill's physicality, was suddenly aware of their orientation. Schläger reacted on instinct, taking a menacing step toward the two men. Jimmy, however, was still in a panic; he raced to the door, blind-sided Schläger on his way through the room, bowling him over. Jimmy opened and then slammed the door shut again.

"Sorry I'm late. Have we started yet?" Jimmy's voice was falsetto from the tension.

Recovering from the knockdown, Schläger took note of Jimmy's gay-follies side before he retreated to his stoop in order to let the theater play out.

Catching the significance of the mock cameo entrance, Bill slid off Carl's lap, and said, "Oh, Jimmy's here now. Over."

Mary-Ellen keyed the mic. JT spluttered in the background, "What the hell is going on up there? Are they turning into a bunch of fairies?"

She instructed JT, "Sugar Lips, you have to say 'over' when you're finished." Her use of the endearment caused brief, floundering chaos in Jimmy's mind, the exact reaction Mary-Ellen might have hoped for as payback for Jimmy's abusive tirade.

JT growled, "Goddamnit, don't call me that. Over, for Christ's sake." Mary-Ellen released the microphone button.

Gathering himself, Jimmy lowered his voice an octave and by way of calming the situation, said, "That was Bill and Carl going over some personal business. Over."

Mary-Ellen engaged the mic. JT said, "That didn't sound like business to me. When I'm up there, I'm going to sort out those two queers. Too much time in the Arctic, I guess, but there's no excuse for turning that way."

Mary-Ellen yelled, "Over." JT cursed before Mary-Ellen released the button.

Jimmy seemed to have deflected his potential personal tragedy over a simple misunderstanding between himself and Mary-Ellen to Bill and Carl. He hoped the strategy might have saved his future plans for Mary-Ellen. He said, "So, now that we're all here, did I miss anything? Should we start the meeting? Over."

JT said, "Make it quick, and no names."

A third voice broke into the call, "Sir, you have to finish your side of the conversation with 'over,' over."

Mary-Ellen keyed the mic. JT said, "Who the fuck is that? Why do I have to say 'over over'?"

The voice added, "No, sir, only one 'over' is required ... and no cursing is allowed. Over."

Holding the mic open, Mary-Ellen reminded JT that the entire NORAD defense network was listening to their conversation. She released the mic after JT said, "Fuck them. Don't they have anything better to do?"

Jimmy started in, "Okay, JT. Can we get back to the bonspiel now? We have security ready here. The bunkhouse has been prepared. We are expecting three teams of government officials for next weekend. Is that still correct? Over."

JT said, "Mary-Ellen, is that correct? Nothing has changed, has it?"

Mary-Ellen winced at her name issued over the airwaves from Moscow to Washington. She keyed the mic to exact her revenge. "Yes, JT, everything is already arranged. I phoned the government inspectors and the auditors with your invitations and they were accepted. The 'boys can be boys' while in camp. Oh, is this thing on? Over?" She held the mic open.

JT was mortified Mary-Ellen had exposed the details of his plan over the wireless. Having attained revenge for her name being dragged into Port Radium's sordid affairs, Mary-Ellen continued, "The donations are already arranged, JT. Oh, sorry honey, I used your name again. We will bring the money to camp with us in ten days. And the last of the gourmet food will come with us, too. We'll send the trophies and the alcohol up next Wednesday. Oh, this thing is on again. Damn ...." She held the mic open.

The listeners heard JT mumbling in the background, "Who gives a shit about any trophy? Waste of money. We should bribe the government scum and be done with it."

Mary-Ellen said, "JT, you know they have to go to the mine site to inspect, that way everything looks legal. Now, remember your language, JT."

"What language? Shit or over over?"

"No, *bribe*. And didn't you want to call them tax deferrals?

Now hush, baby, we're almost done here. Oh, I guess the mic was on again." She continued to hold the mic open.

Again, Mary-Ellen reined in the old warhorse JT, who was hollering and protesting "women drivers" and demanding to hold the mic. Mary-Ellen eventually released the key after saying, "Over."

Jimmy cut in. "Okay, then. It sounds like we're ready to go. I can't wait to see you Mary-Ellen — I have a surprise for you. Over."

JT hollered, "You better get those queers fixed up before I get there, or I'll have a surprise for you."

Mary-Ellen cut the connection with a final "over" just as JT wound up into another vein-popping tirade. The call ended to the dismay of the communications specialists of various armed forces installations across the continent.

Jimmy waved a hand at Bill, who turned the radio power button to OFF. Jimmy said, "Seems like the old man thinks you two are a couple of knob-gobblers, eh? Anything else on the agenda?"

Both Carl and Bill looked as uncomfortable with that comment as they were with their outed sexual orientation, of which they themselves were only somewhat aware. Throughout the radio call, Carl and Bill were sneaking quick looks at each other, wondering about what JT had just said aloud. Schläger drifted off into a predatory and violent fantasy, triggered by the homosexual display, but he'd caught every meaningful glance. If they did not get it, he sure did.

By way of emotional recovery, Schläger returned to business, and said, "We might have a more urgent problem with our geologist."

Jimmy asked, "Now what?"

"He has medical issues. He should have a plane accident. Soon."

"Exactly what sort of medical issues are we talking about?"

Bill interjected, "He's poisoned. Cancer. His doctor in Edmonton notified us after Corey's last trip out. The son-of-a-bitch went and got tested. His lungs are shot. He wants full medical coverage, too."

Jimmy picked up the vial of silver dust from his desktop and began toying with it. "In six weeks we go public on the New York Stock Exchange, but first we have a critical week coming up here. If word of Corey's state of health leaked to our guests, they might have to shut us down, no matter how much cash we throw at them. I don't want this getting out … I've already spent a bundle so they stop asking questions. I don't care how it happens." Jimmy glared at Schläger. "That kid has to be kept away from our guests. Got it?"

Schläger nodded. "There's a plane going back to Yellowknife on Thursday night. The company could arrange a medical exam for Corey, and he could be on that plane, part of the way, at least." He indulged an evil grin.

"No. That leaves a paper trail. Make a different arrangement. Figure one out. I'm not paying anyone's fucking medical bills, I'll tell you that. Anything else?"

Bill and Carl exchanged glances, wondering what other *arrangements* Jimmy was referring to, and considering their new designation as *the two queers*, they were both petrified they were being set up for "the long drop." Carl stared at Schläger, trying to interpret his smirk.

Enjoying his elevated position of power within their cadre, Schläger said, "I think the geologist talked with that cook, the one who used to be surface crew … the guy who fucked up the bus clutch; he's a real mouthpiece. Maybe he should be on the same plane?"

"I sure as hell don't want any troublemakers meeting our guests. Let's make sure he gets the message, too, but first we need him to cook. Bill, Carl, you two watch that guy. Make sure he shuts the fuck up. Be warned, I'll personally tear the heart out of any of you who fucks up this weekend. I want everything, and I mean *everything*, to go as planned. Now, we're done."

Carl flew out of the office. Bill followed, citing some urgent filing that needed doing. He closed the door as he left.

• • •

In the outer office, Carl turned around the second Jimmy's door closed and launched himself into Bill's willing arms. The two embraced and kissed passionately, then they began dry humping, causing Jimmy's office door to bang and slam with rhythmic intensity. They broke their embrace after Jimmy yelled, "What in hell is wrong with that door? Bill, get in here. I want to see Corey's WCB claim." The two lovers pulled away from their dramatic moment, eyes locked, exhilarated, confused, and deeply in lust.

• • •

Jimmy said, "Schläger. Keep an eye on those two. Something fishy is

203

going on there; I can sense it. Now, you get the fuck out too, so I can get some work done."

Schläger left, shaking his head. He passed Bill on his way in. Schläger stopped at Carl's desk in the outer office and whispered in Carl's ear, "Man-love is a dangerous, violent world." Schläger drove his tongue deep into Carl's ear before he left the office.

26. The Hour Before Dawn

Two days later, we had another new "chef." Bald Ed had quit. Ed worked my shift when I joined in on Dave's wake, but he told me he couldn't take the isolation. I understood. After three months in camp, I felt like my mind was full of cement, and though I wouldn't acknowledge it, I wondered if I could make it to the bonspiel. I was counting the hours, not the days, I had left.

The new cook, Cliff, arrived the day after Ed quit — just eight days before the bonspiel. Cliff looked and acted like a friggin' narc. Cops had the imagination of a flat tire and considerably less subtlety, so it could be possible the new cook was an RCMP plant. Cliff evaluated me on the job the night he arrived in camp. While he sobered up, he followed me through my routine and took "mental" notes. He told me JT hired him to be the "chef of the day" for the bonspiel. Cliff was old, maybe thirty, and was an odd mixture of aggressive and a little vague.

"What culinary school did you graduate from?" I asked.

"School? None. I was the steak chef at Mr. Mike's, a bun 'n' run in Edmonton. Saw this ad two days ago and got the job."

"How was your interview with JT?"

"Bun" said, "He gave me a job." He laughed alone at something he thought funny. "I heard the cops came in here. Too bad they didn't bust you and your friends. You'll never make it past Yellowknife; they'll be waiting for you. And you can't bullshit me; you won't be here long."

He shadowed me until four a.m., like the breath of a panting dog in the backseat of a hot car. He left before the breakfast feeding frenzy began, so he missed the best part of my day. The rest of the week, I saw Bun only in passing at the end of my shift until he called me for extra duty to prepare for the bonspiel.

• • •

I started my last Wednesday night shift exhausted and drained. Something besides Bun and the extra hours gnawed at my dwindled reserves. When I left the kitchen Thursday morning, I walked across the top of the ridge toward time alone to be alone. I wanted to quit, but I had to figure a way through Yellowknife without those cops waiting for me. I knew I had to stay in camp for at least a while yet. I hated the place more than ever. I had to find a way to lighten up for three more weeks, then it would be my time.

A dark, ominous inversion swirled above Port Radium and dominated the overcast day. It was May now, and the weather patterns had changed. Storms developed when the warmer south wind piled into the walls of bitter cold fronts that still tried to bully their southern cousins. Sweeping down from the Northwest Passage to assault us, another gale was expected to join a big one that had been brewing right here in camp.

I walked farther west for no reason other than to escape the present, toward the cliffs that overlooked the lake. In a sense, I walked back through time. I drifted past the guest bunkhouse, the curling rink, the new crushing mill, and the leaching plant. I climbed a rusty, rocky rise, and, for the first time, stood in the shadow of the original processing structures. The buildings had decayed in a hollow. The main structure was three times the size of both our high school gyms and was by far the largest building at Port Radium. Derelict and long abandoned, most of the windows along the top of the walls were broken. I was curious and decided to investigate.

The building grew in stature as I descended the ridge on my approach; the foreshortening effect on this Cold War *House of Usher* made it seem much smaller than its actual size. I looked up to a murder of crows perched on the eaves of the roof seventy feet above me. They remained still against a leaden sky. Then one crow launched into a cawing fit. In the isolated swale, that raw sound echoed an ominous, atonal rasp, a flat melody to the low howl of the wind through the broken windows. I refused its warning

Rusty bolts attached a worn metal sign to two posts, brown with creosote stains, near the monstrous bay doors. Double the size of a sheet of plywood, bent and weather-beaten from decades of Arctic punishment, the large black lettering read: Shed 8 CLASSIFIED ENTRY ONLY. The five-foot wide, once yellow and black but now faded, radioactive icon was still legible. This caution, necessitated during a bygone era and so much more required now, spoke of why history remains important. The washed-out paint still impressed me, even more so because of its origin in that other era. Chains and a padlock secured the hanger doors, but the violated office door hung half-open and cockeyed, so I went inside.

The office was in ruins. A combination of souvenir hunters, the passage of time, extreme weather, and animals had caused the destruction. I walked across pages of soiled white vellum scattered across the floor, layers of spreadsheets and summaries that dated back to the forties, accounts of the incalculable destruction and suffering this place produced. I breathed the decay that permeated the stale air. *One step through the looking glass and you can't get back.* Too young to be afraid of knowledge and hungry for experience, I walked through the next door, onto the hangar-sized, wooden floors of the factory; I was ready for history to talk to me.

This place is huge.

Jagged edges, high across the south wall, where windows had once refused Nature, allowed daylight to penetrate and create inside pale, eerie shadows. Three huge wooden vats dominated the factory floor. They seemed to loom above me, each on its own raised, wooden platform. A giant's bicycle-chain curled around rusted gears at the bottom of each vat. When in operation, the chain must have powered the rotation of the vats. A demonic cold warrior's machine, the agitation first churned Mankind's most evil concoction in these industrial cauldrons.

Elevated farther above me, the remnants of a conveyor belt hung down in shredded, black rubber folds. Higher again, were twisted sections of catwalk planks that hung precariously to metal supports attached to steel rafters. From above and deeper inside the cavernous recesses came an intermittent, metallic bang; driven by the wind, a metal brace slammed into a support, as if it were a past reckoning that stole metered moments from the future.

I was fascinated. Despite the warnings of the radiation logos still on the walls and railings, I walked through the entire plant. *This is where evil was germinated — here.* Industrial chemicals were refined, the ore was crushed until it became a grainy consistency, then it was delivered here by the conveyor belts to be liquefied and leached. It was here, in the unholiest of Petri dishes, that military-industrial chemists concentrated their nightmare, spawned from the ugly marriage of military amorality and their contempt for Humanity, the possibility of our annihilation — U-235.

This was the second line of casualties; after the miners, it would have been these workers. The next to fall to cancer were the camp surface laborers. Next, it was the men from De☐ line, the porters who loaded, by hand, ninety-pound burlap sacks of the ore from this factory onto the barges. During and since WWII, they transported the yellowcake to Fort McMurray, then to America. Some of the trains took the poison to Uranium City or to the refinery in Port Hope to fuel Canada's own nuclear power industry. There, the unsuspecting residents lived on tailings dumped in their town for decades. The Canadian dead, cast aside along the uranium trail, joined the many dead of Hiroshima.

In dreadful awe, I uttered, "Manhattan," the curse Corey revealed to me. In this place, so desolate of human spirit, ghoulish scientists incubated the worst of our many crimes against Nature and ourselves. What existed here? Only the conceit of war and the vile arrogance of profiteers and old men sending Death to millions in their beds or to die without purpose on bloody, soulless battlefields. Supposedly an endless power source and useful in a few medical procedures, Uranium, once tasted, was the poisoned apple from which there was no awakening. I stood at the heart of its evil, the waste that kept radioactive poison coming for 703.8 million years ... And then another 703.8 million years.

I wanted to be away from this place, ignorant of its purpose, its deeds, and its lies. My steps echoed off the walls, pursuing me until I rushed out of the building, the echoes never forgotten. However, I was too late; I had touched the alchemist's stone and there was no going back.

Outside, under clouds that roiled above me, I breathed in the Arctic. I wanted the regenerative, pure air. But in Port Radium, none had existed for thirty years and none would for 700 million more years. At the top of the ridge, I wondered what manner of people were the owners who, decades after the war and its atrocities ended, could still be here, subjecting unprotected men and women to the certain danger, simply to acquire more of the poisonous, reviled ore.

In that moment, I hated being a descendant of Canada's legacy and hated it more because we had failed to do better. My chest was pounding as I realized just how impossible it is to change the machine's momentum, grinding to decay Nature's garden with willful, industrial intent. In Port Radium, I was surrounded by a living, cancerous pustule, an expression of addiction to greed, control, and power at its lowest common denominator, where the blood flows from the veins to the bone and into the marrow of our souls, where the daily theft of our humanity is most unyielding and horrific. In the shadows of the monolithic, vacuous factory shell, I stopped in my tracks and crossed my arms, raising one hand to my face, resting my chin in my palm. *Is this the best we can do?* Breathing out deeply, beneath the grey Arctic skies, my eyes cast downward ... I shuddered out the realization the currency of experience is counted in the exchange of lost virtue. So, coming of age is about making the choice to care enough about things larger than ourselves, things that need fixing, and do something no matter the cost. The alternative is to sift through life as just another sand grain through the hourglass. The choice was immense and daunting. Insatiable corporations, lying politicians, laws meant to serve the rich, all of them conspired as authority to crush any common sense resistance in Parliament or in the streets of our own communities. Who are these monsters? What kind of a human is it that would recklessly pursue profit though it meant shackling succeeding, pacified generations further into servitude and have us live in terror throughout our lives?

I raised my resentful eyes to this altar that was now *my* burden and a monumental, disgraceful human failure. "Fuck that," I said. "Maybe I don't win, but I'm going to make some noise on my way through."

• • •

Michael had parked his delivery truck outside the curling rink, so I stopped to meet with the boys. When I entered the small, two-sheet rink, Michael and Frank were unboxing paper plates and cups, and unfolding tables and chairs brought over from the community hall. I pointed at a trunk and a rolled up screen.

"What's that?"

"Hey, Al," said Michael. "What are you doing here? That's Schläger's projector for the bonspiel. Maybe they are showing training films." *Deep Throat*, the cult porn flick after it had made its global circuit, had arrived in Port Radium.

"You gotta see what I found ..." Frank stopped to listen. "The old processing plant from the forties. It's still standing."

"I'd like to see that," Frank said.

Michael and Mouthy Frank followed me over to the plant. I felt less like the Pied Piper and more like the Grim Reaper, but still, they were both impressed. We saw my footprints in the dust on the factory floor, and that worried me.

"This is weird shit," said Michael, after he scooped a handful of ore dust off a railing.

Frank said, "You don't wanna do that. That's the same dust they shipped out in the forties, I bet. In one shot, one huge fuckin' explosion, they say 40,000 people were instantly vaporized, and there have been the same number of deaths and deformed babies ever since."

Michael shook his hands, and then slapped them together. Furious, he cursed, "*Câlice.*"

I said, "I can't find the words for how much I hate these people, y'know?"

"I know that. Me, too." Michael cocked his head off to one side, rolled his eyes, and said, "But what can we do?"

My dander was up. "Enough with this moping around," I said. "Let's go over the plan again at the rink, make sure we didn't miss anything."

Half an hour later, we had sized up the layout, shared and finalized a couple of details, and were ready to leave. Then I became distracted by the ice. The clean curling ice and rows of reflective curling rocks were like an open invitation to try our luck. The three of us indulged until we had scattered all the rocks to the far end of both ice sheets. I enjoyed our moment of fun. I was unable to sleep the rest of that afternoon, but the price of insomnia, I was sure, would be worth it.

27. Bonspiel Day

The next day, the Friday of the big pay-off weekend, a week after my gloomy walk through history, was a crazy-busy day for both the kitchen and surface crews. We expected JT, Mary-Ellen, the auditors, the medical inspector, and a plane full of booze, cash, and other supplies to arrive on the Friday morning flight. Then the pilots would refuel and fly back to Yellowknife to bring in the mine inspectors, two cops, and half a dozen other government officials. Everyone would step onto the ice with their hands out and palms up. We expected the late plane full of "dignitaries" to arrive well after dark and that they would be as drunk as lords.

Leaning over the sink, a dead smoke in his mouth, Ernie scrubbed out the porridge pot. He said, "In May, the weather can go either way, but I predict a blizzard this weekend."

I had six orders on the go when Jack and Schläger came in and stood in front of me. Jack was wet hen angry. "You son-of-a-bitch!."

"What the hell are you freakin' out about, Jack? Don't tell me Mike drove the D9 through the ice again?" Everyone in the cafeteria perked up to listen, and derisive laughing followed my comment, which aggravated Jack even more.

"You know what you did, you and that frog."

"Michael? What? What did we do?"

"You went to the curling rink and threw those rocks. Didn't you?"

"Yeah, sure. What's that, a crime or something?"

"You did that on purpose! You know when rocks sit on curling ice they melt the ice and screw it up. You ruined the curling for the bonspiel. It's too late to resurface the ice … You knew that."

"What a shame," I laughed. I had no idea that could happen; I was never a curler. "Oh well, spilt milk. Now, can I fry you up a couple of eggs? How 'bout you, Schläger? Do Nazis eat eggs?"

Schläger's mouth twisted into a cold, lifeless smile. He said, "Don't worry, cookie, yours is coming."

Jack continued his rant. "JT will be here this morning, and I promise you he's gonna hear about this …" Jack and I parted ways for the last time in a shouting match over a couple of curling rocks.

211

When they left, a smattering of applause escorted them out the door. Someone yelled "Speech," but I declined the implied honor.

The weekend was just getting started ...

I had finished cooking breakfast when Sean dropped by to top off his coffee. I grabbed a cup for myself, too. We talked in private at a dining room table. "So, you and Jan?" I asked.

Sean hesitated, then said, "Yeah."

"What about Donny?"

"We already talked it over; it's Jan's choice. She didn't want to come up here in the first place, but Don talked her into it. I'm glad he did, 'cause I'm in love with her."

"That'll make two of you, but if you're askin' me, go get her, man. We all gotta go where our hearts take us. I think it was over between them before they left Edmonton, and Donny was going to find out sooner or later ..."

Sean left by the back door, where Jan waited. I gave her credit that she tried to make it look like she was sweeping up.

The first time I woke up, it was to welcome Morag. She had found a way to sneak off. When I woke up the second time, I was alone again, and I discovered Ernie was right. The weather deteriorated through the day into a classic, brutal northern gale. Between the construction outside my bunkhouse window, the rising buffeting of the wind, and my anticipation of the weekend, I knew my sleep would be limited. I was back in the cook shack by two p.m. Michael was looking for me and he had a story for me while I drank my first coffee.

"JT's plane arrived just before lunch," said Michael. He was unloading suitcases when two of them somehow popped open in his hands and the wind from the backwash of the engines sprayed most of JT's clothes across the ice, which caused him to splutter like a broken toilet. At the same time, Mary-Ellen watched Frank drop her pink suitcase. It tumbled out of the plane and broke open when it hit the ice. Michael, ever the knight in shining armor, retrieved some of her things, which included a handful of her lacy underwear and a huge, black, double-ender dildo. When he handed the vibrator to Mary-Ellen, her lips blood red and her curls still that cheap, dye-job blonde beneath her black beret, Michael asked, "I think this is yours, or is it yours, JT?" JT's eruption almost drowned out the plane's engines. Michael's time was short, too.

Sex toys notwithstanding, the corporate feast scheduled for Saturday night was fast approaching and the preparations would eat up the best of two days. Bun 'n' Run maintained himself in a state of tizzy. The menu I'd updated would be a challenge for Bun, if judged by the order I put in: cases of crab, shrimp, fresh salad, barons of beef, pâté, steaks, chops, chicken, and more.

"Fuck me. How much can these assholes eat?" Bun asked rhetorically.

Michael was packing in another thirty-pound baron of beef when he answered, "There's a lot of 'em, and they're all hungry."

Later that day, Bill, Carl, and I delivered the last of the specialty items to the kitchen from the special storage shed, where I had lost my battle with the frozen turkey so long ago.

The pilots would have to land the night flight in the teeth of the full-blown blizzard that had kicked into extremes. Anyone flying tonight would experience a true white-knuckler, which I considered a perfect greeting for the jerks coming into Port Radium. Of the two possible extreme versions of conditions in which to arrive at Port Radium, there was the dangerous, nighttime, -55F version that was always impressive on one end of the scale, but on the other was the summer version of a face full of dust, huge, ravenous mosquitoes, and clouds of biting black flies. Each scenario had its charm, but from the probable shape of the ground crew, tonight promised to be even more memorable.

After supper, Sean and Michael met in the pub to prepare for the arrival of the plane.

Much later, while grinding out my regular shift, Morag and I listened to the volume of the howling wind increase. She estimated it at, "a good, old-fashioned screamer." Two hours later, Morag brought me a hot tea while I peeled potatoes over a pail in the pantry. We stopped chatting when we heard a slightly different sound rise above the wind, different from what I was used to when other gales blasted us. "That's an odd sound, isn't it?" Morag agreed. Minutes later, we heard the same sound again, only it was louder. We looked at each other, as if to require confirmation it was a *strange sound*. A low rumble had accompanied the wind. Several minutes passed, and then I heard it again. *Must be the plane.* From the sound of it, this pass was less than two hundred feet above the camp. I put down my paring knife and we went to look outside. I saw the running lights of the plane circle quite low over the lake, and then pull up and disappear into the low clouds.

"That would be scary in this wind ... good thing our cracker-jack surface crew is on the job," I said.

I returned to my chore, but then the plane made a "rattle the pots and pans" low pass.

"Aren't Michael and Sean supposed to meet the plane?" Morag said. The surface crew was definitely AWOL, so I decided it might avoid a messy cleanup operation if I tracked them down. Besides, there was a beer shipment on the plane. "It's time I was getting back, anyway. Give those boys a kick in the rear and get them moving when you find them." She gave me a quick kiss, we grabbed our coats, and we left the kitchen together.

I knew Michael and Sean had closed the bar down, so I went over to the community hall. When I walked in, two empty cases of beer and the bottles strewn about confirmed the boys were well-prepped to receive the plane. A scratchy Janis Joplin wailed out *Ball and Chain* over the record player. Sean and Michael were deeply involved in a game of pool, though they were supposed to be on the ice an hour before to set up the landing strip pots.

They both teetered over the pool table, verging on slobbering drunk, to look up at me when I came in. "Hey boys, do you mind if I turn Janice down?"

Stunned as a turnip, Michael raised his beer and said to Sean, "I think the dignitaries might be here. Al, you wanna check?" Sean laughed like a teenage girl drunk on lemon gin for the first time. Michael said, "Oh, well, I guess the pilots know how to land the thing by now, eh?"

It was Michael's shot.

Sean said, "Y'know, Michael, I think we forgot something. We didn't put the pots out."

"Quiet, please. I am trying to make this shot." He hammered the 8-ball; it rattled around the table and collided aimlessly with almost every other ball. "Perfect. Now we can go. But Sean, you are too drunk to drive. I will drive." They left. I had to fight against the violent wind to close the door before I returned to the kitchen.

The rest of the story came to me in bits and pieces.

By the time Sean and Michael arrived at the shop, the plane had taken another dangerous, low swipe at us. While passing a joint between them in the shop, Michael took credit for pointing out to Sean that it would be impossible to light the diesel bottles out on the ice. Sean agreed, so Michael lit the wicks of the thirty full bottles already lined up on the wooden deck of the truck and then drove out of the garage. On exit, the replaced clutch grabbed magnificently when engaged, and the truck bumped and heeled hard over on the substantial ice curb formed at the garage door. This unforeseen glitch in their plan caused several of the ignited bottles to roll over. These spilled their fuel and ignited other bottles and the wood deck; a perfectly good plan was ruined. The wind provided a robust supply of oxygen as the surface crew sped, truck almost completely engulfed in flames, onto the ice.

When I returned to the kitchen, I found myself confronted by a different sort of flame. Carl and Bill had arrived to drink coffee and gawk at each other. When he'd arrived in camp earlier that day, JT had issued orders, taken control, and organized the weekend. He clamped the lid down on us and tried to muzzle me in the form of Bill and Carl, who JT ordered to act like security guards. He also put Schläger on Corey. Carl and Bill were to spend the rest of the Friday night shift with me because the booze and the specialty weekend food had been delivered to the cook shack. The gala banquet was to follow the curling extravaganza as part of the exclusive blow-out.

At about the same time the truck burned in effigy for the dignitaries, I addressed Bill and Carl, "So, you boys are full-blown gay, eh?" I was unafraid of confronting any number of elephants in the room; I sat down with my cup of tea.

They looked at each other, then at me. Both appeared uncomfortable, and said in unison, "No."

"C'mon, boys. It's just you and me. I'm liberated. You two want to hop in the sack, I couldn't care less. Besides, that's your business."

Carl softened, "Billy, he knows." He put his hand tenderly on Bill's arm.

Bill heaved a sigh of relief and said, "Is it so obvious?"

"Oh, no, no, not at all, I'm just intuitive. I'm guessin' JT is a little weirded out about it though ... Jimmy too, I bet." They both

215

winced. "Right. A little mean about it, were they?"

Carl blurted out, "JT said if we couldn't keep it in our pants, Schläger was going to do electro-shock on us both with battery jumpers." He looked at Bill, his worried eyebrows arched like the entry to a Nazi torture chamber in the basement of a Parisian cathedral. "We're in love."

Bill took both Carl's massive, knuckle-scarred hands in his own. "Don't worry, hon, I'll protect us."

"I'm just so scared of Schläger," hissed Carl, his voice a frightened whisper.

I said, "Yeah, well, JT is a throwback from another era and Schläger *is* a piece of work. But don't worry about him; he has his own instant karma to worry about." I drifted my gaze over to the cases of alcohol. "You boys mind if I initiate a little pay-back?"

Bill asked, "What do you have in mind?" He patted Carl's massive shoulders.

"We have a couple of surprises planned." I looked at the stack of boxes filled with liquor and then back at them.

Bill and Carl both nodded. "As long as we get some of the booty." They both giggled at Carl's double entendre. I snapped my fingers. Murray and Mouthy Frank appeared from the pantry, surprising Carl and Bill. Murray secured the back door with the two by four.

I handed one of the full bottles of scotch to Carl. "Don't you guys have a better place to celebrate?" They looked at each other.

Carl said, "We're supposed to stay. Maybe we could help?"

There was a muffled knock on the back door. "Naw, we got this. You two deserve a night off, together. I'll make sure no one finds out. Go. Enjoy yourselves."

Murray showed the boys out the front door while I let Michael in the back. His voice had attained a high pitch of French-Canadian alarm. "Hurry up. I think Petunia is out here." I threw the door open and Michael jumped inside. I slammed the door shut, locked it with the two by four, and then I poured Michael a coffee. He was high as hell and drunk as a loon. He was the perfect man for the upcoming job. Michael said, "The dignitaries are walking up the hill now with Sean."

"Okay, guys," I said. "It's a go. Don't lose the caps. We have less than an hour before the pilots refuel the plane and then show up here."

I locked the front door. We opened the cases and emptied each bottle of a third of its contents into an empty five-gallon milk canister enlisted for the job. Soon, cases of open liquor bottles covered the table.

Frank, Murray, Michael, and I began to top off the opened liquor bottles with white vinegar and the urine Michael, Frank, and I collected over a couple of days. We had stored our effluent in used milk jugs. Michael raised a refilled bottle, sniffed the air, waved his hand over the opening, and said, "This one smells like stew."

I held my bottle up against the overhead light. "Chateau Port Radium, May '75, I believe, perhaps a whiff of pork."

Murray compared the last unopened bottle of scotch and the refilled bottle. He said, "The color is pretty close. We did this to a bully in high school; he couldn't stop puking for a week."

Frank said, "That had to be pretty miserable."

"And that was after they pumped out his stomach."

Frank said, "With this brew from the lake water, there is a possibility of intestinal parasites. We can only hope."

We repacked the bottles into their respective cases to finish up. Michael had brought a pickup he'd commandeered after the unfortunate incident during the plane's arrival. I said, "Remember, Michael, two cases go to Mary-Ellen's room, right now, for her rounds. Then you gotta hide the rest, in case they come looking."

"I got it, boss. I have a hiding place picked out."

"Frank, you have to make sure Ernie gets a case to deliver to JT. Okay then, no one tampers with the rest of this shipment. We don't want to tip our hand and spoil the weekend." Murray volunteered to help Frank. We checked for Petunia, but she was elsewhere, so we packed the booze out to Michael's pickup.

There was no night-shift crew during the bonspiel weekend since the entire focus of management was to pamper the dignitaries. Besides, working miners created dust that inspectors might balk at, and that might hamper JT's plans.

I had one thing left to do after I was finished with the pilots.

They arrived for a late meal after securing the plane, about three a.m. They must have envisioned themselves as a soon-to-be crumpled ball of flaming airplane wreckage.

217

"You should have seen it," said the shaken, angry pilot. He sat in front of his huge steaming plate of mashed potatoes, hamburger patties, and corn niblets slathered in rich gravy. They talked out their ordeal as I encouraged them to eat their stress away, prepared to dole out a hefty second plateful. "The burning truck swerving down the ramp and all over the ice. Those guys could only place two lit bottles on each side of the runway before they abandoned the truck, which was going up in flames. After we landed, we watched it burn down to the axles." He took another forkful of potatoes and gravy, and I urged him to wash it down with scotch. "The truck's fuel tank exploded just seconds after our last pass overhead. We were on fumes so it was land or crash. I don't know how we brought her in."

The co-pilot chimed in, "The ball of orange flames … when the truck exploded … that was just enough light for us."

"Lucky for you that happened," I said. Both men looked at me with twisted doubt on their faces. "Eat, drink," I encouraged them. "Hot food will help you avoid going into shock." I had laced the gravy with the extra strength Ex-Lax bars I'd ordered from Edmonton; there were no free rides this weekend. Though the self-pitying pilots lamented the tale of their arrival, I was proud of our crew; in the end, Port Radium's finest had served them well.

Between the three of us, my opinion was unique. "Lucky? How?" asked the incredulous pilot. "This was a seventeen-hour day, fourteen of it in the air, in these conditions, too!" The pilots recounted how the passengers endured buffeting winds that threw the plane around the entire night flight. The unhappy trip was so much worse for those who had to share the few airsickness bags in the plane. The pilots summed up Michael and Sean's efforts, "Those dumb, drunk bastards damn near got us all killed!"

"Did the beer shipment make it through okay?" I asked.

"The beer? Yes …"

"Thank God."

When the pilots left the kitchen, I gave them each a "special" bottle of rum to enjoy "on JT."

Sean dropped by to sign off for the night. He told me that as the passengers deplaned and their luggage was unloaded, they were unimpressed when several suitcases sprang open. Into the night, curling garb and underwear disappeared across the ice before the brunt of the full-blown gale that screeched across Great Bear Lake. Sean led their march past the orange glow of burnt wreckage and up the "stairway to heaven." The group trudged through the bunkhouses, receiving generous heaps of verbal abuse when they awoke sleeping men. The party arrived weak, and possibly hypo-thermic, at the guest bunkhouse high on the far ridge. Sean said, "They dove into the booze like they'd been wandering in the desert for forty years."

At 4:45 a.m., it was finally my turn. I went to Bun's bunkhouse and kicked his door open. The room reeked of stale cigarettes and whiskey. I yelled at the idiot, "Thank you for the offer, but I am refusing all over-time. There is no law in this territory that says I have to accept involuntary over-time. You have fifteen minutes to get into the kitchen, or 140 hungry men, a bunch of airsick curlers, and JT will require your explanation. Now, you go right ahead and have a nice day."

I left as Bun whined from behind bleary eyes and tousled hair, "Aw, c'mon, buddy, you have to cook."

"The fuck I do, *buddy*." For full effect, I slammed shut and then kicked his door open again to ensure I would wake his neighbors. I shouted over his protest, "I didn't mean to call you a common idiot. There is no other idiot like you."

Ernie told me that after his inadequate breakfast of toast and burnt coffee, JT demanded from Bun and Stalin how they'd spent the food budget, "because it certainly is not obvious at this breakfast table." JT was still storming angry because of the curling rink ice, Mary-Ellen's exposed dildo, and the AWOL breakfast cook. JT launched a full tirade in the cook shack and stripped about six public pounds of flesh off Jack's hide, too.

"If the rest of this weekend does not proceed absolutely flawlessly," JT thundered, still outraged after his inspection of the truck wreckage smoldering on the ice, "you will rue the day you and that stuttering moron of a partner of yours ever came to work for me."

Jack departed the cook shack in a sullen, dark mood and stalked the bleary-eyed surface crew to bully them and vent his outrage.

Over coffee that afternoon, Corey gave me the rest of the details, word for word …

He waited outside the main office while JT stormed loud enough inside that Corey heard every word clearly. JT threatened Carl and Bill; he accused Carl of mincing when he walked and pursing his lips at JT. "And you, Bill, shuffling around like you have a roll of quarters shoved up your rectum. What in hell is going on in this camp?" JT had no idea how close his observation was to the truth.

Corey was next up on JT's pogrom list. Once inside the Manager's office, JT released his fury on Corey. "Now, you sniveling twerp, I hear you have a cold."

"It's more than a cold. It's cancer. From radiation poisoning. I don't think …"

"Let me tell you this," JT cut Corey off. "I'm not paying off WCB for nothing here. If you think for one minute that I'm going to let you hit me for a claim, you better think again. I gave you this job, and this is how you repay me? With a WCB claim?" JT held a handful of pages up to Corey's face.

Already demoralized and weak with pain, Corey wilted under JT's cruelty but refused to retreat. "The radon in this mine is highly poisonous, and you know that, you've always known that. You failed to protect the men; you've sent them to their deaths."

"You dare lecture me about men?" JT turned apoplectic. "What do you know about men? Did we cave in when the men we left behind at Bataan marched to their deaths? Did we cry over the men in the trenches and fields at the Somme or for those men left decomposing in the elephant grass in Vietnam? No! We sent them to war and they took their medicine. Boys became men, the ones that came home, at least. Well, except for the head cases. And I see that's what we have here. You're fired. Take *that* to WCB. Now get out of my office and be on the Monday plane, or I'll put you on it myself."

Jimmy said, "Schläger will make sure you are on that plane, Corey."

JT said, "Jimmy! That's how you deal with his type. Corey, send those two queers back in here. I'll straighten them out, by God, or I'll put them on the same fucking plane and the Devil can have them. Schläger, hand me those battery cables."

Jimmy asked, "Do you want to take care of that cook, too?"

"No, let him be for now. He can work the weekend and then Schläger can deal with him any way he wants."

I hated the sound of that; *Mash* had morphed into *One Flew over the Cuckoo's Nest.*

Corey concluded, "I figure I'm getting a short trip and a long drop over the ice. They're coming for you, too. Watch your back."

28. Mary-Ellen

By Saturday morning, Mary-Ellen had started her rounds. "Well, Herman," she said, slipping him the envelope stuffed with cash. "We meet again. I've missed you since last fall."

The pudgy, bespectacled WCB inspector, Harman, sat on the edge of the bed in front of Mary-Ellen. He was a chinless, pale version of a man of little repute, less class, and no style. But he was important to JT because after Harman managed to cheat his way through a year of Alberta Community College and then forge a two-year diploma, he begged his reluctant but influential uncle, the Director of some government department in Yellowknife, to hire him as the Mines Inspector for the territory.

Harman had looked forward to this ménage à deux for months. It was and would be the highlight of his life and the final nail he would drive into the coffin of his failing marriage.

In Port Radium, Harman was still a dignitary, the WCB inspector who signed off on the mine. Mary-Ellen was on her knees between Harman's legs, doing what she did best. Pitifully, within seconds, their transaction was complete.

• • •

Mary-Ellen wanted desperately to leave Harman's room. She purged at the sink, like a cat coughing up a hairball, while he counted the few hundred dollars in his envelope.

"Mary-Ellen, I have something to say, and I've given this a lot of thought."

This dweeb is so fucking earnest. She refused to look at him while she applied more lipstick. "I haven't told my wife yet," he said. "But I'm leaving her. And ..." He faltered.

She turned and glared at him with her flat, uninterested eyes that offered no flicker of connection.

"I ... I'm in love with you," he said. "I want you and I to be together ... always." Harman fumbled in his shirt pocket and held out a small case.

She took it from him, opened it, and said, "That's nice, Herman, but it's 'me', not 'I'."

"My name is Harman. I know it's you ..."

"No, I meant you said 'you and I' not 'you and me' ..."

222

He looked up at her, completely lost in her grammar correction. "Right."

She rolled the ring around in her fingers to calculate its pawn value and mentally compared it to the other fake jewelry that adorned her fingers. *Why is it always this way with these losers? First, that moron Jimmy tried to pawn that cheap knock-off on me, and now this ...*

She had left Jimmy, minutes before, humiliated and emotionally shredded because she refused to indulge in more than professional contact with him. She had screeched at him, thrown the Zircon ring back in his face, and laughed when he'd slumped to the floor and cried fake convulsions.

"Get up, you blubbering loser," she'd said. "Even your asshole father has more pride than you do. And you can take that crap ring back to the Five and Dime and get your beer bottle money back. It's not worth my time to pawn it." She tossed a packet of Kleenex at him before she slammed the door on Jimmy's hopes and ill-conceived plan.

And now this one ... There's only one way to deal with these backwoods droolers.

"Listen, Harvey, I could never be a home wrecker, and by the look of this ring, you couldn't afford me anyway." She tucked the ring into her cleavage; after all, twenty dollars was twenty dollars. Mary-Ellen gave him the full flash of her dismissive smile. "I have my own plans, too, and they don't involve living in a trailer in Yellowknife, waiting around for a sniveling Pillsbury Dough Boy."

"It's Harman," he protested. "I'm saving for a house." He sobbed through the sentence.

"Wonderful ... keep saving. JT expects to see you at dinner, Harry." Mary-Ellen patted Harman on the top of his head before she walked out of his sad, empty life.

• • •

Harman suffered the intense rejection pain that even his abuse of barbiturates and alcohol was inadequate to block; the final crash of the door slamming behind Mary-Ellen, he knew, would haunt him for a long time. He slumped down onto the bed, so recently the scene of his pleasure, took the cap off the bottle of scotch, and drank a mouthful. He flinched at the taste. "Even the scotch is bitter here," said Harman aloud, utterly heartbroken as he talked to the walls. Though tears of self-pity flowed down his cheeks, his gaze drifted over the envelope and out the window.

Harman drank half the bottle, alone in his life and his room. By ten a.m., he had begun to vomit. Harman thought he had Delirium Tremens when the movement outside his window, in the Murphy tailings dump, caught his bloodshot eyes. He followed the progress of the oddly-shaped dog until it scuttled beneath the curling rink skirting. Harman was the first dignitary to document Petunia's return to camp.

• • •

A fallen angel but still a trooper, Mary-Ellen carried on and performed her own dressing-down duties without enthusiasm. She had no illusions about enjoying any part of her day servicing men she loathed. The same tawdry, sexual payoff that left Harman such a vacuous wreck played out in other guest bunkhouse rooms throughout the day. Mary-Ellen was no nuclear physicist, but she knew her job and earned her pay. After she'd dispatched Jimmy and Harman, she delivered sex, booze, and sealed envelopes to the RCMP officers who were already drunk and aggressive, then finished off before lunch with the company accountant. Mary-Ellen had a full slate of afternoon appointments scheduled with the health inspector, the fire inspector, a government auditor, and the pilots. Her last appointment was tentative. Both pilots had come down with a touch of the Port Radium lower intestinal flu. Having enjoyed a second heaping helping of doctored gravy the night before, both men deferred her affections until later, if, as the co-pilot put it, "a guy can ever get off the fucking toilet."

Though Mary-Ellen fooled herself about her prowess as a *home-wrecker*, she knew it would take several days before each of them would have to explain to their unsuspecting wives or lovers the raging gonorrhea brought back from Port Radium. However, even sharing that STD would be the least of their relationship problems. Before coming into camp, Mary-Ellen had failed to address the inflammation that nagged at her throat, due to JT's demands on her professional calling, and was sure she had also initiated an epidemic of genital warts.

29. Stew

I slept until mid-Saturday afternoon. The gale had passed. I needed to be in full form for our big night. I dressed quickly, went right to the kitchen, and began my shift early to pitch in. Bun wanted to shake my hand as his offer of reconciliation, but I declined his gesture as mine held a coffee cup. All day he cooked his heart out, but it took Jan, Ernie, and Morag and Genna to make it all work; they had already assembled platter after platter fit for a banquet at 24 Sussex Drive.

At one point late in the afternoon, the Cigar Lips senior and junior spot-checked the kitchen, trailed by Carl and Bill. JT instructed Jimmy, "Now, boy, you'll see the results of a stiff rod. Never spoil the child, I say. Just look at Carl and Bill. I say, treat men as men, they stiffen up and take matters into their own hands. That's the stuff that built this country." The moment the father and son left the cook shack, Carl and Bill fell into each other's arms to comfort themselves after their earlier re-indoctrination session with JT.

Throughout the afternoon, the rest of us had whirled around the kitchen and coordinated the timing on each prepared entrée. Any odd ends of vegetables or meats went into my stew pot, which rendered down through the afternoon to a sadly recognizable, consistent gruel.

Under the watchful eyes of Carl and Bill, Michael had delivered the special alcohol to the curling rink before noon, so it was available for the early games. All afternoon, the official agenda of scheduled inspections also continued. Michael reported a "stomach flu" had hit the guests hard, and he had spent the day shuttling the queasy dignitaries between the visitor's bunkhouse toilets and the curling rink, where they resumed quaffing tumblers of alcoholic beverages.

Between rounds of drinks and curling matches on the pock-marked ice, the mine inspector managed a brief visit to the Echo Bay mine. Michael tagged along and he told me the inspector hardly lingered over the benign V-700 radiation counter. Before he rejoined the festivities at the curling rink, Michael asked the inspector if he wanted to stop at the Eldorado mine, which was flooded for the weekend. The man said, "No fuckin' way I'm goin' in that hole!" He protested between intermittent bouts of projectile vomiting. Corey said it was possible for the company to have current Eldorado data, but the "tried and true" liquid paper over original dates and signatures forged with current dates solved the nuisance of the paper trail; facts would have proven counter-productive to JT's plans.

The other civil servants performed similar lightning-fast cameo appearances at other buildings. The auditors drank scotch in Jimmy's office for an hour. The Safety Inspector relied on Harman's nod to confirm mine safety. No one visited the nurse's station or Corey's lab. The Health Inspector walked through the cook shack looking for a half a cup of coffee to doctor his rum.

When the official chores were completed, JT's plan called everyone to rev up the curling extravaganza. He also announced he would allow the community hall cafeteria to open at six p.m., a magnanimous hour earlier than usual, and that we could have opened beer there, too. Ernie was the hall bartender.

We had our own plans, which were well underway, though we were careful to wait until the scene at the curling rink was at full throttle.

That afternoon, Sean and Don had raided the office storage room and packed an ancient amplifier and microphone into the community hall to boost the existing sound system. By four p.m., Ernie, a trusted member of the kitchen corps, refused to accept payment for a beer at the community hall. The news spread through camp faster than an Australian bushfire in the outback, so Big Puppy Don and Chattering Ernie slung free, ice cold bottles of beer across the counter often enough to wear out their arms. Eddie the Wrench fiddled with a toolbox, some electrical tape, and a roll of wire and rigged a way to pipe the record player sound through the amp. Eddie cranked Derek and the Dominoes, Dolly, the Stones, Janice, Hank, and the Beatles throughout happy hour and into the night. Mouthy Frank made sure anyone who did not want to join us in the hall knew cold plates, sandwiches, tea, and coffee were available in the cook shack.

We planned to deliver a special surprise to our people, which they would enjoy right after we delivered the hot food to the drunks at the curling rink.

By five p.m., Bun and I were finished in the kitchen. I broke my personal vow and bumped up the heat on the stew, which I had doctored liberally with my secret ingredient. And, of course, there would be bread. We had the platters of choice menu items set for delivery at five thirty.

"You'd better get going," I said to Bun. "They'll expect you, as the master chef, to make an appropriate entrance and entertain the diners. Frank, can you take Bun over to the rink?"

Mouthy Frank nodded, but Bun was no ordinary fool. He looked at me with a wary eye. He said, "If you think I'm going to fall for that one …"

"Hey, what are you worried about? Carl and Bill are here." They looked up and waved at the mention of their names. "Michael can help them bring the food over." I corrected the swanky tilt to Bun's chef hat. "Now, if we're going to do this thing, let's do it right."

A pawn to his own nattering and fretting, Bun believed my "load of barmy," as Boiled and Burnt Les might have said and which Liz might have confirmed. Frank hustled Bun outside and into a pickup, just as Michael returned from a delivery run to the curling rink. "Those dignitaries," said Michael, "are a pig. They are all drunk from this afternoon."

"Sounds like fun," I said. I noted a whisp of rum on his breath. "Let them have their bonspiel, right?"

Michael took a swig of his coffee cup and smirked back at me. "I listened to those idiots all day; I needed some courage of my own."

Having joined the rest of his ilk at the rink, Bun was finally out of our hair. Under the mooning eyes of Carl and Bill, Michael, Aussie Murray, who had been sticking close to me all afternoon, and I loaded the food into the pickups; one destined for the community hall, for our side, the other for the curling rink. Bill and Carl escorted Michael and Frank to the curling rink. I drove the second pickup to the community hall. It took both Murray and me to lift the half full milk canister of hooch out of the truck and into the hall, where plenty of volunteers had already set up the tables and chairs.

At the curling rink, Frank, Carl, and Bill off-loaded their feast and packed it through the back door of the deserted kitchen. Carl and Bill watched from the door while Michael detached distributor caps and wires from engines on the few trucks and the bus. Sean, who waited at the curling rink, joined Michael and took any sets of keys he found in the vehicles and tossed them out on the tailings.

When Sean gave them the pre-arranged signal, Morag, Genna, and Jan set up the last of the open bottles of tainted liquor on the bar and then our giggling and bouncy co-conspirators slipped out the kitchen door of the rink. Murray waited for them in his pickup and drove them and Sean, who jumped into the back, to the community hall. Outside the hall, Murray invited Carl and Bill to join our festivities, so they piled into the back with Sean.

Just as the girls arrived at the hall, Eric Clapton's bluesy, magical riffs poured out of his heart as he expressed his love for Layla. Jan, Genna, and Morag entered to a standing ovation from the hall full of men, already half-baked on hooch, weed, and free beer. Laid out on the kitchen counter were two barons of beef, chops, steaks, two whole stuffed chickens, several fresh veggie platters, three kinds of potatoes, huge bowls of fresh salad, loaves of hot garlic bread, a conga line of condiments, and the desserts JT had flown in, intended for the consumption of the monarchy at the curling rink. Murray and I refilled the hooch jug at the end of the buffet counter and encouraged everyone to take a big glass, compliments of JT and Jimmy.

We served the women first and then dove into the food and free liquor. Sure, it was a mix of rye, vodka, scotch, and rum, but it was still free booze at the Arctic Circle. A little ice added, mixed with water or apple juice, and it crossed the palate with the subtlety of an exploding truck! Everyone loaded up full plates with all the trimmings. We piled it on and enjoyed our first great meal as a group in a couple of months. Each bite tasted better than the previous, especially knowing we had stolen our feast.

After he finished his meal, Ernie left the hall as planned, jingling his ring of keys on his way out. He nodded at me before the door closed behind him.

Throughout our dinner, Michael had an impish grin on his face. After I administered a third degree, he finally told me what he had been up to during part of the day. "This morning, when I did my first delivery, I spiked their pepper."

"At the curling rink? With what, cayenne or something?"

"No. With dust from the plant. Now they can choke on their own dust."

"Holy shit. Well, with my secret ingredient, which promises relief from constipation, and your radioactive dust, it should make for a long and interesting evening for JT's crowd." I clinked his glass with mine. "*Salut, mon ami.* I guess we know what the rich are eating tonight."

When Ernie returned, he gave me his double thumbs-up and slipped me a fat envelope.

Everyone was served and limbered up, so I thought it might be the right time to toast Dave, our departed comrade-in-arms. I wanted part of this night to include a celebration for "Dusty" Dave Rhodes. All agreed heartily and good cheer filled the hall. We shared the rest of the hooch and polished off the banquet grub within the hour. Inspired by Michael, I ended the dinner with another toast, "Here's to what the rich folk are eating tonight. Here's to …" I held up my full glass, as did the eighty or so other satisfied revelers in the room who joined me to yell out, "stew."

Even as the sounds of our party grew louder around me, I grew quiet, struck by the measured distance between consequences and actions, and pondered why the leap over the chasm was so difficult for some. From a stool near the bar, I watched ordinary men enjoy the company of their working friends. I felt like we were acting out our own version of the film *The King of Hearts*, as if we were the gaggle of cheerful, if oblivious, lunatics escaped from the asylum, left alone in the town rigged with booby-traps, who thoroughly and innocently enjoyed the new freedom provided by the desertion of the frightened citizens.

JT planned this night to be an arranged exchange of cash and sex between elitists. Fountains of booze would flow throughout the weekend festivities before a dull flight returned the condemned visitors, hung-over and morally compromised, back to dull desk jobs. Our crew knew the night at the Port Radium curling rink promised to be a far different adventure.

• • •

Different, for sure, but the events at the curling rink were hardly dull.

Disturbing sounds filled the banquet room. Outside, dignitaries draped over railings retched off the front stairs. Harman, unable to hold his burden long enough, retched on his hands and knees outside the locked bathroom door. The bar keys and the keys to the bathrooms were misplaced. Some showed signs of passing out from too many doctored drinks, the strain of projectile vomiting, and no food. Both once pristine curling sheets looked like the floor of an emergency room unable to contend with a particularly virulent outbreak of botulism.

Bun could only produce a huge vat of tepid, greasy stew and a dozen loaves of stale, white bread. From behind the bar, which his guests still mobbed, JT refilled tumblers with whatever liquor he found. The girls gone and Mary-Ellen refusing to pour drinks, JT said to no one in particular, "Where the fuck are Genna and Morag?"

Happy Hour threatened to unravel into the triage chaos expected during the Black Plague. JT was out of his controlled element and beyond livid that the girls had disappeared. Distressed at the social shambles displayed before him, he fired his employees a couple of times each. JT had tried to attract Schläger's attention, but he was busy assisting the drunken Mine Inspector tangled up with the drunken Auditor. JT was enraged when he realized the two men were dry-humping each other like two dogs in heat, and he roared furiously when he realized Schläger was taking Polaroid's rather than pulling them apart. JT retreated in disgust to the head table and drank a sullen tumbler of tainted whiskey. He believed the success of the weekend pivoted on his next decision; servers or not, he had to feed these men. He yelled above the din, insisting Bun fill everyone up on stew.

At the command, the intoxicated crowd, those who could still stand, complied with their host's wishes and formed a weaving line along the bar. Stalin pulled the Auditor and the Mine Inspector apart and escorted them to the end of the food line. Bun waited at the other end of the counter, ladle in hand and his hat jauntily askew, to serve the guests as they filed past. Assured now that the drunken diners would eat their fill and reclaim some composure, JT sat at the main table, where he struggled to gather up whatever semblance of decorum remained before the swaying mob. He accepted a platter of stew bowls and bread delivered by Jimmy. JT was pleased at the fruit of his efforts; the dignitaries had settled at their tables and slurped and dunked bread into full bowls.

JT called for order by ringing his spoon against his refilled tumbler. However, when he stood up to address the crowd, he spilled his bowl of lukewarm stew onto Mary-Ellen's chest and into her lap. Unaware of what he had done, JT waved down the smatter of applause. As he prepared to speak, Mary-Ellen scored the silence like a whizzbang at Vimy Ridge when she screeched, "You fucking great ox." She stood up, knocking her chair over backwards, and stormed over to the end of the dais.

Schläger further silenced the crowd when he chose that moment to run his homemade film through the projector. Unmistakable footage of Jimmy displayed across JT and on the wall behind him. Jimmy's camouflage pants were pulled down around his ankles, he was chained and on all fours, and he howled at each stroke of the vicious whack delivered by a half-naked, muscular ghoul in a black leather mask. Schläger had brought his home movies of Jimmy's army hazing into camp.

Misunderstanding why the crowd became subdued, shocked even, and why Jimmy wept into his hands, JT took a moment to light a cigar, protesting, "Please, the spotlight is unnecessary." When he began reading his prepared speech, he managed only a few sentences before becoming aware he was competing with a growling Doberman Pinscher. JT stopped reading, looked askance at Mary-Ellen, and said, "Would someone please let that dog out."

Harman, who misconstrued JT's request, was the first responder to reach Mary-Ellen before others of the drunken horde followed suit. Almost as one, they leapt from their chairs to wipe at the stew that JT had spilled over Mary-Ellen. In the melee, Harman was knocked into Mary-Ellen's arms, his mouth gaping.

"Oh no. Once is enough for you, scum," Mary-Ellen said. She utilized the brown belt she held in karate, and chopped Harman viciously in the windpipe. He gurgled like a dying man, dropped to her feet, curled into the fetal position, and rolled beneath the white sheet covering the dais. There, his dining experience deteriorated to a gagging series of self-pitying sobs.

Having dispatched Harman, Mary-Ellen turned her cold wrath on the rest of the crowd and stopped them in their unsteady tracks. "You pitiful bastards," she howled, unloading her contempt for them. This appropriate and loud epithet called the guests to an inebriated halt. Even the RCMP officers, drool on their chins, retreated.

Taking advantage of the suspension of the riot, JT addressed the deficiency in the meal. He raised his glass of urine-laced whiskey and spoke about what he knew. "Never forget, the boys at Bataan would have killed for this meal. Let's empty our glasses in their honor ..." Of them all, only Schläger and Jimmy had ever worn a uniform, but everyone returned to their seats, found their drinks, and toasted the 40,000 boys and men who'd died after General MacArthur deserted them in the sweltering Philippine jungle.

As they drank, the film sound track erupted again with the vicious barking of the Doberman. In the small world under the table where Jimmy hid, he reacted to his irrational fear of dogs and vomited involuntarily into Harman's horrified face. Jimmy heard Mary-Ellen say, "Here we go again, the fucking war." At the sound of her voice, Jimmy rolled out from under the dais, gained his knees, and stared up at Mary-Ellen.

Her comment caught JT's attention. He watched her swipe the stew off her white velour top with a bar towel. By way of recognition for her devotion to the weekend's success and no doubt because he was affectionate with whiskey, JT said, "Fill your glasses, men, and let's have a special toast for Mary-Ellen. Without her, this day would have come off a disappointment. To Mary-Ellen." He raised his glass.

Jimmy was unable to join the toast; the film that still played on the wall had transfixed him. He watched himself on screen, passed out cold as the ferocious, aroused dog had his way with him. The dignitaries applauded and cheered and drank from full tumblers to Mary-Ellen's health. He looked at her, pleading with his eyes, but after Mary-Ellen winked at him, Jimmy slumped back under the dais.

Mary-Ellen turned her glare toward JT as the rippling applause diminished to a thin smatter. She lit a cigarette and went to sit and smoke alone, at the end of the bar, while JT rattled on about A-bombs, the Japanese, the Russians, the Viet Cong, the "A-rabs," the Chinese, the Cubans, and world domination through military aggression funded by citizens, which filled the pockets of tax-exempt corporations. By the end of JT's speech, many of those gathered in the room had doubled over due to the sudden onset of violent, lower-intestinal cramps.

When the reel of film ended, Jimmy regained his chair, in shock and thoroughly humiliated. Soured and defeated, he raised his tumbler, and shouted, "And here's to Port-fucking-Radium," just before he passed out in the stew spilled on the table. In the background came the distinct sound of retching; the three-hundred pound Health Inspector had succumbed at Mary-Ellen's feet. The full effects of the spiked food and drinks had advanced an already terrible toll. In the shadows of the festive decorations and subdued lighting, Merle Haggard croaked the redneck anthem, "We don't smoke mary-wanny in Muskogee..."

His speech concluded, JT sat down to finish his bowl of bland fare. He took a peppershaker and shook the spice onto the stew, then ate a mouthful followed by a bite of bread. He raised his eyebrows and announced to the rest of those in the mob who were still conscious, "It's not too bad with pepper, and pepper is great for the digestion."

The sycophants spiced their stew, prepared to eat anything that might help with their digestion. After they mopped up what was in their bowls, most went for more. Many refilled their drinks before the urge returned to stagger off and vomit more brackish bile onto the curling ice, or suffer through cramps of violent diarrhea outside the rink. There, Nature provided them a tender mercy; the gale, similar to the dignitaries, had blown itself out.

JT said, "I see the projector is ready. What have you got for us, Schläger?"

Schläger gladly replayed his home movies. The shocked guests, for the second time, watched the highlights of Jimmy's hazing. JT commented after a brief glance, "War films? I love them." Bun refilled JT's bowl. As the film played on the wall behind him, JT peppered his stew liberally, and then jammed stew-soaked bread into his gaping maw. Jimmy was still passed out, blind drunk, when Schläger started the second reel.

● ● ●

In the community hall, Fleetwood Mac's *Rumours* played in the background. I stood up and called for order.

"Quiet, quiet. Eddie, kill the music for a minute." As pre-arranged, Eddie turned down the amplifier and changed the record. The room settled. I continued, "You know we lost our friend, Dave, a couple weeks ago. One of his final sentiments was in his song. You know the tune."

Eddie queued the track. John Denver sang in the background. Don was a far better singer than I was, but we shared the microphone anyway. Don accompanied the record on guitar, and we sang the first verse and chorus of *Country Roads*. Then we turned off the record and started with Dave's words to the same tune. At first, only Don and I sang, but soon I gave the microphone to Don because everyone in the room joined in or hummed along. When it was over, we sang the song again after repeated and good-natured cries of "Encore!" There wasn't a dry eye in the house, as the old saying goes, which was damn close to the truth.

The third time through, Corey and the twins left. Corey had been quiet all through the meal. Genna and Morag helped him stand, and then they draped both his arms over their shoulders to help him walk. After the song ended, one big smoke break erupted. The last of the hooch was gone, so Ernie and Donny cracked open beers like they were born to it. Jan and Sean jumped in behind the counter to help serve. The music blared again; this time it was the Rolling Stones' *Sympathy for the Devil*. I followed the three of them outside as our vibrant crowd sang along and never missed a single chorus of "woo oo."

When I walked into the sugar shack, Morag and Jenna were sitting on the edge of the couch in the darkened living room. Corey was flat on his back, a bloodstained face cloth was over his mouth. He looked at me, and I saw fear in his eyes. Morag watched me closely. Corey coughed, spitting more blood into the white cloth.

"Holy shit. This doesn't look like the flu. When did it get so bad?" I asked Morag.

Corey swallowed, and then wheezed when he whispered, "This year. I needed medical to cover my bills, so I stayed working here. The company refused, said this was from smoking. I've never smoked in my life. I shouldn't have come back to camp. I'm definitely poisoned. Again." He cried softly. I watched him drift into semi-consciousness.

I asked Morag, "Isn't there something we can do for him? He needs a Medi-Vac. Now." Her eyes saddened.

Genna said, "Can't. They're all too drunk. He'll have to make it on his own until tomorrow, then he's flying out."

My thoughts raced. "He'll be on the Medi-Vac manifest, so he'll arrive in Yellowknife, at least. Schläger can't touch him if the hospital knows Corey's coming in."

Genna wiped Corey's forehead with another cold cloth, then folded and placed it on his brow. "He doesn't deserve this. He never did anything to hurt anybody."

Morag said, "He's sleeping now. We've seen this before with Corey. He'll be better when he gets treatment at the hospital tomorrow. They'll put him in an iron lung; it helps heal his insides. I just don't know how many more times he can stand this ... I know I can't." Genna unfolded a blanket over Corey, took off his shoes, and made him as comfortable as she could.

Genna said, "God, he looks so helpless. I hope he'll be okay." We stood over him in the subdued living room shadows. The light over the kitchen stove was the only light on in the house.

I put my hand on Genna's shoulder and said, "He can rest now. He'll be in a doctor's care soon."

Genna said, "I'm going to sit with him for a while." She lit a joint and continued to tend to Corey.

I said, "We should watch him tonight, together, for any changes." Morag's hand reached down to my stomach and hung on my belt, gently, she directed me toward the kitchen.

"Corey is in good hands now," she said, pulling me into her bedroom. "Quickly, this will be our last chance." Her tongue teased at my ear. In the muted light, I lifted Morag onto the dressing bureau and kissed her full on the mouth. She undid my belt and ground her pelvis into my leg. I unbuttoned her shirt. She writhed on the bureau as I explored her the way she liked. She leaned back, arched her body, and reached toward me as she moaned at my mouth and touch.

Then there was a loud knock on the boot room door. We froze in situ.

"JT here! Hello the sugar shack."

The old wart hog had found us. The kitchen doorknob rattled. We broke for cover. I had only my long johns on and Morag was naked. We looked at each other and laughed silently. I couldn't run dragging my jeans around my ankles.

Genna yelled from the living room, "Oh, hi, JT. One minute until I'm decent, and I'll come."

Morag said to me, "Poor girl ... I already did."

JT said, "I was wondering why you girls left the party. Is everything okay? Why the fuck does it smell like a burning mattress in there?" I heard the door rattle again.

Over her wicked giggle, I whispered to Morag, "You could lose your jobs, too. Remember?" I reached for my jeans, hopping around the bedroom on one foot. Try as I might, my turned-out jeans would not cooperate.

JT, who had a key, hollered again from outside the kitchen

door, "Girls? It's cold out here. Why is this door locked? I'm coming in."

Morag watched me as I tried to wrestle my jeans on, and whispered frantically, "There's no time for that — you have to go now. Quick, gather up your clothes. Here you go, out the window."

Morag manhandled me as I bunny-hopped across the bedroom. She opened the ground floor window. I turned to face her, and said, "This seems pretty damn convenient. Just how many times have you used this as an escape hatch, anyway?"

"Shut up and go!" Morag pushed me out the window backwards. I dropped three feet and tumbled down the icy snow berm. My coat, runners, and shirt followed me. I sorted out my coat, tore off my jeans, pulled on my runners, and whispered, "We have unfinished business. Can you come over tonight? My old room?"

We heard Genna stalling JT in the kitchen; he roared when he saw Corey on the couch. Genna was trying to convince JT she had burned a snack of late-night pancakes.

"Yes ... Kiss me, you idiot." I stood up to kiss her. "Now, passionate boy," Morag said, "go, before we lose our jobs."

Unconcerned about my lost dignity, I said, "Bring Genna, too."

I was carrying my rolled up pants under my arms when I ran away from the house in my long johns. I raced past the kitchen, but cut through the community hall on purpose, where I received a standing ovation. I hollered at Michael to follow me, then zipped along the series of boardwalks and through bunkhouses to Michael's room.

He found me ten minutes later. I was dressed and sipping on a beer. He turned his mouth down when he stared at me. I had the distinct impression Michael was judging me. He sat on his bed and I on mine, the gulf between us only three feet, but it felt wider than that. Something was wrong between us; our connection had turned gloomy, testy. He had a story to tell, so I listened.

"You knows, haf'er you lef' dat dinner," he said. I realized I heard his accent again. *What the fuck?* I had forgotten how he struggled with English. "I was out for a smoke an' I saw dat Mary-Ellen walking to 'er bunk'ouse so I followed 'er. I didn't let 'er see me, but I could see 'er. She was a t'ief an' went in all da rooms of dose dignitary, den came out an' I seen dose envelop in her 'an'. When she wen' to 'er room, I wen' an' knock on 'er door. She was surprise an' tol' me to go, but I tol' 'er I was in love an' can she let me in? She says she can not love me an' I ask can we 'ave some sex den an' she says, 'No,' but I touch 'er sof'ly an' she respon' so I touch 'er some more an' then she kiss me on de lip so I touch 'er breas' an' she says, 'Wait ha minute. I need to freshen up firs'.' When she goes in da bat'room, I fin' 'er envelope in 'er mattress. Jus' like we tink. So I look in de envelope an' she 'as paper but no money. I lef'. I know you wanna go to school. Who 'as da money?"

I'd be damned if I'd let money come between our friendship. I took the envelope that Ernie slipped to me at our banquet from my inside coat pocket and handed it to Michael. He looked inside and whistled when he saw the bribe money. "You have it, Michael; you keep it. They'll figure out the food and come after me. And don't worry about me, I'll pay my own tuition."

Michael tucked the envelope under his mattress. "For sure, my friend. They have their eyes on you." We were right with the world again.

A soft giggle and a quiet knock interrupted us. I mouthed to Michael, "Is it Mary-Ellen?" No, it was the twins, and they let themselves in.

"We wanted to thank you for a great night."

"How's Corey doing?" I asked.

"Don and Jan are taking care of him. They're breaking up. Finally."

The girls took a pillow off each bed and we helped them stuff the opening over the doorway. They wedged a chair up against the door handle while Michael and I hung a blanket over the window. We cracked four beers. I turned on Dave's lava lamp and turned off the overhead light. Morag lay down beside me and propped her head up to sip her beer. She gave me a quick kiss when I bumped her.

Across from Michael and Genna, it was clear in the wavering half-light, they wanted to be alone. Morag and I looked at each other and silently slipped out of the room. "Michael," I said, before closing the door, "I'll be back in a couple of hours."

In my own room, I turned to Morag. She pulled me into her with one arm and took my hand in hers to place it strategically on her person, and she said, "You need to make love to me."

"Aw, do I have to?" I pretend whined.

"Stop talking now, boy, and start gettin' busy."

Some time later, we were lying naked under a sheet, Morag was smoking, I was stroking her red hair, wondering if all the lasses in Scotland had such fine, red hair.

Morag said, "Michael thinks he had them all eating radioactive dust instead of pepper. I hope no one dies."

"It won't hurt my feelings either way."

"You don't mean that."

I said, "We'll be fired this morning." Morag lifted her head and rested it on a crooked arm to look me in the eyes. "I can give you my parent's phone ..."

She said, "Don't," and placed a single finger across my lips. "Hush, now, we are great friends and this has always been wonderful, but don't we both know that when one of us leaves, it's over?"

I felt a sadness ... the empty longing for her had begun with those words, I hoped we would both soon find someone new.

"I can't stay. I have to go see how Genna and Corey are ... kiss me. I'll miss you."

I was unable to summon sleep.

I was halfway between exhausted, exhilarated, satiated, and disturbed. Something still nagged at me. I knew that Michael and I were out of a job. No one had to tell either of us that, but the way I saw it, any escape from this hole still breathing was a good out. We marched into our plans for this night knowing JT and Jimmy would come hunting for us by morning. I was still outraged for Corey and the many that lived sick or died after working in this camp or anywhere with uranium in the picture. The infuriating fact remained that the perpetual crime of this mine continued for decades because owners and our government ignored or covered up the risks. But their kind would never stop; obscene profit was their common, amoral bottom line. My indignation kept me awake.

The hallway filled with the sound of tramping feet that, no doubt, heralded the approach of the firing squad. He was sleeping and alone. A fist pounded on the door. JT hollered, and the door burst open. The backlight from the hallway darkened their faces. JT, Schläger, and Stalin moved in on us like a pack of dogs. Carl and Bill trembled in the hallway behind them.

Schläger spouted the obvious, "There he is."

"Jesus," I said. "What happened to you guys? You all look like shit on a griddle." It looked to me like they had imbibed a lot of the unique liquor, and I hoped they had also peppered their Ex-Lax stew.

"That one was in the sugar shack," said JT. "Bring him with us."

I dressed and was then marched by the idiots outside and over to Michael's room. Fortunately, Genna had already left and Michael was snoring like a baby, the lava lamp shadows waving on the walls as if manifesting spirits from days past. At our intrusion, Michael woke and turned on his reading lamp. In an instant, he was up on one elbow, methodically flicking his knife open and closed. He said, "JT. How come you look like shit? Can you pass me my pants? I got a hard-on ..."

JT said, "I told you this one was dangerous." He recoiled and raked his heel down one of Stalin's shins. Stalin yelped and fell backwards into Schläger, who shoved him off. Stalin hobbled down the hallway, one hand held to a knee. JT roared again, "I want you two out of here on the ten o'clock plane ... Or else. Jesus H. Christ, I gotta take another crap." The old boy turned to yell at Bill and Carl, "And you two queers can get the hell out of my sight." JT stormed away to the toilets, where he would find I had already removed all the paper from every stall.

Schläger said, "We'll sort this out, you two and me, in Edmonton."

When they left, I secured the door with a chair. I said to Michael, "I've had it with this place anyway."

Michael said, "Yup, that JT and Jimmy, they sure are assholes." He'd put in a long day and rolled over to return to dreamland.

30. Ernie

I decided to go to the kitchen one last time and make myself a cup of tea.

On my way to the cook shack, I ran into Ernie, who was about to start his shift. We both swatted at early mosquitoes, proof that spring was here and that the Arctic winter would eventually crack. As usual, the early birds lined up at the kitchen door, eager for coffee and breakfast. Bun was late; the doors were supposed to be open a half-hour earlier. More men arrived for the daylight meal. A few growled at me and there were inquisitive looks, so I said, "The new cook will take care of you guys from now on. I quit."

Almost on cue, Bun emerged from his bunkhouse in his street clothes. His shirt tail was caught in his fly, which was half open, he had cross-buttoned his shirt, and he was definitely still drunk. He stumbled down the stairs and crumpled awkwardly to the mud at the bottom step. Everyone laughed. He rose up on one knee, faltered, stood up, and then staggered toward the kitchen. Deputy Frank stepped out of the front of the lineup at the cook shack door. Frank met Bun and barred him from the top step. The deputy said, "If you got the best cook we've had in camp fired, you're done for …"

"It was Jimmy who fired him," said Bun. Then he turned and retched over the railing.

"Frank, buddy," I intervened, "I'm not fired; I'm quit." The men in the lineup elevated their grumbling and threats. "One word of advice, Bun? If you can't handle your drink, then stop. Oh, and don't burn the eggs."

Ernie took me aside, and said, "This might get ugly. C'mon, let's go have a beer. I got the flu today. I understand there's a fair amount of it going around camp this morning. Schläger might even be on the hunt for you. You can hang out in my room for a while …"

A cold beer sounded good, so we left for Ernie's room.

Ernie locked the door behind us. He crossed his double-wide room, opened a mini-fridge set up on the floor beneath his desk, pulled a couple of bottles from inside, popped open a beer for me and one for himself, and sat on his bed to roll a cigarette. "You don't smoke these Port Radium cancer sticks, eh? Just that happy cabbage?"

"Yeah, I smoke some pot. But I work when it's time to work, too, and people can get the hell off my back about how I spend my leisure time."

"I feel the same way." He lit his smoke with a wooden match that filled the room with a sulfurous, acrid stench. "I like to blend mine with my Drum tobacco. Helps with my chronic backache. I find the tobacco hides the odor."

"So I hear ..."

I sat in a comfortable chair, sipped my cold beer, and looked around. Ernie had his place set up comfortably, for a bunkhouse. Someone had knocked out the shared wall between the adjacent rooms long ago. He had a single-burner electric stove, and a well-used, metal coffee percolator sat on the single coil. A second small fridge, a flip-top record player, and jars of jam and marmalade were arranged on a table. A tiny lamp sat on the table, and a metal wash bowl hung from a nail on the wall. Ernie had other functional items in his orderly kitchen, such as plates, cups, silverware, glasses, dish soap, tea towels, and a wooden box converted to a cupboard where he stored cans of cream, a bag of sugar, and dried soup packets. Ernie's room was immaculate. His oasis was a smart setup where he escaped from camp life.

"So this is how you manage to miss so many meals in the cook shack."

"When there was a doctor in camp, he stayed in this room. I've been here for four years now."

A black and white photograph of a skinny, young pilot hung on the wall over the table. A man in a captain's khaki uniform stood on a jungle path. He smiled, but all his teeth were missing. From the looks of the vegetation, he served in a jungle somewhere.

"That you, Ernie?"

"I volunteered to fight with the Aussies in Burma in '44. When the Japs captured me, they tortured me. They tortured anyone they captured for being cowards. Those guards were sadistic animals. My mates took that picture a couple of weeks after we escaped the jungle camp. The guards pulled my teeth out with pliers. It was my record, for evidence, in case I didn't make it. They pulled 'em out for the fun of it."

His false teeth chattered and his eyes rolled around the room as he relived some part of his painful memory. He grew agitated, took off his left shoe, and pulled off his brown wool sock. He exposed a ghastly set of scars, torn up from each of his toes. His toenails were yellow, twisted, and deformed. I looked away.

"Jesus, Ernie. Maybe next time you give me a little warning when you do that, okay? That's horrific. Fuck."

"Sorry." He put his sock and shoe back on, and tied the lace. "The other foot is the same. But that's what the Japanese did to me when they captured me; both feet. Everyone got the same treatment— if they didn't shoot you outright. Every nail pulled out. And they waited in between each nail so you would suffer more. They pulled up the foot to increase the pain. They laughed at me. They took a week on each foot to drag it out. They didn't want to capture us, they wanted to die in glory fighting us."

I felt both sick and humbled when I heard what this man had endured.

"They were monsters. And we had no medical supplies, either, 'cause they stole our Red Cross packages. I lived through it, but it took weeks before I could stand up, let alone walk again. If you couldn't work, they put you on half-rations, so you starved on half a cup of rice a day while you recuperated. They took our shoes, too, so we would pick up staff infections and die that way. Most never made it through, but if you did, you worked until you starved to death. There was always malaria and dysentery. I was in that camp almost twelve months."

He opened us each another beer. I studied his thin, lined face.

"I've been in worse situations," he said.

"You must have been happy when they dropped the bombs?"

"We didn't know what was going on … Except there were mass executions of the enlisted men. Every day more men were marched into the jungles, but only the guards came back. That lasted for a week. They knew something we didn't. We were told they were going to a different camp, but we knew that was bullshit; they were killing the witnesses. That was the worst time of all. The last morning, it was our turn to march into the jungle, but the guards were gone. They left in the night. They were the cowards. We outlasted them. The first day, no one left the camp because we thought it was a trick. We waited them out. Finally, the hunger got to us, so we broke into their quarters and their officer's mess. That's where I got this." Ernie pulled a Japanese ceremonial sword from under his mattress.

Light flashed up and down the curve of the long, razor-sharp edge when he removed it from the gold-embroidered scabbard. White tassels dangled from the handgrip. I looked at the sword in both disgust and fascination and imagined the terrible role it played in that Japanese POW camp.

"When anyone flew over us, our officers worried we might get strafed, so we left the camp with whatever food we could scavenge. We decided as a group to march thirty-five miles to the coast. We lost men during the march, but at least they died free. It took us five days, what we used to do in a day. We never saw the enemy. When we made the beach, an Australian steamer picked us up. The Japanese didn't believe their Emperor had surrendered, so we dodged patrols on the ocean until we made it to Adelaide. We weren't allowed to go home until they fattened us up. I was there for three months then took a long trip to Canada on a British merchant ship. A typhoon hit us near Midway when we were there for fuel, but we were lucky. We dodged some of the largest waves when we hid behind the island. Boy, was I glad to step off that boat in Vancouver."

"I bet you were. Pretty tough story, Ernie." I stood up, asked with my eyes if we would have another beer, and on Ernie's nod, I opened two more of the dozen or more still in the fridge.

"Others had it worse," he said as I handed him an open beer. "Thanks. I suspect they'll be looking for you soon. If that ain't enough beer to keep you settled, I have this ..." He lifted the grey wool blanket that skirted his bed; he had more beer and a case of whiskey.

"Great stash, Ernie. How'd you manage that?"

"Corey always brought in a bottle or two for me, and I have a key to the cook shack warehouse. Management always thought it was Errol and Mike who stole their booze." I clinked my bottle against his, and we downed half a beer on JT's tab.

"You asked if I was glad they dropped the A-bombs? Well, on the battlefield, that made some kind of sense. I saw so many men die for no reason. The Japs in those camps were war criminals, most of 'em. But not their women and children; they weren't criminals.

Tojo was the one I hated. Besides, they did not drop those bombs to end a war. The Japanese sued for capitulation six weeks before they dropped the bombs. The Emperor tried to surrender. Truman and his generals ignored him. The Russians wanted to take Manchuria and more of China before Stalin would stop fighting. It was their big land grab."

"No, those bombs weren't dropped to stop a war, they were dropped to *start* a war. I'll bet Stalin and Roosevelt planned it in Tehran in '43. When the war ended, the worst of the SS Nazis went to work for the Americans and the Russians. Did you know that? Probably not, right? It was the big secret. They should have gone to Nuremburg and then the end of a rope. But the US and Russia wanted to dominate the world. Besides, if you had no enemy, how could you keep making money at war? Besides, they told us Russia was our ally. That was the old shell game, "the enemy of our enemy is our friend" bullshit. Then, morning after peace was declared, the Russians were our mortal enemy. I mean, how many top Nazis scientists built the A-bomb and rockets for our side? Even after the war, if you said anything, there was a knock on your door or a bullet in the back of your head. The CIA and that drunk Senator McCarthy took care of anyone who asked too many questions on our side of the pond. Read your history: Stalin sent 25,000,000 Russians to war or Siberia and damn few of them came back. Then the US needed a place to put their war toys to work, so, when China and North Korea took their media coverage pot shots at South Korea, the US invaded. The rest is Laos and Vietnam history. Christ, even the French got involved in Indochina. War is big business. The US dumped all their war toys into Asia, then went out and told the American citizens they needed more."

"Hold on a second there. You're saying the Korean War was like a Vietnam?"

"They're all the same, just they let some wars get bigger than others. And they always have the Middle East to fall back on. Remember, Eisenhower told us he couldn't control the bomb-makers and US oilmen calling the shots. The generals are supposed to do what the president says, not the other way around. They still spend billions building bombs and rockets even if there ain't no war going on. And they killed the one president who wanted peace, wanted to put all that military hardware and ingenuity to work going to space.

Why? Because he fought in a war. And LBJ escalates Vietnam before he's even elected president. Nixon was just a glorified mafia puppet. Now Ford wants to put billions more into Vietnam. Why? I never trusted that fucker since the Warren Commission. And why did they kill the Kennedys, then the black guys? Because those men were pacifists and leaders who would not lead the US into war. Nixon would never interfere with the Rand Corporation, or DuPont, or General Dynamics. No wonder their own citizens burned American cities. I've been to war. I support anyone smart enough to avoid a fight. No one should profit from making war."

I let the rant atmosphere settle a bit before I asked, "So, this little slice of heaven even played a role, right?"

"You better believe it. Port radium, the hottest place on earth? I'll say. There's more radiation poisoning in this camp, still, today, than there is at Hiroshima."

Ernie reached into the drawer in his bedside table. He pulled out a small, tin case with a Canadian flag embossed in gold thread on the top. Inside, were three medals and a silver pin. I held the case while he explained, "This one's a Theater of Service medallion; the middle one is a Merit medal they gave me for helping others in the POW camp; the last is an Uncommon Bravery medal for participating in a raid where we took out a Japanese radio tower in the Burmese jungle."

"What's this pin? May I?" He nodded, so I rolled it in my fingers.

"That? Well, that one is special. It's an Office of Strategic Services pin. Look on the back. Someone, probably the guy who gave it to me, chiseled the number '101'."

"Oh, yeah. What's that mean?"

"They'd have cut my hands and head off if they'd found that on me, but I had it pretty well hidden. You can guess where."

I inspected the pin. I said, "They'd have murdered you for this?" I handed the pin and the case back to Ernie.

"I was rescued by those guys from the 101st when I was shot down over Burma. They trained different from me. I was demolition, they were intelligence. The Japs captured us after I lived with the OSS in the jungle for two months. Eventually, the OSS guys were tortured. The guards beheaded them in front of us, maybe even by that sword you were admiring. By that time, I had problems of my own. I got

245

this pin," he rolled it around in his fingers, "from the OSS radio operator. They were not supposed to carry this kind of stuff, but some did, and he gave me this one in case I ever met up with his parents. I never did. I kept it ever since." As an afterthought, he added, "If I had the money, I would go back. I don't know why, exactly, but I would like to see it again. I hear they have tours now and veterans go all the time. Just to see it … But I don't think that's ever going to happen."

When a veteran tells that kind of story, from the heart of experience, he speaks with enlightened truth. I felt admiration and respect for Ernie. This skinny, comical man had lived through a lot and lived to tell about it. In fact, fight and live through that, whatever story you tell, however your politics fall, in my book you have earned the right to your opinion.

Ernie crystallized into simple language the battle that had tormented me since I had arrived. There were obvious, horrible wrongs in this world, but the worst of them was that we allowed the largest corporate lies to destroy our ethics, to weaken the natural bonds shared by all humanity. Of course, the establishment shot some of us dead in the streets, and the cops beat and jailed others at civil protests. Multi-national corporations, who controlled the media, falsely conflated morality and ethics with the twisted notion that profit was king. More than anything, I wanted to become a journalist and do my part to change that. I had questions about those many witnesses who died before they could testify about what they'd seen and heard at Dealy Plaza in 1963. Why did we stop fighting for the truth? Because so many died when our own politicians and domestic, clandestine agencies divided and subdued or killed us. Re-crafted history, and the vested authorities, served witnesses indignity and threats, until all we had left was the hope that one day the tide would turn. And those who benefited directly from the biggest of all the lies? Simple logic dictates they must be the wealthiest and most powerful people in the world today.

Ernie said, "So, what are you going to do?"

"I'll head for the coast. Logging will be going full bore by the time I'm back. I'm happier, and probably safer, in the bush. Mining camps aren't for me."

"You know, I hated you for that porridge pot every morning. It took me hours to clean it most days, but the guys ate well after you started in the kitchen. You did okay." I laughed at the mention of the porridge pot. Ernie said, "Dave was a good man. Let's drink to him."

He reached under his bed and pulled a bottle of Wiser's 18-year-old whiskey out of the case. He poured us each a couple of fingers into clean glasses. We toasted to "a good man gone." I swallowed the drink in a single gulp, which made my eyes water.

"You know, Ernie, Dave's lava lamp would look really good in here."

I felt okay again, but I was knackered. Ernie fixed me up with a quiet room in his bunkhouse. I sacked out behind the locked door and sleep came quickly. I felt warm, protected, and safe. I slept until Ernie shook me awake two hours later.

"You don't wanna miss the plane."

31. Petunia

The DC-3 engines rumbled while the pilots went through their pre-flight routine. They both looked ill. "Nonsense," said JT, responding to the worried enquiry of the Health Inspector. "These are my boys and they could fly circles around Charles Lindbergh himself, if I asked them to." The Health Inspector looked doubtful as the pilot stumbled out of the plane and ran toward the power plant bathroom, again.

Michael and I milled around with the horribly bleary-eyed and blanched dignitaries, who could have been mistaken for the cast in *The Night of the Living Dead*. Some of them still retched up the dregs of their cocktails and stew. Stalin was there, looking worn out as he limped from guest to guest to shake vomit-stained hands and pat shaky backs and slumped shoulders. He offered sympathy and airsickness bags to the passengers. I heard him repeat, "Must be a touch of flu."

I had a thank-you card out and pestered the guests to "sign it for good ol' JT." Weak from their long night, no one protested. Besides, signing the card was the easiest way to have me leave them alone.

Sean drove Donny and Jan to the plane. Don and Jan had quit, too. When Jan told Sean she was leaving, he quit on the spot to go with her. I asked Mouthy Frank why he quit, and he said, "The band is breaking up anyway." Ernie drove my sweet Morag, and Genna and Corey, who looked awful. Michael and the twins helped Corey onto the plane and into a seat. By then, the pilot had returned to the plane and had followed them inside.

JT, the old rifle butt, looked surprisingly chipper. For him, I guess it only took a cigar on the crapper in the morning and he was all set. When Stalin tried to assist JT into the plane, JT barked, "Get your hands off me and go do something useful."

Mary-Ellen glared at Michael and me the whole time she was on the ice. She nudged me aside before she boarded the plane. Her hand on my arm, she said, "I know you have the money. What do you say to an even split?" Her hand snuck a convincing handful of my crotch, most likely for the purposes of emphasis and empty promises.

"Much as I appreciate your enthusiasm … Not so long ago, I might have gone for it." I twisted away from the tender attentions of her last, desperate ploy. "But no deal. Hey, did you sign JT's card?"

"I don't think so, baby," she said, with a haughty sneer. "I only deal in cash." She hooded her eyelids to look me in the eyes. I watched her pink tongue lick around her lips. "Too bad," she said. "You would have had fun." *Said the viper. No thanks.*

Sean joined us, so she released me to light a cigarette. "Soon as we load your bags, we can fly. Can I help you with those?" He took my hockey bag and guitar for me. Mary-Ellen seemed miffed she had to lug her own gear to the plane.

"I thought new guys walk?" I said to Sean. I still remembered the cold welcome Michael and I had received three months, one week, and one day ago.

"New guys and whores walk; neither of you two are new here," said Sean. Mary-Ellen looked away sharply and pretended she had not heard him.

Nice one, Sean.

I had pestered everyone to sign the card. Most of the walking wounded were already on the plane, so it was time to wave goodbye to Morag and Genna, who waved back and made exaggerated winking gestures. Standing on the ice, I took my last look around the darkest hole in Canada, disguised as it was beneath the sparkling snow that reflected the Arctic sunshine. I wondered at the crimes committed in this place. The sheer magnitude of the long-term damage done to this once-pristine lake, the world, and to the collective Canadian soul was immeasurable. It was a difficult resolve to know of a scar on this landscape that was so dangerous. Nature's sad loss touched me with this tragic song of desolation and sorrow on her ruined shores.

A pickup honked and careened dangerously along the lake road. Those of us waiting to board turned away from the plane. The truck swerved onto the ramp, down to the ice, and toward us. An arm waved out of the driver's window; it was Jack. He raced dangerously close to the wing of the plane and slid to a stop. M-M-Mike exited the passenger door to help a man swaddled in bloody blankets out of the truck. Jack hurried around the truck, and they assisted the injured man to the plane. Blood-soaked gauze wrapped around his head still oozed red. He had been in a terrible accident. The injured man dripped a red trail from each of his thick hand bandages as they led him past us gawkers to the plane ladder. From what I could smell, he must have fallen into a full septic tank.

While M-M-Mike helped the victim struggle up the metal rungs, Jack jabbered at us and explained that these were the least of the man's injuries. He was over-excited, but what I understood was that a savage attack had occurred at the curling rink earlier that morning. Petunia had let herself in through the open door, where she had feasted on the last of the stew. When she had eaten her fill, as wolverines do, she defecated on the remaining food in the kitchen, all over the bar, and on the tables and chairs. She tore up the carpets beyond repair, happy as a large cat on scratching post.

While JT sat on the toilet that morning, he dispatched Schläger to find his prized WWII lighter. JT was sure it had fallen out of a shirt pocket at the rink. When he burst in on her, Schläger must have surprised Petunia during her raucous frenzy. In the relatively confined space of the small lounge, she would have reacted to the raised anxiety of the intruder as if he was challenging her. Wolverines are aggressive and defend their territory furiously. So, naturally, Petunia attacked Schläger in a vicious and savage flash of claws and teeth. Apparently, she tore into the source of his testosterone and her outrage, removing his testicles and most of his penis.

I imagined how Schläger must have dropped to the floor and screamed in agony. His many other severe injuries suggested, once down, she'd leapt on his chest, biting repeatedly and with bestial fervor. Polar bears, grizzlies, and wolverines don't quit when they have their quarry down; that is when they get started.

Three hours passed before anyone missed Schläger. Jimmy went to look for him, and when he found Schläger, he had curled into a fetal, unconscious ball, was drenched in his own blood, but was till breathing. Jimmy revived Schläger and helped him to the pickup, and then raced past the abandoned infirmary to the office. He injected the gored Schläger with three full vials of the morphine kept in the office safe. Jack field dressed Schläger's hideous wounds with gauze, pillowcases, and half a roll of duct tape. When M-M-Mike arrived, he and Jack raced with their emasculated charge for the plane.

Jack said, "She must have had at him for a while. She gnawed off an ear, most of his fingers, his nose, his lower lip, even his eyelashes. That sucker will lisp for the rest of his life."

M-M-Mike popped his head out of the plane door, and said, "B-b-before she ran off, Petunia s-s-shit all over him."

There was a new sense of urgency to take off, so we made haste and I, in only one sense, left Port Radium behind forever. Schläger passed in and out of delirium and consciousness. I wondered if he, or what remained of him, would make it to Yellowknife alive. M-M-Mike had placed him into a seat at the rear of the plane, across from Mary-Ellen and JT. Schläger's fumes must have been horrendous. A new round of dignitary retching began as the stench of Petunia's calling card filled the back half of the plane.

When we were airborne, JT lit another cigar and bellowed at Mary-Ellen, "The joke's on me I guess," his face full of smiles. "All's well that ends well. Look, I found my lighter. It was in my jacket pocket. I had it all the time." He laughed good-naturedly at his own folly. "Don't worry Schläger, you'll be all right," said the old goat before Schläger passed out again. "A man like you? A few stitches in Yellowknife and you'll be back on your feet in no time and charming the ladies again."

I turned from the interior distractions to look out my window. The warmer spring temperatures had melted the pristine, white Arctic blanket into a patchwork of mottled, iron ore mounds, a pattern as unpredictable as Nature herself. It was spectacular, fragile, and harsh, this land that required both self-reliance and community strength from each of us, a land teetering in the balance and so vulnerable to the extortions of industry. I felt Nature's grace granted me leave, because She let me return to my life but changed forever. I was in awe of the people who, for millennia, lived in harmony with this wild, dangerous, precious world. But Port Radium was proof that when we persecute Nature, we lose. So far, I thought, Nature has been tolerant of our arrogance, but for how much longer? The Polar bears are dying out, the herds of caribou are gone, the wolves silenced, our oceans polluted, and the polar ice sheets are melting. How much longer can She endure our abuses before showing all of us Her teeth and claws?

I shuddered again at the violence of Petunia's attack. From across the aisle, though the occasional repugnant waft of feces mixed with cigar smoke reached our seats, Michael gave me a "thumbs up." He waited until we were in the air before he told me he'd given the envelope full of cash and Dave's lava lamp to Ernie. He could take that POW camp tour now, but I knew which token he would value more.

I returned Michael's gesture. *Thumbs up, indeed.*

When the ambulance met Corey at the Yellowknife airport, I expected the paramedics might sense something odd about our group. It might have been the half-dead head of Port Radium security swaddled in bloody bandages, or the government men and RCMP officers who staggered about on the runway with black tongues and symptoms of severe dehydration and dysentery, or perhaps it was both pilots sprinting across the runway for the airport toilets. It was then I knew Corey would be in the best care. Before the ambulance attendants whisked him away, I showed Corey the *thank you* card and whispered my intentions. "You and Michael planned on getting yourselves fired – for me. So they'd make you fly out with me, to protect me, didn't you?"

"Safety in numbers, yes. Getting fired was nothing; don't even think about it." The paramedics were in a hurry; I caught the urgent glace from one of them attending Corey. "These good people are about to take you to the hospital and you will soon be in Edmonton. Good luck, buddy."

"Getting fired *was* something. You and Michael took advantage of their weaknesses – greed and control." He raised his hand to shake mine.

I said, "Why don't we let that be our secret, okay?"

Corey laughed until he coughed. The paramedics lifted him into the ambulance, but he regained control first, and said, "Go to journalism school."

We said goodbye with that handshake and a nod.

A second ambulance took Schläger away forever. Life is unfair and cruel — he would survive. However, I was appreciative that my Port Radium denouement would always star Petunia's decisive and triumphant scene. Surely Schläger's departed genitals would require many operations, the results of which precluded any future sexual assaults, and, for his remaining days, his missing parts would necessitate his relieving himself through catheters and tubes into a bag. Of course, with the medical coverage JT provided, the chances were slim that Schläger would receive more than a few closing stitches, perhaps a transfusion, and a couple of codeine tablets before they rolled him out to the Yellowknife parking lot.

Most of the dignitaries departed at Yellowknife. The wives that bothered to meet them appeared shocked at the sight of their bent, weary spouses. The wreckage from the indulgent weekend was as plain on their faces as were their black tongues.

Harman was the last of them to stumble out of the plane, and he left alone. Forced back into the empty, confined corridors of his pitiful life, his wife's lawyer met him at the bottom of the ladder. I overheard the smirking lawyer explain, "Your wife asked me to tell you that after she found the receipt for the ring in your suit pocket, she emptied the bank accounts. She packed up the kids and the dog, and left Yellowknife forever. I'll add that she also took most of the furniture, at least half of your future income, and a substantial chunk of your pension. You're lucky she left you the bed." He handed Harman the divorce papers.

It is an unfortunate reality that I could not be witness when the rest of those criminals opened their thick, sealed envelopes to find inside blank strips of paper rather than the cash they expected. However, it was easy to imagine their reactions. It was also an unfortunate reality that Karma only sometimes works instantly, but we can dream, and from those dreams can come vision, and from those visions, change. The key is to press on, never forget, and hold high the banner of truth.

32. Edmonton, Again

Mary-Ellen changed her seat to sit apart from JT. No doubt she felt jilted, angry, derisive, and kept to her own world for the rest of the long flight to Edmonton. The last two government inspectors retched intermittently the entire flight, which was music to my ears. We flew over ice-free lakes, brown, plowed fields, and green pine forests increasingly clear of snow. I was excited when we finally spotted Edmonton on the horizon. When we landed, JT and Mary-Ellen departed in separate taxis. Though the breeze was warm and the sun was shining, their arrangement looked icy.

Our gang shared hugs and handshakes at the airport. Before Michael and I found a live music honky-tonk to begin our debriefing process, I mailed a special delivery envelope that contained the signature card and a lengthy list of complaints and statements I had already gathered from our crew. I sent the package to a Calgary newspaper, away from Edmonton but still in Alberta, where we hoped someone might investigate Port Radium. I thought the signatures of the government officials would lend credibility to my accusations. It was worth a shot.

Michael and I shared a hotel room. Don, Jan, and Sean planned to meet up with us on Wednesday at the company offices in Edmonton. The gale from the east, Mouthy Frank, took a red-eye flight back to Ontario. God knows why, but I kind of missed him.

When we picked up our final pay cheques, I was sure that the only reason JT paid Michael and me anything was because enough of us were in the office at the same time to outnumber the old bugger. After the company reimbursed themselves for my airfares, my beer tab, and company store credit, I had only a few dollars to my name; the airfare charge was a particularly bitter pill to swallow. I doubt JT wanted anything more to do with us now that the bonspiel was over. Besides my statement, JT handed me a letter from Murray, sent in the company mailbag. I waited until all of us were together one last time before I read it.

I thought about hitching to the coast, but I bought a one-way bus ticket instead. I put $50 on my friend's kitchen table and two cases of beer in his fridge. He asked about my "Québécois friend." I told him, "Michael's okay, once you get to know him." After that, I

spent what little remained of my cash in the bars, saying farewell to
Michael.

I still dreamed of a career in journalism, but would first have
to find a logging job when I returned to BC. Michael's plans were
sketchy, but he was in no hurry to discover how wanted he was in
Winnipeg.

When we met up with Don, Sean, and Jan, Sean started in
first: he told us Corey was going to stay in hospital for another week
in Yellowknife before he transferred to Edmonton General Hospital.
Sean and Jan let it slip they were "shacking up." Donny, Jan's ultimate
fifth wheel, even accepted that because, well, he really loved her.

We ordered a second round before I read Murray's letter out
loud.

May 7, 1975

Hi Everyone, hope you're all too drunk to read!

Everything here is as boring as before you left, but
quieter! Your plane was the last flight to take off from the lake,
which is covered in pools of water now. No sign of Petunia yet,
so she got away with it! I'm going to finish my contract and then
head for the Mediterranean ... Al's stories got to me and so I will
drink the same beer as him (St. Miguel), "The best beer in the
world," says Al. I intend to do my own research lying around the
beaches in Torremolinos.

Want another true Port Radium story? The day after you
all left, M-M-Mike finally finished the D9 rebuild. We celebrated
that. We need the cat so it can plow the airfield and maintain it all
summer so I can leave! Anyway, Mike's first order of business
was still lifting the failed water pump from the Eldorado
mineshaft. While Jimmy waited at the mine, Mike walked the D9
cat over the back road to the top of the main vent. Mike
detoured (always a good idea) out to Garbage Lake to shove the
mine waste farther out on the ice, and, yes sir, walked the D9
right back through the ice where it sank to the bottom. Guess
what? Even after months being re-built, it still doesn't float!

Carl and Bill helped rescue Mike again. They pulled him
out. Mike and Jack were loaded, drunk as millionaire cowboys, on
the next plane out of Port Radium. Jimmy was still yelling at M-
M-Mike and Jack even after the plane left. But you know Jimmy

... He took the bull by the tail, faced the situation, walked out on the yellow ice with a cable and hook, stripped down naked, and jumped into the chemical muck. He sank twenty feet to the D9, secured the chain, and then popped up at the surface of the processing sludge. He was near dead and covered in yellow-green goo when Carl and Bill pulled him out. They pulled the D9 off the bottom a second time!!! It's back in the shop again. One day, that's all they got out of it! Still no water pump in the Eldorado mine but both Jimmy and the D9 now glow in the dark!

Anyway, stay out of trouble or don't get caught!

Your Friend,

Aussie Murray

PS: Ernie says he plans to tour Malaysia and Eddie is staying on for another contract — insanity!

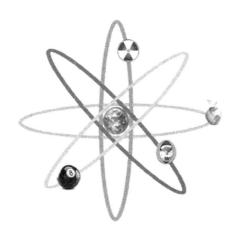

Afterword

"Of all the world's nuclear powers, Canada is the last hold-out on talking about its nuclear legacy and how so many things went terribly wrong," says Gordon Edwards, a Montreal mathematician and president of the Canadian Coalition for Nuclear Responsibility.

There might be those who question the facts that radioactive tailings emitted radon gas in the camp (and in Uranium City, Saskatchewan, and at Port Hope, Ontario), that this would have been impossible because the chemical processes involved would have extracted the uranium before the tailings were used to ballast the bunkhouses. This assumption could only come from the ignorant notion that U-235 is not part of a decay chain, which, of course it is. So, the problem is two-fold: the concentration-extraction process seizes only the U-235 isotope existing at the moment of processing. The process leaves behind the other isotopes of uranium that will become U-235. The second issue is that the uranium-specific leaching process leaves behind hundreds of thousands of years of equally deadly radioactive remaining elements from the tailings. What the reader has to understand is once the U-235 has been concentrated, the uranium remains deadly and toxic virtually forever. The first half-life of U-235 is 703.8 million years.

As of June 30, 2015, Canada had an inventory of just under 2.6 million used nuclear fuel bundles. At the end of the planned operation of Canada's existing nuclear reactors, the number of used nuclear fuel bundles could total 5.2 million "spent" bundles. A bundle of rods is spent after just 5% of the uranium is used — the rest remains in the bundles as highly toxic nuclear waste for more than 1.4 billion years or two half lives.

In January 2017, David Suzuki reported, "By 2022, it will simply be cheaper to build and provide a gigawatt of wind power than the cheapest fossil-fuel alternative and solar will be just behind. Bottom line: renewable energy can power Canada, create jobs, generate wealth and fight climate change."

What about nuclear power's low greenhouse gas emissions? Carbon foot-print? There are dozens of writers who support nuclear power, though one wonders why. Below, two such supporters discuss the expansion of only a single uranium mine and the effect it will

Alfred Cool

have on the environment. Consider this admission by Brook and Heard, made before they dismissed the environment issue in their blog, which ignores the critical problem of nuclear waste:

> ...carbon dioxide equivalent emissions could peak at 4.7 million tonnes per year (tCO_2-e). The Environmental Impact Statement acknowledged this would add almost 10 per cent to South Australia's forecast emissions in 2020 under a business-as-usual scenario

So, how is Canada benefitting from all this nuclear waste we have already generated? What are the numbers? First, the good news. When I extrapolate all the nuclear power benefitting households that could have been generated in Canada using existing nuclear rod bundles, the total amounts to 2,600,000 (spent rod bundles) x100 (households) = 260,000,000. Spread over Canada's 13,320,000 households, that is enough power, say nuclear supporters, to have provided for 20 years. Sounds great!

What the supporters of nuclear power don't tell you is the mountains of deadly nuclear waste created during and after processing lasts for more than 1.4 billion years. That alone, the consequences of nuclear waste, is a terrible enough return on the dangerous resource to stop using it to make light bulbs shine.

Our generation should be ashamed of what we leave behind.

But if we could have powered all the households in Canada for 20 years, without polluting, why did this not happen? Where is all that uranium going? Well, consider only 5% of each fuel rod is used before it is considered to be "spent." That's right, the rest is waste. How many $Trillions of dollars that could have been spent on renewables like SOLAR and WIND generation and batteries has been wasted on uranium over 75 years? In addition, the shelved nuclear Cold War warheads require regular replenishing in order to maintain the deterrent against nuclear attack. The cold warriors have blown it; nowadays the big money is in dealing guns and ammunition to both sides of any conflict.

What about the fantastic claims a thimble of uranium will provide household power forever? That's where the destructive notion nuclear power is good was germinated. The same propaganda

258

exists today. I give you Fukushima, White Sands, Inkai, Kazakhstan, Hanford, Argonne, Australia's Radium Hill and Rum Jungle mines, Chernobyl, 3-Mile Island, Chalk River, WIPP, radiation-poisoned bullets in Iraq deforming future generations, aquifers destroyed by fracking for uranium, stolen uranium around the globe, 47 more nuclear power plant or storage facility accidents since the fifties, and with humble respect, Hiroshima and Nagasaki.

Supporters will tell you new plants will never meltdown or explode because of new technology. TEPCO now has 5 million gallons of water sitting above one of their plants in case of an emergency. Wow! That sounds safe ... TEPCO spent $5 billion to build in their new "safeguards" at one plant alone. Too bad they didn't do it right and put that money into renewable energy. To my knowledge, plate tectonics still exist and the next earthquake is building now ... earthquakes scare humans and scared humans make mistakes under pressure, just like at Fukushima and Chernobyl, and when the power cuts off, how useful are computers?

Let's consider the ironic notion of recycling uranium. Some scientists propose the remaining uranium and plutonium in the rod bundles can be recycled. Says physicist Edwin Lyman, a senior staff scientist at the Union of Concerned Scientists (UCS), a nonprofit that advocates for a healthy environment and safer world, "We do not think any reprocessing scheme existing or proposed can mitigate the serious concern of proliferation and nuclear terrorism. Commercial spent fuel has plutonium in it and you can think of that as an ore that could be mined for fissile material [bombs]."

Nevertheless, advocates including researchers at Idaho, Argonne, Los Alamos, and Oak Ridge national laboratories point to a reprocessing future of so-called fast-breeder reactors, which use plutonium to generate electricity—and in the process of fissioning generate yet more plutonium, a theoretically inexhaustible source of energy. "In theory, it could produce a self-sustaining energy supply," Lyman acknowledges. "But in practice it's never worked."

In 2016, Canada granted Kazatomprom and its partner, Canadian uranium mining giant, Cameco, "an option to obtain UF6 conversion services at Cameco's Port Hope facility and to receive other commercial support from the Canadian company." We should all be very concerned.

Both Eldorado and Echo Bay mines remained operational for seven more years. Men and women worked in the murdering radon dust and radioactivity until the owners had enough silver, copper, and U-235 to buy their way onto the NYSE. And yes, the owners became rich; they sold the false legacy of Port Radium lies on Wall Street and in government offices in Canada, where no one is ever overly keen on knowing the facts.

3 months, 1 week and 1 day. That is how long I lived in Port Radium during the winter and spring of 1975 — working eleven-hour or longer shifts.

The fuel for Oppenheimer's Little Boy and the nuclear dawn of the Cold War came from those isolated rock outcroppings on the lake named The Great Bear.

I bounced around in several jobs while in camp: I was a member of the surface crew, a driver, and then a cook. In one sense, I came of age in that camp. I flew in young, naïve, and fearless, seeking only to leave healthy and able to pay for my first of a four year degree in Journalism. I found out I had much to learn about how open minds and youth are threats to people who use money to wield control. I flew out thoughtful, defiant, and broke because the company found a way to steal my wages.

This story is not about money or lost wages; it is about right and wrong, and what we leave for the next generations. Experience is the tough schoolmaster that earned me the right to formulate my opinions. Before I went to Port Radium, the media educated me about nuclear energy. Despite the bias, I was neither for nor against it, but I was always against those who profited from war. My grandfather spent four years as a machine-gunner in the trenches in France throughout WWI. From as far back as I can remember, he warned me to distrust generals and politicians. He is still right, except I took his advice further and grew to loathe those who put him and millions like him in the mud, stole his health, his innocence, and his youth. They called WWI the "war to end all wars" and WWII the "necessary war." Yeah, sure. If it is wrong to make profit from war, and it is, then the disgrace of Port Radium was that it was the nuclear source of Mankind's worst immorality.

Before I worked in the mine, the thirty-year Cold War fueled the need for more uranium for weapons, and then carried on for another dozen or so years. At risk of committing the crime of repeating myself, I'll remind the reader that in 1961, America's SL-1 Idaho Falls reactor melted down; in 1979, Three Mile Island nuclear facility was a half hour from total meltdown; Russia's Chernobyl nuclear facility exploded in 1986; and Japan's Fukushima nuclear facility exploded in March 2011 and to this day, the Fukushima Daiichi Nuclear Power Plant, which has been inoperative for 6 years, still produces 100,000 gallons of radioactive water every day. TEPCO thinks this might continue for at least another 40 years. Machines and computers cannot clean up the 3 melted reactor cores, which will remain deadly for 1.4 billion or more years. These were the results of trivial equipment failure complicated by human failure. At Hanford, WA, 75,000,000 tons (est.) of highly radioactive solid and liquid waste continues to poison the soil and leak into the groundwater, leaching from buried silos into the Columbia River. Hanford whistleblowers warn of a pending "hydrogen event" are charged and lose their jobs or worse. As of 2013, eighteen world states have access to nuclear arms. Fifty major accidents have occurred in nuclear power plants. Today, more than one hundred incidents of hijacking of nuclear fuel occur worldwide every year. In 2014, the ten billion dollar nuclear Waste Isolation Pilot Plant (WIPP) in New Mexico, the showcase depository for the mountain of nuclear waste at Los Alamos and US nuclear power plants, shut down because of human error. A "Hydrogen event" necessitated the closure. At the time of this writing, the WIPP facility is still trying to reopen. The cost to taxpayers is estimated at $450 million. The nuclear snake has encircled all of us and is devouring its own tail.

Port Radium ranks as Canada's worst nuclear environmental disaster the US Freedom of Information Act has yet to uncover. Tied to Fort McMurray, Alberta, Uranium City, Saskatchewan, and Port Hope, Ontario, the remote site was the supply source of the Canadian government's on-going radioactive waste disaster. Since then, Canada's nuclear power industry has escalated as a global threat. Uranium is an expensive and dirty power source. To present uranium otherwise is the equivalent of putting lipstick on a pig.

The amount of nuclear waste associated with nuclear power and nuclear arms is atrocious. In Canada alone, imagine four lanes of the 401 Highway from Port Hope to Ottawa gridlocked by loaded dump trucks. Imagine each truck transporting eight tons of

Alfred Cool

radioactive and chemical waste. First the Canadian government and
then privateers left millions of tons of waste behind when they fled
with their profits from the once-pristine shores of LaBine Bay on
Great Bear Lake. Imagine thousands of Canadian miners and workers
and indigenous men with cancer, dying horrible deaths since 1932.
Imagine the Canadian government turning a blind eye to them and
their families, blaming instead the tobacco companies. That denial
and abandonment is the on-going legacy of the uranium industry in
Canada. The "necessary war" ended in 1945, but the mine operated
under the auspices of the Canadian government until 1982. Today, in
addition to 2.6 million spent fuel rods, an estimated 200 million tons
of radioactive waste remain spread across our nation.

What is U-235? It is an isotope of Uranium. U-235 is fissile.
It can sustain a fission chain reaction. It is the only fissile isotope
found in significant quantity in Nature. Concentration processes,
chemical alterations, and enrichment of the isotope makes it more
dangerous than dynamite sweating TNT in the shaking hands of a
shell-shocked war veteran. The alchemy of men converts U-235 to a
deadly fuel for bombs or into a deadly fuel for power plants. What is
a half-life? It will take 703.8 million years before Canada's
200,000,000 tons of nuclear waste radiation is as potent as
100,000,000 tons of deadly waste. That is a half-life; the deterioration
term remains the same. 703.8 million years after the second half-life
begins, Canada will still have the equivalent of 50,000,000 tons of
deadly nuclear waste. That is 1.4 billion years from today. The
product of the decay chain eventually produces the heavy metal lead-
206, but during it's deadly decay, U-235 mutates into Neptunium,
Thorium, Protactinium, Actinium, Radium, Francium, Radon,
Astatine, Polonium and finally heavy lead. Nature cannot reverse
man's tinkering; U-235 remains deadly for all time.

Going forward, the only significant commercial use for
uranium is to fuel nuclear reactors to generate electricity. The only
military application is topping up nuclear weapons potency or
applying uranium to bullets, which is what happened during the
second Iraq war. As of August 2011, there are 440 reactors operating
worldwide, 60 new reactors are under construction, over 150 nuclear
power reactors have approval and await construction, and over 340
more are proposed. Canadian corporations, Cameco, acquire over
30% of the uranium needed to fuel the world's reactors, and Cameco

does so in Afghanistan by the means of In Situ Leaching, a method more commonly known as *fracking*. Today's decommissioning standards for nuclear power plants are those developed in 1981. It cost $1.24 Billion to shut down Vermont's Nuclear Power Plant. It is a myth that spent nuclear rods can fuel commercial reactors. The carbon footprint to re-use spent nuclear fuel rods is well-beyond any benefits and the technology does not exist.

Sixty kilograms of enriched U-235 fueled the Atomic bomb exploded over Hiroshima, Japan on August 6, 1945. That bomb and its fallout destroyed 90% of the city and killed at least 80,000 people. Much of that uranium came from Canada. Much of the heavy water required in the enrichment process of that uranium came from Trail, British Columbia. We continued after 1945. As of 2011, the global industry produces 59,370 tons of uranium every year; Canada produces 26,000 to 29,000 tons of that volume. The connection between what happened in Hiroshima and what is happening now is not difficult to make. In 1945, the white flash and annihilation the use of nuclear weapons produced and the shocking loss of life and destruction was calculable. Whereas today, the slow process of nuclear poisoning we experience requires more diligence to detect and considerable political courage to report, though, ultimately, it is just as deadly.

In Port Radium, I was at ground zero of that terror. Many times I felt I was an innocent miniature of myself, one peep away from discovery, being devoured, and then forgotten. I had wandered into the midst of giant, angry demons colluding with wicked sorcerers. I saw the disconnect between what we preach and what we practice, that there is distance between truth and reality. One picks sides; I tried to close the gap by taking responsibility back from those who would force even more separation and double the veils snuffing out the faint light of truth. Despite landing on the moon, Man has not travelled so far from those days when our distant ancestors huddled through the nights, cold and afraid of the leopard patrolling the entrances to our dark caves.

My journey was enlightening. I walked hopeful footsteps along a risky Canadian path. I delayed my post-secondary classes in lieu of travel and then found the job in Port Radium. Sometime later, I realized that I'd acquired in that isolated, wonderful landscape something far more valuable than money for school; I'd brought back an education. To this day, I am thankful Fate intervened to change my future. When I finally returned to school, it felt like a job, but was one I undertook to learn how to write this story. That irony concisely epitomized my wanderings. I was destined to discover in the vast, white purity and freedom of our far north my nation's moral degradation, where industry was hard at work grinding our own national legacy into shame. Proliferating nuclear reactors around the world and the fuel needed for them to operate, Canada played and plays a major role in the sinister connection to Humanity's darkest moments. Exposed in one brilliant, terrible flash, history became finite, indelible, and Canadian, and scorched forever our iconic maple leaf with our own scarlet letter – U.

Scientists estimate that at our current rate of consumption, within 300 years we will deplete all the uranium in the world as a non-renewable fuel resource. The radioactive waste we leave behind, depleted or otherwise, for following generations will continue to poison the planet for more than a billion years. Who among us has the right to make this decision?

I have read the government and the corporate denials; the lame explanation it was cigarette smoking that killed uranium miners, workers, and transporters, not cancer from unprotected exposure to radon gas attached to dust particles. This refrain, begun in the forties, is still popular with too many consulting "doctors" and our own government. To be fair, the government warns people to take precautions — now. Decades late and after the third publicly funded, extensive (15 year) site remediation project and after all the buildings were burnt to the ground and heavy equipment was dropped in the lake or down a Port Radium mine shaft, a pamphlet still declares no human should remain more than three months during any year on the Port Radium site due to the still measurable levels of surface radiation and radon emissions. There is no such tobacco warning posted in Port Radium today.

The People

"Before the mine, you never heard of cancer…" Paul Baton, 83, Déline Elder.

Declassified U.S. atomic weapons and energy program documents reveal that both the Canadian and American governments knew, in the early '40s, about the deadly hazards of uranium extraction. Yet for two decades, Ottawa failed to warn thousands of miners and natives of the risks they faced daily. Source: Nikiforuk

'The Village of Widows" "Déline is practically a village of widows, most of the men who worked as laborers have died of some form of cancer." — Source: Cindy Kenny-Gilday

Radioactive tailings used as road cap and bunkhouse ballast. Why would anyone do such an unspeakable thing?

Port Radium produced 37 million ounces of silver, 10.5 million pounds of copper and 13.7 million pounds of uranium oxide. 1932-1982

WASTE: 1.7 million tons of radioactive and chemical waste left behind at the mine.

In Canada, we have 200 million tons of this radioactive waste, called uranium tailings. As Marie Curie observed, 85 percent of the radioactivity in the ore remains behind in that crushed rock. Source: Dr. Gordon Edwards.

Cameco produces 29,000 tons of uranium every year in Kazakhstan by fracking; spewing the radon gas in the atmosphere. They have forecast a global need to rise to 2,000,000,000 pounds of uranium required per year by 2030.

Nuclear power is the most expensive and dangerous power source known to man.

440 nuclear power plants are operating in the world today. Wikipedia reports, "As of 2014, there have been more than 100 serious nuclear accidents and incidents from the use of nuclear power. Fifty-seven accidents have occurred since the Chernobyl disaster, and about 60% of all nuclear-related accidents have occurred in the USA."

Fukushima update (2016) "The reactors continue to bleed radiation into the ground water and thence into the Pacific Ocean," Gunderson said. "When Tepco finally stops the groundwater, that will be the end of the beginning," referring to the water flowing into the leaking basements of the reactor buildings."

TEPCO estimates another 40 years are required before the site will be decommissioned. Signs of Fukushima radioactive contamination are being detected in British Columbia and California.(2017)

Declassified Documents: the Cover Up

The federal government [of Canada] owned Eldorado Mining and Refining and regulated the uranium industry. It privatized the firm in 1988.

Although the Atomic Energy Control Board and uranium companies have long argued that little was known about uranium's hazards, evidence from U.S. and Canadian archives and survivors of the era tell a different story.

Unlike Ottawa, the U.S. recently (1998) declassified 250,000 documents on its atomic weapons and energy program, which reveal that government officials and scientists in both countries actively discussed uranium's hazards in secret. Yet publicly they remained mute.

The perils were well documented. As early as 1932, Canada's Department of Mines published studies on Port Radium that repeatedly warned about radon's poisonous affects n the lungs and "dangers from inhalation of radioactive dust."

The department's own blood studies on Port Radium miners lead it to conclude, "… that a hazard may exist in the breathing of air containing even small amounts of radon."

Notes Robert Bothwell, a University of Toronto historian and author of "Eldorado, a lengthy history of the Crown Corporation:", "The profound and deliberate falsification of nuclear hazards began at the top."

In 1945, a federal research team from Montreal sent to monitor radon in the mine found conditions at Port Radium "appalling." They reported, "...the radon content seems to be so high as to be definitely dangerous to the health of those working in the mines." Source: Nikiforuk

Wilhelm C. Hueper, the founding director of the environmental cancer section of the U.S. National Cancer Institute in 1942 reviewed 300 years of radon data on European miners. His conclusion: radon gas in cobalt mines routinely produced lung cancers that systematically killed more than half of all miners 10 to 20 years after their employment.

When Hueper began to issue similar warnings to U.S. uranium miners on the Colorado Plateau in the early '50s, "the mine operators and politicians got all excited," says Victor E. Archer, an epidemiologist who started the first cancer studies on U.S. miners in 1954 and is now a professor of occupational medicine in Salt Lake City at the University of Utah.

When Declassified U.S. documents also show that the U.S. Atomic Energy Commission told Hueper, a world expert on lung cancers, that references to occupational cancers among uranium miners were "not in the public interest" and "represented mere conjecture."

Archer: "The Canadians knew about the same things that the U.S. did and in general tagged along with the Atomic Energy Commission." In fact, Eldorado management and the Canadian government regularly received updates on radon and lung cancer studies on American uranium miners throughout the '50s.

Neither government nor mine owners wanted to scare miners away or implement better health safeguards that would force uranium prices up, says Archer.

"In 1976 after depletion of this ore body, Echo Bay Mines re-opened the former Eldorado mine shaft #1, and mined silver from its workings until depletion in 1982.

1940-1960, Radon measured in Eldorado mine recorded at 1,000+ times World Health Organization safe standards.

"In the early days of uranium mining, little was known about the health effects of radon, so there was no or little radiation protection. Ventilation was poor or non-existent. Consequently, uranium miners were exposed to high levels of radiation.

This resulted in high rates of lung cancer among early uranium miners."

Source: Radon and Health (2012) Sec. 3.2 Health Effects, pg. 7 © Minister of Public Works and Government Services, Canadian Nuclear Safety Commission

Not so! In 1945, a federal research team from Montreal sent to monitor radon in the mine found conditions at Port Radium 'appalling." The conditions remained unimproved through 1982.

The Canadian government sent two physicists to the area in the mid-'50s to check on radon levels at Port Radium's sister mine on Lake Athabasca — a mine with much lower grade ore — they found lots of radon. However, according to one retired senior civil servant, that report, like Hueper's concerns, never saw the light of day.

"We printed it in green covers, which means declassified, and sent a copy up to Chalk River. In addition, the next thing I knew we got orders from the assistant deputy minister to collect every copy and get them back to the department because not one was to go out. That report was squashed." Source: Nikiforuk.

Sources

1.Wikipedia, Declassified U.S. documents - US Atomic Energy Commission
2. Minister of Indian Affairs and Northern Development and Federal Interlocutor for Métis and Non-Status Indians — Port Radium Remediation Plan 2005 note: 2-11 image of mine site & ventilation
3. Radon and Health (2012) Sec. 3.2 Health Effects, pg. 7 © Minister of Public Works and Government Services, Canadian Nuclear Safety Commission
4. Echoes of the Atomic Age, by Andrew Nikiforuk, Calgary Herald 2009
5. The Human Health and Ecological Risk Assessment stay at the site for up to three months per year
6. Wilhelm C. Hueper, the founding director of the environmental cancer section of the U.S. National Cancer Institute 1942 Occupational Tumors and Allied Diseases (Springfield, Ill.: C. C. Thomas, 1942).
7. V. E. Archer, whose epidemiology studies on American miners finally broke the official silence in 1961
8. Vol. 14, No. 2, Mar 2007–0 THE ETHICAL ISSUES IN URANIUM MINING RESEARCH IN THE NAVAJO NATION
9. 1993 recommendations of the Joint Federal-Provincial Panel on Uranium Mining in Northern Saskatchewan
10. Cindy Kenny-Gilday The Village of Widows
11. URANIUM: Known Facts and Hidden Dangers (1992), invited address by Dr. Gordon Edwards at the World Uranium Hearings, Salzburg, Austria September 14, 1992
12. "Canada well on its way to a renewable-energy future.", The Globe and Mail, Dec 2016, Christopher Barrington-Leigh
13. Giustra, Kazatomprom, Port Hope, et al, "http://www.world-nuclear-news.org/UF-Cameco-and-KazAtomProm-to-restructure-Inkai-2705167.html", May 2016
14. Dr. Edward Lyman, Edwin Lyman | Union of Concerned Scientists, 2009 https://www.scientificamerican.com/article/nuclear-waste-lethal-trash-or-renewable-energy-source/"

15. Nuclear Fuel Math, Nuclear Waste Management Organization, https://www.nwmo.ca/en/Canadas-Plan/Canadas-Used-Nuclear-Fuel/How-Much-Is-There, and https://www.nwmo.ca/en/Canadas-Plan/Canadas-Used-Nuclear-Fuel, and https://en.wikipedia.org/wiki/Spent_nuclear_fuel, 2017

16. Ken Buesseler, "PBS Newshour," a marine radiochemist with the Woods Hole Oceanographic Institution (WHOI) and director of the WHOI Center for Marine and Environmental Radioactivity. 2014

17. Wellerstein, Alex, "Restricted Data – The Nuclear Secrecy Blog, "When did the allies know there wasn't a German bomb?"

18. Barry Brook, Ben Heard, "Crbon Offsetting of Uranium Mines," https://bravenewclimate.com/2012/05/06/carbon-offsetting-uranium-mines/, May 2012

19. "The Nuclear Option," NOVA, 2017 https://www.youtube.com/watch?v=bBAZc-nQISw

20. "Pandora's Promise," 2013 https://www.youtube.com/watch?v=t10mJkG8bPA

21. Stefanie Spear, "3 Myths From Pro-Nuclear Film 'Pandora's Promise'", 2013 https://www.youtube.com/watch?v=t10mJkG8bPA and http://www.foe.org.au/pandora

22 "From Jimmy Carter to George W. Bush: Presidential Policies and Involvement in the Debate over the Arctic National Wildlife Refuge, 1977-2009", Gisle Holsbø Eriksen, UNIVERSITY OF OSLO, Fall 2009

Alfred Cool

Uranium Half-Life

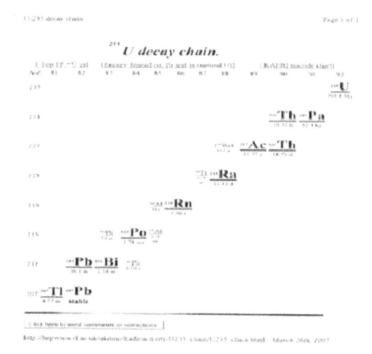

Made in the USA
Columbia, SC
02 March 2018